D1462223

Much to Your Chagrin

Much to Your Chagrin

A Memoir of Embarrassment

SUZANNE GUILLETTE

ATRIA BOOKS
New York • London • Toronto • Sydney

ATRIA BOOKS

A Division of Simon & Schuster, Inc.

1230 Avenue of the Americas

New York, NY 10020

First Atria Books hardcover edition March 2009

ATRIA BOOKS and colophon are trademarks of Simon & Schuster, Inc.

For information about special discounts for bulk purchases, please contact Simon & Schuster Special Sales at 1-800-456-6798 or business@simonandschuster.com.

The author and the publisher gratefully acknowledge permission from the following sources: page 195, excerpt from *The Collected Essays, Journalism and Letters of George Orwell, Volume III: As I Please 1943–1945*, copyright © 1968 by Sonia Brownwell Orwell and renewed 1996 by Mark Hamilton, reprinted by permission of Houghton Mifflin Harcourt Publishing Company; page 405, "Everything" from *Monologue of a Dog*, copyright © 2002 by Wisława Szymborska, English translation copyright © 2006 by Houghton Mifflin Harcourt Publishing Company, reprinted by permission of the publisher.

Designed by Dana Sloan

Manufactured in the United States of America

10 9 8 7 6 5 4 3 2 1

Library of Congress Cataloging-in-Publication Data

Guillette, Suzanne.
    Much to your chagrin : a memoir of embarrassment / by Suzanne Guillette.
1st Atria Books hardcover ed.
        p. cm.
    1. Guillette, Suzanne—Anecdotes. 2. Embarrassment—New York (State)—New York—Anecdotes. 3. New York (N.Y.)—Biography—Anecdotes.
I. Title.
    CT275.G843A3 2009
    974.7'043092—dc22
    [B]   2008016637

ISBN-13: 978-1-4165-8597-8
ISBN-10:   1-4165-8597-4

For Gwendolyn Beatrice, 1907–1989.
With so much love.

AUTHOR'S NOTE

As Patricia Hampl once said, "Memoir writing is not best understood as a transcript of reality." Along these lines, the story that follows here is not an objective, journalistic account of a particular time in my life. Rather, this story is an effort to recreate a singular kind of reality: my emotional reality, for which I have consulted no outside sources. Character portrayals strictly reflect my inner experiences at the time. Because of the extremely subjective nature of the book, I have changed numerous identifying details of characters in it, including names, physical characteristics, locations, and, in rare cases, even events. In one or two instances, I have created composite characters, to best streamline the narrative arc. Finally, *Much to Your Chagrin*, my meditation on embarrassment, practically begged to be written in the second person; apropos to the subject matter, I found it much easier to say that *I* did not do these things—*you* did.

PART I

What is life, but a series of inspired follies? The difficulty is to find them to do. Never lose a chance: it doesn't come every day.

—GEORGE BERNARD SHAW, *PYGMALION*,

1913, ACT II

1

YOU'RE LATE—AGAIN. YOU still haven't decided for what it is you are late, but that hardly matters. You are just late. Looking frantically around your room, you know what you should do, although that thing about follow-through has really been biting you in the ass lately.

You are getting dressed and packing bags and watering plants—all at once. The phone rings, and you ignore it. You are half naked, topless in a red prairie skirt, holding a glass of water in one hand and your toothbrush in the other. Looking at both hands, full, then over to your nosy senior citizen neighbors who seem to appreciate it when your blinds are up, especially at times like these, you smile and put the toothbrush down. It's not the old men who stare most often. It's the ladies with their high-waisted shorts and tight gray curls. There is all of Edison Avenue—a narrow Bronx street lined with nondescript telephone poles and empty, turned-over trash cans—between your bedroom window and their three porches, which are side by side but not connected. You always think you're safe to be naked and they always think they're safe to gape. You never do seem to close those blinds in time.

As you empty the glass into your indoor window box, careful not to douse the leaves of your precious and temperamental African violets, you reach blindly toward the cord and yank it until the blinds fall far enough to cover what would most likely be a view of your boobs. You do the same at the other window, and now you are safe, safe to figure out what the hell it is that you are going to do once your bags are packed and your top is on and you are settled into the front seat of your beat-up car. But the knowledge of what you *should* do is already fixed in the pit of your stomach.

You've always been adventurous, often resulting in a hesitancy to make plans with too much notice, much to the chagrin of your more organized and routine-driven friends. "Maybe" has become your favorite word. Of course, you like routine, too, just not the kind that gets in the way of your dazzling, if fanciful, world of possibility. Spring, with its budding flowers and warmer airs of optimism, is all around you, and you live in this world more often than not.

Option A is driving straight to Boston, where you will spend the weekend with Annabelle, your older sister, and be her date at the wedding of her friend, who also happens to be the ex of one of your exes. And yes, you both dated him at the same time, for a period of weeks until he stopped calling you and you started seeing them together everywhere. (Your attempts to ignore them would have been successful if she wasn't so damn nice.) After spending five years with him, she broke it off, found a new man, one you've never slept with, so you consider you and her to be cool now. You will drink a lot of wine this weekend, and possibly smoke cigarettes, too, so you wonder if, in the best interests of your lungs and brain cells, Option A shouldn't be postponed as long as possible. Option B would be a perfect, ready way to delay the debauchery that seems to be picking up new momentum now that it is May and you have fallen in love with New York again, now that it is one week from graduation and you have broken up with Ondra, your sexy, albeit long-distance Czech lover, via a transatlantic phone call and the invaluable help of a Czech-English dictionary. Yes, Option B would be perfect, if only your head were in the right place.

Option B consists of stopping by campus first, to meet with a literary agent; it's part of a program set up by the directors of the writing program you have been attending for the last two years. The format is open, though—you could easily skip off to Boston with an apologetic phone call. Last week, as part of the same program, you met with another literary agent on campus. She was a very pretty brunette with perfect hair who was solid and striking and demure. While you are not demure (as you once overheard a former supervisor say, much to his embarrassment—yes, there was a red face—because you knew from his leaned-in kind of smile that he liked you anyway), you rather enjoy this quality in other females. "Demure" is Southern, high-necked sweaters, pearls, someone who knows when to keep her mouth shut. "Demure" is lady. You are not a lady, not exactly. But your favorite word in the Italian language is, indeed, "donna." Sometimes you relate to this word, feeling the heft of your thighs in shorts when they stick to a vinyl seat or the greasy, bony flatness of your décolletage in V-neck sweaters. Today especially, with your curves and your flowing skirt, you are all woman.

Which is precisely why you should not choose Option B. You are not comfortable yet in this skin. You are getting there, but are still miles away from understanding what, exactly, this means, to be a woman.

OUTSIDE, THE SUN is shining and the sky is blue and limitless, beyond the brick houses, beyond the American flags on the porches, and yes, even beyond the slack telephone wires. The ladies are sitting on their identical suspended white benches, heads now turned toward one another. Now that you are outside, they pretend like they don't even know you're alive. Their profiles are so strong and stark that you feel like you've interrupted something precious, like they are transfixed by their own personal goings-on and aren't *at all* nosy. Why would they be so intrigued by you anyway? Eddy, the downstairs neighbor, is far more interesting, you think, remembering the time he invited you to a barbeque and you almost went, until you heard a fight erupt in the backyard. His voice rang out, presumably directed at the man who was departing, "Oh, yeah? Your wife's a crack whore, and where's my five thousand dollars?" The next morning, you saw Eddy on the front steps and gave a mostly sincere apology for missing the party, to which he responded, Budweiser in hand, "You missed a gooooood time." Yes, Eddy is surely more interesting than you, some small-boned, nameless blond girl with blue eyes whose bedroom light goes off around nine most nights and who, thanks to two back-to-back, ridiculous-in-their-own-ways long-distance relationships, has barely had sex for the past eighteen months, if you don't count the self-servicing. (And you don't.)

You make a point to look up at the ladies until they look back. Despite carrying a heavy overnight bag and unsuccessfully balancing a cup of coffee, you wave, knowing that this gesture isn't genuine, that this full palm-raising just as easily could have been your middle finger. They nod. Eddy comes rambling down the sidewalk, gut hanging over his cut-off shorts, in his leisurely every-day-is-Sunday swagger, complete only when you notice the cigarette butt dangling out of his mouth. "Hey, doll," he yells at you, as you walk toward him to get to your car. "When're we gonna hang out?"

All is normal.

As familiar, though, as this landscape is, you know you can't stay here forever, and so Option B rises from the rubble of indecision as the winner.

THE AGENT'S NAME is Jack. His is printed above yours, which is scrawled next to the number "1." So you are Jack's first appointment of the day and, even though you aren't focused on writing or your career at the moment, a small thrill washes over you. *First.*

The fifteen-minute drive from your house had been glorious. Heading through the stretch of the Bronx where there are beach reeds and sun and sky on the right and sterile towers and bleak strip malls and industrial vistas on the left, you'd done what you always do: squinted your left eye and looked to the right, just far enough to enjoy the space and yet not too far to have an accident. The drive is familiar to you, since you've done it many days over the last two years. Sometimes you have moments on this stretch, heading home at sunset, and remembering other moments—an amorphous stress that went away with the spread of pink clouds, an excited thought of seeing your now-ex-lover that seemed to gain momentum in accordance with this highway's curves—that were not more or less than any other ordinary moment in your life, but you've had enough of them, on this road, to think that they should add up to something. You shake your head at the implausibility of having memories about the present, in the present.

But that's exactly where you are when you run into the graduate center, dressed in the flowing skirt, gold lamé flats, and a belly-exposing shirt, worried that you might be late. From the information sheet, you see that Jack's meetings are all being held in the front room. You pause for a moment to brush the wisps of your dark blond hair out of your eyes and take a deep breath. Breaths can be long and your thoughts drift to all the fun you'll be having later in Boston with Annabelle, the large iced tea that you will purchase before getting on the road, driving by your favorite bridal shop in town. These are all pleasing thoughts, but nothing is more pleasing than the vision of your perfect silk shift wedding dress and the surest knowledge that you will not have the occasion to wear it anytime soon. You are still relieved, very relieved, to have dodged that bullet.

"Jack?" you say, when you walk into the front room and see a man standing near the far windows. The room—with its fireplace and couches and lone computer—is otherwise empty: all the students have gone.

He smiles, big. *He's done this before,* you think. You walk toward him, your hand already extended, as he says your name back. It is not posed as a question.

You continue to move closer and suddenly the panic has set

in so acutely that he might as well have a fuzzy circle over his face, the kind that court TV uses to preserve witnesses' identities. Despite having devoted the last two years of your life to writing, despite the fact that you haven't yet figured out a plan to start repaying hefty loans, you have prepared nothing.

After a minute of awkward, standard pleasantries, he looks at you and says, "We should go outside." Again, not posed as a question.

"Kind of warm in here," he elaborates, loosening his tie.

You turn on your heels toward the door and try to remember what it is that you're trying to sell to him, going over the list of five book ideas in the generic agent-letter you wrote. He has read them, plus your samples, probably recently, and you haven't even considered what it is you might like to talk about. As you hold the outside door open for him, you take in his dress: lavender shirt, with matching tie just one shade darker, well-tailored navy suit. He's tallish, preppy-looking, with green eyes, a full Roman nose, and mid-length dark hair that he tucks behind his ears. You surprise yourself with the thought, *So not my type.*

Once you've spilled outside to the green lawn and you're both situated on a stone wall, energy comes from nowhere. Maybe it's the sun or the cloudless blue sky. Maybe it's the premise of this meeting that you haven't done crap for. Your head is dizzy and you are buoyed by this feeling that comes up every now and again, a feeling that you are not quite in control of what might come out of your mouth next; yet this feeling, when it surfaces, always seems like the most delightful thing that's ever happened to you. Every time. Something else takes over and you're suddenly saying things that are probably not appropriate, like telling people at a work function about the time you were arrested for disorderly conduct or responding with the exact truth when asked what you're talking about, even when the topic is as off-color as anal sex and you even have the audacity to term it "butt-fucking." Yep, this is one of those times. God help you. No, on second thought, God help *him.*

"So," he says, a smile poised on his charming face. "The good news is . . ." He's pausing here, sitting quiet and still for dramatic effect. You look at him, eyes wide.

". . . you can write."

Any other day, this might have bothered you and your internal dialogue would have then become really loud, as in, "Uh, duh. You *are* meeting me as part of the writing program I've been enrolled in for the last two years." But the volume of snarky-you is turned very low today and so all you say is, "Thank you," but not in an overly grateful way.

At this, he says with a postured familiarity, his head cocking to the side, "So tell me . . ."

When you were a little girl you had friends, more than one, who would ask you during sleepovers, just before bedtime, "Will you tell me a story?" There was a quiet confidence then, your head not wanting to rest on the hard floor of another family's house. And you, so happy to have been asked, so unfamiliar with taking center stage because at your own home you were too busy observing the laundry list of why the needs of everyone else in your family all seemed so much greater than yours, you would say with a cowgirl's swagger, "Pick a topic. Any topic." And whether it was butterflies or brothers or barbeques, you would talk, talk, talk, noticing as your friend drifted off to premature sleep—almost immediately. Yet you continued on because the story was far from over.

So when Jack, hands folded carefully in his lap, asks you about boxing—the topic on which you wrote your thesis—you talk nonstop. The stories come so easily, are so rehearsed in your head that this process, entertaining people, doesn't require that all-obstructing presence of thought. You spew details: the all-women's gym in Boston, with the teacher whose occasionally soft voice belied her combat boots and weathered face; the unusually sunlit gym in Prague, where no one spoke English except for one adorable young man with green eyes, and his was pidgin at best; the beloved Bronx gym, a mom-and-pop operation whose walls were varnished with years of dried sweat, where your sparring partner was a senior citizen named Willy, who always amused you with the same opening line, spoken in his faint Puerto Rican accent with a mild lisp: "You gonna kick my ass-th today?"

Jack laughs in all the right places. In the offering of more details, you wonder if your stories are really *that* good, or if he's just an easy audience. The difference is meaningless to you. If there were to be a transcript for this conversation, it would reveal nothing of consequence—a laugh here, a "Really?" there. No, what matters, what really matters, is that here you are performing in your über-feminine dress, gypsy earrings dangling, talking about throwing a mean one-two punch and therefore casting yourself—because who else is going to do this for you?—as bold, lighthearted, and, yes, a study in contradictions.

On a less inspired day, you might have looked at him from your perch on the stone wall and, with slumped shoulders, squeaked, "Love me, will you?" For now, you are in love with this version of yourself, and this is enough.

Jack speaks authoritatively about the market for boxing books. He's gently pessimistic. "Publishers tend to like them, but they don't sell."

"But the thesis isn't a book."

He purses his lips and even though his mouth is closed, you can see him running his tongue along the outside of his bottom teeth. Jack, whose agency makes a 15 percent commission on deals garnered for his clients, then responds, "Well, what is, then?"

"Well, I'll tell you," you add with a playful exasperation normally not revealed to strangers.

You fly through the other ideas, the ones that Jack is sure to dismiss. There's your fascination with human rights workers, secondary traumas they encounter on the job, and how this potentially complicates the way they see themselves in the world. (Here you are able to drop in the bit about spending a month in Africa.) There's the desire to follow the first U.S. Women's Olympic Boxing Team on their historic journey. (Here you are able to drop in the bit about traveling to Colorado for the sole purpose of attending the USA Boxing Nationals.)

Jack nods and offers occasional feedback, for example, "That sounds . . . interesting."

But he is waiting for something else, the last idea on your list, the one that was improbable just last week, the one you'd only decided to include at the last minute for the sole reason that people seemed to like it. You have spent the last week telling yourself that this idea—as dissimilar as it is from all of your others—is something you could spend a little time with, at least until you figure out what it is you really want to write about. After two years of school, the only answer you can come up with when people ask you what you want to do is, "Uh . . . write books?"

Jack is patient. While you hesitate, he tells you about his childhood in the Pacific Northwest, sage advice his mother gave him on choosing a college, that he has an unpublished book of his own. In a flash, you see a stark image of the apartment he shared with his ex-girlfriend after college, seeing its loneliness through his eyes, imagining faded white walls that needed paintings, photographs—anything to fill them up. When Jack has shared just enough, you realize you like him and his easy, familiar way. A lot.

So you start from the beginning. This book isn't even your idea. One night, you came home from the gym, stood there in your sweaty clothes, and couldn't wait to tell Davida, your full-figured Puerto Rican roommate with impeccable posture, about your latest gaffe at the gym. This time, it involved a hasty snack before your workout: two underripe pears. You didn't realize that these two underripe pears didn't really agree with you until you were exactly three minutes into jumping rope in the windowless, and therefore stuffy, gym.

Jack looks on with amusement, so much that any vestige of reason has officially evaporated from your mind. Is it you, or is he sitting even more rapt than before?

You jump up in your puffy skirt and start to mime your most recent embarrassing moment.

Almost winking, you say, "I have a lot of these, you see."

Davida has pointed this out, on numerous occasions. In the midst of her trumpet-ringing laughter ("hahaha-haaaaaaaaa, hahaha-haaaaaaaaa"), she told you that you should put together a collection of funny, embarrassing stories. Maybe Colin Powell had one, when, during a very important meeting—possibly with the Queen of England—he struggled to keep control of his bowels? Maybe Donald Trump's hairpiece had blown off in the middle of a busy New York street, only to be nabbed by a bichon frise being walked by some old lady? Davida was laughing hard. A novelty book, she said. Funny, embarrassing stories—something you'd see by the checkout counter of Urban Outfitters. Everyone will be able to relate. She even gives you the title: *Oh, Shit!*

You're standing before Jack, reenacting the jump-rope scene, and how you blamed your gas on Ron, the older heavy man who was known throughout the gym for his distinctive scent—and not in a good way. Ron, always working out in his high-water khakis and scuffed loafers one size too big, is one of the nicest people you know. And still, when the knots in your stomach were undeniable, you scooted closer to him while keeping pace with the click of your plastic rope, a completely unprovoked action. He was shadowboxing in his characteristic slow-motion way, and as he was throwing a left jab, his nose wrinkled. Arm hanging, he moved only his head, ever so deliberately in your direction, staring for a long minute before walking away. You felt terrible. Even if you farted in the face of your trainer, he never would have believed it was you anyway. You're a girl, a cute girl, and girls just aren't supposed to do things like that.

You are pleased with yourself, telling this story to Jack and owning up to your uncouth ways. Somewhere far beyond this moment, this meeting, you think you're a riot. Life is not the

carefully followed recipe it seemed to be when you were deciding whether or not to break up with your fiancé; no, life is an
amusement park, and you have a map of all the fun rides.

Somewhere, mid-pretend skip, you see Jack sitting there.
On a mini-scale, it's like your daily walk to the subway, where
you just try to get from point A to point B, until one day, small
pieces of your everyday surroundings—fake ivy on a storefront,
Art Deco design on the corner apartment building—emerge in
relief, as if you'd never seen them before. Good lord, Jack is
appealing. You see him as a world unto himself and you wish
you hadn't been talking so much. His chin is arched in your
direction. His eyes are open, even smiling. His legs are crossed
wide and everything about his body language is saying, "I'm
here." There is something in his eyes that tells you that, despite
the (presumably standard) engaged face he put on from the
start, this is no ordinary meeting—for you or him. Your need
to know more is great.

You stumble a little, end your story prematurely, and sit back
down, uneasy with your new awareness of Jack.

"Um, yeah, so . . . that's how it started . . ."

His body is close and you see great things, sitting with him
on the stone wall on this brightest day. In this moment, Jack
is not a faceless audience or even a professional connection.
He's actually *thinking* things right now; you see that in his expression. He has gone somewhere else, and you're certain that
he's not making a mental note to pick up his dry cleaning after
work.

Jack is good with the dramatic pause. He stops for a minute,
with a big smile on his face as he refocuses his eyes on you.

"Look"—he clears his throat—"I love it."

This is delightful.

"This could be huge," he continues.

You feel like the time you dove into a hotel pool in Miami and were surprised by a blast of classical music playing underwater.

Jack sees lots of possibility, and even recommends that you look at similar books of compiled stories. His ideas are big and his enthusiasm for your new project, bigger. Was this really happening all because you farted in the gym two weeks ago? To a complete stranger, you have just mimed what it was like to jump rope, have gas, and blame it on the outcast. Oddly enough, you are tickled.

"Okay, then," you say. "I'm going to start collecting stories this week."

The clock is ticking. He's already a few minutes late for his next appointment and so he hands you his shiny black card and says, "Let's get together. I'm away for a couple weeks, but maybe in early June when I'm back."

You thank him, excited. Neither of you can stop grinning.

2

PEOPLE WHO DON'T have embarrassing stories are untrustworthy. Or at the very least they aren't telling the truth.

Last night you got duped into a blind date when your friend Maria called and said that her perfect Italian boyfriend had a perfect Italian business partner and you had to meet him. She warned you that he was shy. But you found Marco, with his confident demeanor and close-talking body language, anything *but* shy. (Which, incidentally, was fine with you.) He'd walked with his hand on your back after knowing you for all of five minutes. *How did she mistake this man for shy?* you thought. But maybe Maria was right, on some level; after all, Marco pleaded the fifth on having any embarrassing stories.

The best moment of the night came before you met Maria and the men. You'd dragged yourself from bed, where you had lain all day with a stack of books and magazines. It was the birthday of Ted, your ex-fiancé, and you couldn't help but remember where you'd been the year before on this very day, at the barbeque held in his honor. At the end of the night, you covered up the pasta salad, kissed him on the cheek, and went to bed as he stayed basking in the backyard spotlight and holding court with his friends that you'd only met that night. Later, a tipsy Ted climbed into bed, curled in toward you, and whispered, "Thanks, baby. That was so awesome." Today, in your bed with your books, you remember feeling happy for him and recognizing it as completely foreign because the happiness was suddenly very far from your own sense of personal satisfaction.

In your head, driving down the West Side Highway on your way to Maria's apartment, you remembered Ted again and wondered with whom he was celebrating this year. Your five-year relationship had ended a little more than nine months ago, and you still weren't over it—despite all your efforts to move on, which had included getting involved with Ondra, the boxer you'd met the summer before in Prague, when you'd gone there to take a writing course as part of your graduate work. In fact, you'd gone to Prague that July without any desire to meet anyone—not even new friends!—because ever since you and Ted had gotten engaged that May, you knew deep down that marrying him wasn't right. Of course, he knew it, too, and so you had spent a miserable couple of months wondering who was going to say it first. Only, your mind was not so clear, which was why you intended on having some much-needed solitude while you were away, to figure things out. But the unexpected happened one afternoon when you walked into a dingy boxing gym in Zizkov and met Ondra, who was already mid-workout, his black shorts and black T-shirt drenched with sweat. Taken by his broad Slav nose and easy demeanor, you didn't argue when, after you changed, he picked up your wraps and started to loop them tightly around each of your hands. Suddenly you had a boxing partner, who had a mean uppercut and gentle spirit. Then one day, looking forward to what had become daily afternoon training sessions, you absently left your engagement band in your room, next to your journal. Despite the denial of your obvious feelings for Ondra, there was regrettable overlap between the two relationships. Before you knew it, you had broken off the engagement to Ted, and nine short months later Ondra was suddenly using the phrase "fiancé visa" (in talking about a move to the States). With this phrase, you broke out in hives and realized, *Well, I guess this needs to end, too.* When it came to committing to another person, you had some serious limitations.

And so there you were, alone on Ted's birthday. Now that the relationship had ended with Ondra, there was a clearing. As you drove down West Side Highway, all of your old feelings about Ted bubbled up to the surface. You were feeling a little melancholy, a lot nostalgic, wondering how long you could last on this blind date with Marco, when you rounded the corner and took in the vastness of the Hudson River. Every single time this view amazes you, the moment your car emerges from the tree-shrouded stretch of road, opening to the view of luminous cityscapes, competing billboards, two distinct states, and one glorious, albeit polluted river. This was no ordinary river, you thought as the pink sky fell all over the horizon. Just then, you decided to turn up the volume on the radio. Rod Stewart sang out, "Young hearts be free tonight . . . time is on your side . . ." You'd never paid much attention to this song before, but all of a sudden *you* were the young person he was singing about. There was time yet, for love—for more heartbreak, even. There was time. You rolled down the windows and tuned out the cars zooming around you, wanting only to cry, and not because you were sad.

The date was fine. Marco was nice, as well as tall and handsome, with curly hair and stylish red-framed glasses. You all went to dinner, and from the start you liked him well enough. He told you about being an engineer, moving to New York after having lived in England, and about his American mother who, with his Italian father, had raised him and his sister outside of Rome. You told him about your new book of embarrassing stories.

At the end of the night you offered to drop Marco at home, since you were driving anyway and since Maria and her boyfriend had already disappeared into one another behind Maria's refrigerator. When you pulled in front of Marco's house in Williamsburg, he reached for a pad of paper in your console and scribbled his number on one half, then asked you to write yours on the other half. You were ho-hum about the prospect of seeing him again and he could tell. With a smirk, he said, "I'll try to come up with some embarrassing stories."

"You!" Melody shrieks when she sees you the day after your date with Marco. Never one to hold back, Melody is one of your most outrageous friends, always has been. You haven't seen her in months and in her fancy midtown hotel room, you toast with champagne from her minibar. You sip as she changes from her suit to something more nighttime. Glass in hand, you notice the faded nub of a stuffed animal on her bed.

"You still have that thing?" you say, loud enough for her to hear from the bathroom.

"Wha—" she says as she emerges, her voice raspy. Upon realizing you mean her precious friend, she continues, "What?"

But it's more incredulous and pointed than her first attempt at the question, which had been merely curious. "I travel a lot—and he keeps me company!"

When you smile, one eyebrow raised, she shakes her head and says, voice lowering playfully, "Okay?"

Melody stands there, brushing her long, straight hair. Even though she grew up in Massachusetts, her blond hair, skinny tanned legs, and enviable big breasts scream, "California!"—which is where she now lives. She's here on business, in town for an annual television conference. She placed phone calls to you today from Tavern on the Green and Daniel.

There is a knock on the door. One of the girls in Melody's department needs advice. You overhear her saying, "We have less than twenty-four hours to finalize this deal and now he wants to change everything!"

Melody's voice turns serious. "What did you tell him?"

You don't hear the answer, and suspect it wouldn't make any sense to you even if you did. You tune in to the sirens outside for a minute, then back to the hum of the air conditioner. The girl sounds stressed.

"Well," Melody says, "you just go back and tell them . . ."

After the girl leaves, Melody apologizes, "This job is never-ending."

But you aren't bothered one bit. In fact, you are impressed. Melody now holds a remarkably high position, with a great deal more responsibility than she did the summer you two spent on Cape Cod, wearing walkie-talkies as hostesses at one of the resort area's busiest clam bars. After nights of telling vacationing families to walk down the ramp and take a right at the captain's wheel, you drank beer and skinny-dipped, while spending the days on the beach, floating out to sea on a king-sized air mattress that wasn't exactly meant for the water. On one unusually sad day, she picked you up at the bus station; you were returning from your grandfather's funeral. Looking out the window, you'd said, "I really don't want to go to work today." Before you knew it, she picked up the phone, dialed in to say that you couldn't make it to work that night and, oh, yeah, that she couldn't, either—ever. You spent the rest of the summer playing Trivial Pursuit on your front lawn—where you liked to do solo hits from your homemade gravity bong while gazing at the view of the ocean that would have been idyllic if it weren't for the unsightly Three Seasons Motel across the street, with its stucco walls and swells of unhappy families rambling through the parking lot. Once, you even heard an exasperated father telling his chubby son, "We are having a good time, dammit!"

Every time you see Melody, at some point you both start in on, "Those were the days . . ." But you imagine that for her and her demanding job, this kind of reminiscing means something that you, with your quasi-bohemian life, recent grad school career, and string of nonprofit jobs, can't quite understand.

Outside, you walk toward Central Park. Neither of you cares where you go—you just want to catch up. Cars stream by unnoticed. New Yorkers bustle to and from restaurants, hotels, bars. Souvenir shops are packed with crap and not customers.

A man with dark eyes and a crocheted cap approaches. By now you are standing across from the park and have stopped on the corner to figure out where you should go.

"Let me guess," he says. "You aren't from around here?"

"No," Melody answers. "I'm from California."

"Thought so—in town for the television conference?"

"Yeah!" her face brightens. "How did you know?"

"Just a guess—me, too."

Even though you are, technically, now from around here, you don't say anything. You don't have to. Melody explains everything, and you remember how easy it is, as a youngest sibling, to fall into the steps that older siblings like Melody create.

The man introduces himself as Ben and suggests that if you're looking for a nice, quiet place, the Stone Rose is a decent lounge just down the street. In fact, he's meeting friends there himself. You and Melody have a quick conference with no words and determine that the likelihood of him infringing on your girl-time is slim to nil. He seems nice.

As you walk, he asks Melody more about her job. She asks him about his. You find out that he writes for a flailing new sitcom, a spinoff you've heard about pretty much only for its bad press.

"Oh," Melody and you say at the same time, only she sounds interested and you sound disappointed.

"I used to write for *Roseanne*," he counters, which results in the excited, collective "Oh!" he probably expected in the first place.

The host of our nonparty, Melody gestures to you and tells Ben that you are a writer, too. But you haven't published anything. You are embarrassed a little, which is perfectly ironic when Melody describes *Oh, Shit!* for you.

"Wow, that's great," he says as you three reach the roundabout at Columbus Circle. The Stone Rose is inside the Time Warner Center and as you wait for the light to change, Ben points up to the wall of windows to show you where you will be going. Sunset is five minutes old, and dusk's light reflects off the new building's all-glass exterior. You are standing there remembering the Robert Polidori photographs of this same building, wondering how something so new can seem like it's been there forever, when Ben abruptly turns to you, his hands open in emphasis, "Oh, my God. My friend has the greatest embarrassing story, and he's coming tonight."

"Really?" Both of your eyebrows raise.

As Ben nods his head vigorously, Melody adds, with some false trepidation, "Um, one of her most embarrassing moments happened in front of me."

Ben's presence recedes and you look at her. She's already laughing. There was a time when you forbade her from telling this story (although even then she interpreted that loosely, as in she didn't tell this story to anyone with whom you had the primary relationship). But this is the spirit of the book, coming clean, embarrassing stories as catharsis and entertainment. It's not a closeted embarrassing story anyway. You went through a period of telling it often yourself.

Now, as you look at Melody's big grin, you are aware that the moment that once checked you into the hotel of shame for an extended stay—that very same moment—was still living as one of the great joys of Melody's life, and probably always would.

INSIDE, MELODY ORDERS two glasses of champagne from the bar. Far from just a "decent lounge," the Stone Rose is fancy, its eastern-facing wall of windows overlooking Central Park. As Melody grabs the glasses, you turn your head and admire the full moon, until you are distracted. The waitresses are all wearing short black miniskirts with knee-high boots, and you have to assume that a free gym membership is part of the employment package.

Ben finds his friends, leaving you and Melody to settle in on the bar stools. Moments later, a boisterous man in a suit walks in and greets Ben with a big hug. Ben waves you and Melody over, introduces you briefly, and then says, "So Seth has the best one—come on, Seth, she's writing a book about embarrassing stories."

Without asking any questions, Seth starts—before he even has a drink in his hand. Although Seth is an average-looking guy with brown hair, brown eyes, and glasses, his face is extremely kind. He's the sort of person who looks as if he is always waiting for the right occasion to crack a smile.

"Okay, so, a few summers ago I'm at a Mets game with two female clients and my sister."

"Wait," you ask. "What do you do?"

"Lawyer. So, it's the perfect night. Mets are winning. Company's great, and I have a few beers and hot dogs."

You look slyly in Melody's direction. She's intent on Seth, but you can tell from the half-giggling expression on her face that she knows where this is going, too.

On the way home from the game, Seth drove downtown to drop his sister off first. One block away from her apartment, a sudden pang sharpened in his stomach. He had to go to the bathroom—immediately. Trying to play it cool in front of his clients, he cracked the window of his brand-new Saab convertible with leather interior and took a deep breath. But the pain didn't go away. Against his fervent wishes, a little poof of gas escaped. With his window now rolled way down and the pro-liferation of Dumpsters on the street, Seth figured he was safe. By the time he was parked in front of his sister's house, he realized that he couldn't just run up to use her bathroom because he was wearing shorts and now uncertain that the earlier pains were merely gas. Whoever made up the edict "Never trust a fart in Mexico"—okay, well not exactly an edict, but it should be—could have come up with that brilliance just as easily after having overindulged in concessions at Shea Stadium.

Seth started to sweat. He said a hearty goodbye to his sister, while silently cursing the extended conversation she was having with one of the clients. *Yeah, yeah,* he thought, *who fucking cares about emailing the name of your fucking hairdresser? If this conversation doesn't end soon, you're going to need the name of her therapist, too.*

Maintaining his composure—with the exception of sudden jerky movements—Seth finally drove away and tried to make small talk: "So, ah, tell me about your trip to Kauai."

The short ride to Chelsea was challenging. The gas pains were coming in more frequent waves and Seth found himself leaning back involuntarily. When he got to their neighborhood, Seth pulled over. At this point, he was sure that they at least smelled something.

When one of the clients leaned in to give him a kiss, he put his hand up abruptly.

"Night!" he said, as if there were an unspoken rule about not engaging in physical affection when one has poop in his pants, or, um, shorts.

As soon as the ladies were safely on the street, Seth sped away, moving quickly block by block, running red lights and taking illegal right-hand turns on red. By the time he got to the West Side Highway heading north to his apartment on the Upper West Side, Seth was nearly folded in half in front of his steering wheel. Sixty more blocks to his bathroom, Seth looked up at the full moon hanging in the sky and thought, *Please God . . .*

Lucky for him, Seth's God answered. Somewhere in between stomach spasms and now-audible yelps for help, a calm arose in Seth: *I can let go now.*

With that, he did, relinquishing control of his bowels and going number two all over his fine all-leather interior. Still driving, Seth felt an incredible sense of relief. At least the pain was over.

When he pulled off the highway, Seth was eager to get rid of the newly soiled clothing. He stopped his car on Riverside Drive, rolled down the window, lifted his body up just enough to wipe away the evidence with the dry spots on his shorts, and threw the clothing into the park.

Since it was late on a Sunday night, Seth figured that no one would be walking around in his neighborhood, that he could park his car and race up to his apartment half naked. But Seth seemed to forget momentarily that this is New York—late is never as late as you think, even on a Sunday.

Crap, he cursed when he drove up Columbus and realized that there were still plenty of weekend revelers walking the streets. Couples strolled home arm in arm from restaurants. Old ladies were walking their dogs. A frustrated father walked his crying baby in a stroller, hoping that movement would quiet the child.

In another panic, Seth pulled up in front of his apartment building with an idea. Fortunately, his residence had a doorman.

"Psst! Mamadou! Hey, Mamadou!" Seth yelled out of his window at the doorman, who always appeared positively at attention, even when no one was looking.

Mamadou walked over to Seth's car, but before he got too close, Seth said, "You're never going to believe this. Someone stole my shorts!"

"Oh, my," said Mamadou, his face frowning in concern.

"Yeah, listen, can you run up to my apartment and grab me a towel?"

"Poor Mamadou," you say to Seth. By this time, the four of you—Ben, Melody, Seth, and you—are huddled together, the circle only opening when one of you takes a step back to make room for your laughter. Or get further from the idea of imagining the horrors that Seth has just described; you're not sure which. When Seth tells you that Mamadou hasn't looked at him the same since, you ask, "And a towel? Why not ask for another pair of pants?"

"Look, you don't exactly think clearly in these situations."

"She knows," Melody says with a giggle.

After giving Seth's story its appropriate due, Ben turns and says to you, "Wait—so what's yours?"

You are not so in the mood to share. Somewhere over the last ten years, this story stopped inspiring the amusement it once had. Now it's just gross. But since you initiated this conversation, you can't back down now.

"Well . . ." you begin, taking a gulp from your nearly empty champagne glass. "When I was nineteen—"

"Sure, try to blame it on youth!" Melody says. When you

shoot her a look, she says sweetly, "Another round?" and lifts her index finger to the bartender to indicate more champagne.

When you were nineteen, you had some troubles. You don't tell your new friends this part, but it was a difficult time. You were confused about who you were and what you wanted out of life. After growing up in a middle-class suburb, your first year at an expensive college proved unsettling, to say the least; once, during your first semester, you did the math and discovered that 45 percent of the females on your floor had already had some form of plastic surgery—nose jobs, liposuction; one particularly frail girl had even had her hip bones shaved. One of these girls had once referred to you, to your face, as "the pretty girl," and since you took this to mean that she didn't find you at all interesting or funny, you took her comment as a personal slight. When you met Melody, you began to feel some semblance of comfort again. Sure, Melody is a bombshell, and she's also smart. Ever opinionated, she has been known to launch into a heady, in-depth analysis of why physical humor makes her laugh so much and why, sometimes, in the face of very dark things, laughter is the only response.

Melody passes you a drink and nods to encourage you. You tell Seth and Ben about that summer briefly, mentioning your irresponsible party-girl ways. They stand there, waiting. Abruptly turning to Seth, you say, "Well, let's just say . . . ah, I did what you did!"

"Whoa, whoa, whoa," Melody says, waving her hands. "Are you going to deny me the joy of hearing this story all over again?"

Remembering the very moment you'd lost control of your own bowels, thanks to a vicious hangover and upset stomach, you start to tell the story, very reluctantly. After all, you *had* lost it in the front seat of Melody's car, while she was driving. The smallest part of you still feels like you owe her.

By the time you are finished with all the graphic details—the basics of which are extremely similar to Seth's story—your new male friends are laughing, but not as much as Melody. You're glad she's here because the success of this story is largely dependent on *someone* being amused. She tells you not to forget about what happened when she finally got you back to her grandmother's house.

"Oh, you mean how you drove the rest of the way home laughing with your head out the window?"

"Yeah, that and how my cousin Alan from Ireland was looking out the front window, waiting for us."

You add that, after you'd spent a good three hours in the bathroom cleaning up, you emerged to find two melon-scented Yankee candles lit on the floor just outside of the bathroom and how, at that very moment, Melody just happened to be walking by with a lit stick of incense and a spray can of Lysol.

"Oh, hey," she'd said, feigning innocence. "Everything okay in there?"

LATER, SETH PULLS you aside and you spend some time talking about lust, boxing, and then finally *Oh, Shit!*

"This is really great!" he says. "Not only is it funny, but it's also a way of talking about something that no one wants to talk about."

You elaborate, telling him that this is exactly why you're doing it, acutely aware that some of this is B.S., considering

that you haven't done any work on the book yet. Seth interrupts.

"Can I tell you something?" he asks.

"Sure." You brace yourself.

"In the strangest of ways, I kind of feel like I've just had sex
with you."

Any other day, in any other bar, this would have felt like
a pick-up line. But looking out through the spacious windows, you get an unexpected glimpse of this new project. The
moon—you never see the moon like this in New York—is slung
low over the treetops in Central Park.

When you don't say anything, only smile, he asks, "Do you
feel like that—I mean, after having shared your story? After all,
these are kind of intimate."

"Well, honestly," you say, "no. I do not exactly feel like that."

He doesn't know that, for you, because of the number of
times you've told this story and others of its ilk, you don't really see it as all that personal or even embarrassing anymore.
To you, embarrassment is the extreme dismay that arises when
something you've so desperately hoped to conceal is revealed—
and not by your own choosing. Stories like these, though, over
time eventually stand on their own as just mere facts of a life.
Gross facts, but facts nonetheless.

3

Now you're the expert. Between your family and friends, a big game of telephone has begun and now everyone wants to tell you his or her most embarrassing story. Your mother calls you to say, "So, I went to get some chili at Wendy's . . ." This week on the news, there's been lots of publicity about a woman finding a severed finger in her very own yellow Wendy's chili container, but you decide not to mention it. What your mother hasn't heard won't hurt her—you hope. Your mother is easily the most excitable person you know. Always, always, she is enthusiastic about her ideas, like the time she got jazzed up to tell you the myriad ways she planned to cook the pot roast she got on sale at the local A&P, for the low, low price of $2.69 a pound. ("Can ya beat that? What a deal!") In every email she sends you, there is at least one sentence that is written in ALL CAPS. Recently, she called to tell you that she'd seen the editor of the *Paris Review* on *Charlie Rose*, extolling the virtues of nonfiction. "There's hope for you!" she'd screamed excitedly into the receiver, fully intending this to be encouraging. Often, her unbridled delivery makes you smile—which is exactly what you do when she calls with this latest story about Wendy's chili.

She's chatty, and instead of taking notes, you opt to focus on how nice it is of your mother to take such an interest in your work.

One morning, Dan calls with a good one. Dan is your best friend, the person you've known longest on this earth ever since the date of your birth, when you two "met" in the hospital nursery. Dan was one day old. When you are together and people ask how long you've known one another, either you or Dan cites this history, in the most specific terms possible. And then you both sigh and look into each other's eyes, as if to say, "Hey, you. How's my soul mate?" Dan is a bright and upright man, who also happens to be a real charmer. Ten years ago, you'd walked with him through a department store and watched in awe as saleswoman after saleswoman turned his way either to wink or wave or say, "Hiiiiiiiiii, Danny." Of course, this is an old memory of Dan, who was just a teenager at the time. But the point is this: he is witty, good-hearted, and easy to adore. Today, Dan lives in Berkeley, where he studies architecture. Daily conversations are alternately mundane (Dan's curry recipe, how you might let your hair grow longer this year); philosophical (are there substantive differences between the love one has for one's family and the love one has for one's friends?); emotional (the appalling dearth of public-space recycling receptacles in New York City!); supportive ("Tell that ho to leave you alone!"); and goofy (in-jokes, such as singing "On the Road Again" with a faux-French accent . . . *just can't wait to get on ze road again* . . .). In short, you love Dan to pieces and if you two weren't orientationally discordant you'd be married by now. But facts are facts: you like men and so does Dan. On this particular day, he calls you when you're at home sitting on your bed: "Want to hear something funny?"

Like you would ever say no. You put aside the stack of bills you've been flipping through. "Well, yeah."

The night before, he had been hanging out with a group of people at the Bear's Lair, a favorite Berkeley haunt. One of his classmates, a young woman named Marcy, was nervous because she was going to meet the girlfriend of her crush, also one of their architecture colleagues. Marcy knew that John had a girlfriend, but her crush-from-afar was a source of giddy, innocent joy—the last thing she wanted was for Stephanie, his girlfriend, to come along and ruin her little fantasy of John's all-consuming love for her—which, clearly, based on their limited interactions in the studio, had no footing in reality. So, when a group of people met up for drinks last night after class, Marcy tried to act nonchalant when she heard that John was on his way—with Stephanie. Upon their arrival, John introduced Stephanie to everyone, and Marcy, in a very poor effort to act "cool," thrust out her hand and said with a tad too much exaggeration, "Hi! I'm *Stephanie!*"

Relaying this story to you as he's driving, Dan says, "How Freudian is that? I felt so bad for Marcy. She basically shouted, 'I'm in love with your boyfriend!' "

Though you don't know Marcy, you cringe *for* her.

"Anyway," Dan says, "how are you?"

Thinking comparatively—silently glad you're not Marcy—you say, "Fine. Just fine."

AND EVERYTHING IS fine, more or less. You're embarking on this new, postgraduate chapter of your life. You've finished school and secured a temporary gig at a premier health organization, working in research and proposal writing. You don't love fund-raising but hope that the job will provide you with enough security while you get the rest of your life in order. It will only be a matter of time until *Oh, Shit!* is in good enough shape to whip into a proposal and be sold. In your head, you keep the very ambitious goal of having it finished by summer's end. And then you can get going on the other ideas you've been wanting to explore.

Temp, schmemp, you think.

You remember a moment, weeks before, in the final meeting you'd had with one of your professors; you'd looked at her, her face so free of wrinkles that you wondered how it was that she could be any older than you. Hoping for advice, you told her about *Oh, Shit!* You knew this was probably not highbrow or literary enough for her to get excited, but you were still fishing for encouragement. Her eyes moved distantly across the room, where an empty birdcage hung near the wall of books. She said, "Well, then it seems like you've got the next phase of your life pret-ty well mapped out."

Even though, yes, that's what you were going for—a plan— the reality is this: it is now the beginning of June, and although you have a handful of stories, you have no real strategy and have produced no actual writing. To make matters worse, the newly unattached you just wants to have fun and enjoy the balmy weather. Since breaking up with Ondra, you have officially freed yourself from all romantic obligations—a feeling you haven't had since long before you met Ted. On one level, this freedom bleeds into every area of your life, heightening your aversion to anything that could be construed as mandatory, necessary, requisite, or compulsory. Hell, you haven't even picked up a newspaper or listened—with any kind of real engagement—to public radio in weeks. Lucky for you, summer is about to hit full swing, just in time to complement your carefree, untethered mood. Suspecting that you aren't going to be writing anything (of consequence) anytime soon, you still want to make an effort, however minor. So you pick up the phone and call Jack.

You're sitting in front of your therapist and the topic of *Oh, Shit!* comes up, because you're going to meet Jack after your session ends. Elaine has never been one to hold back. In her middle age, she is petite and pretty, with an expressive face. Elaine is very generous with you and has been a helpful influence, even if you sometimes question her rambling messages on your answering machine that go on to explain that she was out of the office because her two-year-old daughter had a doctor's appointment. You knew all of two personal bits about your last therapist, Dr. Nick, whom you'd seen for six years: he liked opera and he had a cat. You discovered the latter piece of information during a phone session, when you heard a "Meow!" in the background.

Elaine's mouth twists, ever so slightly, when you say that you are writing a humor piece about embarrassing stories. Your eyes drift off to her bookshelf, and you pretend to be interested in the same titles you've perused for the six months you've been seeing her. You notice a heavy incidence of the eating disorder variety.

"Well," she counters, "I can think of a lot of embarrassing things that people would not find funny."

You nod your head, buying some time while you try to figure out which corner of the human mind she's coming from.

"Yes, of course," you say, the false assuredness in your voice implying that you've already drafted the *Oh, Shit!* manifesto (which, by the way, you haven't).

"I mean, I have this one patient who's, like, the most beautiful woman you've ever seen," she continues, her head shaking in vigorous emphasis. The last part of the sentence sounds like *beautifulwomanyouveeverseen.*

"Uh-huh," you say, wondering when it is you're going to get back to the talk of planning your life after school. Transition—and heartbreak—brought you to Elaine in the first place, when you were trying to figure out what life in this new city, without Ted, was going to look like. Ignoring the fact that life is a perpetual transition, one phrase has infiltrated almost all of your thoughts: *Once I am settled . . .*

"I mean, *beautiful,*" Elaine continues. Again, more emphatic.

"Uh-huh . . ."

"And she was born without a leg, which is, in fact, a great source of shame and embarrassment, and—"

"Elaine," you interrupt. "I'm asking people about funny things that have happened *to* them. If the person doesn't offer it as something they now see humor in, it doesn't fit."

In your head, you try to guess the root of Elaine's disapproval. Does she really think that you'd include a story in which someone tells you she saw the "funniest" thing, a woman without a leg who got herself into some silly jam? Elaine doesn't know you that well, but surely she knows you well enough to realize that you aren't *that* much of a jerk. Besides, you have been in therapy for a good portion of your adult life, long enough to know that you aren't supposed to worry about your mental health professional judging you.

"No. I know. I know." Her voice sounds weary. She's not accusing you of anything, and yet there is something about *Oh, Shit!* that has struck a nerve.

You stare at her.

"It's just . . ." She sighs, not ready to let it go.

You take an upright stance, sitting across from her, where you can see her empty Diet Coke cans and Starbucks iced coffee containers next to her chair by the window. You take in a small breath and make a conscious effort just to listen to whatever it is that she has to say, even if this whole conversation is beginning to annoy you.

"There's just a lot of things in this world that people are ashamed of—sexual traumas, weird family situations—things that aren't at all funny. I see it all the time in here." She gestures around her office, seeming to forget that you, the client sitting right in front of her, have spent most of your time "in here" talking about your own "weird family situations."

When you say nothing, she adds, "That's just something that, you know, I'd want you to be . . . aware of."

You have fully tuned her out at this point, and have chosen to sit there wondering what about the topic is bothering her so much that she had made all these associations and assumptions without actually having asked any questions. From what you know about Elaine, this is unusual.

Her mouth is still moving, her gestures becoming stronger. *Nah,* you think. *She's just worked up.*

When your session ends, you are relieved, even excusing yourself a few minutes early. You wonder if this line of questioning is a strategy of Elaine's—are you supposed to confront her now? Is this about your way of slowly processing the events around you and coming, sometimes very late, to useful conclusions?

You've explained nothing to Elaine about the feel-good, cathartic element of *Oh, Shit!* or the fact that, by talking about things that were formerly traumatizing and viewing them in a more humorous light, it's a lesson in how not to take oneself too seriously. This is fine. You don't pay your therapist to brainstorm about your work.

That's what Jack is for, only you're not paying him and you're not sure how interested he actually is. Over the phone, he told you not to worry too much about talking to people about *Oh, Shit!* It is a unique idea, yes, but you have to get your stories from other people. It isn't exactly the kind of thing you can keep under wraps. After taking the elevator to the lobby and waving goodbye to Frank the elevator guy, you pick up your cell to call Jack. You leave a message that you are on the Upper West Side and you're hopping in a cab. You'll be there in a few.

WHEN YOU WALK into the Algonquin's lobby, you are flooded with memories. Hotel lobbies are fun in general, and this one has never disappointed you, with its antiques, Oriental prints, and dim lighting. When you peer over the partition between the lounge and the front desk, you see Jack, sitting alone at a table for two. He's wearing a button-down again and mindlessly fingering the base of his martini glass. Before he sees you, you yank down your black pants, which have bunched up around your upper thighs. You wish that they were just a hair looser—

since finishing your thesis, you've been boxing with less frequency and eating with abandon. At least your top is not too revealing, you think, thankful for your pink blouse's high neck. You'd like for Jack to take you seriously, even if you are meeting him at seven-thirty for a drink at a hotel.

You nearly trip over the fluffy gray cat near the bellhop, which throws you off balance. Jack spots you just as you are regaining your stride.

He stands immediately, and greets you with a kiss on the cheek. You are happy for some familiarity, even if Jack is still a mystery to you. You know he is charming and handsome and . . . not much else.

"I love this place," you say, as you hoist your heavy bag from your shoulder and place it on the back of your seat. "The magazine selection in the rooms is killer."

He raises one eyebrow—a quirk you will come to adore— and you explain, "I stayed here once, after a wedding in Woodside, Queens, at Donovan's Pub."

You don't mention that you had stayed here with Ted, when you were both living in Boston—or that you and Ted had some of the hottest sex of your five-year relationship in one of those rooms with the killer magazine selection.

"Great wedding," you say instead, with the confidence of someone who has a subject to avoid. "Bride and groom were in their sixties and neither had ever been married. The feeling was that there was no other reason, except true love, to do it now . . ."

With the mention of "true love," Jack's expression turns from polite interest to genuine appreciation. He has a sweet, faraway look on his face. Clearly a romantic. "That's wonderful," he says.

You like when he says "wonderful." His voice is strong, velvety, with the smallest undercurrent of vulnerability. You see awe in his eyes, and are not sure if it's because he likes the idea or if he's thinking of something else.

The tuxedoed waiter approaches and you order a beer.

"Um, anyway," you say after the waiter walks away, "how are you?"

"Oh, it's been the busiest week," he tells you, sighing. "Look at these bags under my eyes. I mean, this is *ridiculous.*"

His delivery is amusing. With a smirk following his comment, he seems to be aware that it is not, in fact, ridiculous for someone living and working in New York, one of the most overworked cities in the world, to look worn-out. Indeed, there are circles under his eyes, but no more than would be average for a man his age—you're guessing late thirties, early forties. Besides, none of this detracts from his appeal. In fact, you have one of those involuntary flashes where you see yourself giving him a hug and telling him that everything is going to be okay.

When you nod, he adds, "This week has been so hectic. Last night, there was a book party. Plus, I have two clients visiting from out of town. Just can't escape my work."

You pause for a minute—you *could* feel guilty, since you, too, are technically hoping to become one of his clients. But Jack cuts short your Catholic tendencies by saying, "Hey, I can't complain. I love what I do."

When he says the last line, about loving what he does, you notice that he shakes his head, and even sounds a little Southern, despite the fact that you know he's not. Conversation moves quickly, and not in a task-oriented manner. He talks about his own past with writing, how his first job out of college was in the mail room at a prestigious agency, how he really, really doesn't like exercise. You tell him about your disconnectedness with your family, but you don't go into detail. You don't admit that, actually, at this point in time, you feel very disconnected from them. In your head, there is a deeply embedded belief that if you don't have an absolutely swimming relationship with all of them, then you are flawed, very flawed, and therefore unworthy of any kind of intimacy. Even though with this thought you've screwed yourself straight out of the gate, you are not about to go into specifics with Jack—or anyone—because, frankly, you still don't get it. You don't understand the disconnection, mostly because you've spent so much time being overly connected, at least emotionally, to the point where, in certain memories, you're not even sure where your feelings begin and their feelings end. For example, David, your brother closest in age, was diagnosed as a young child with some amorphous "developmental disability," one that you never really understood the nature of, except to understand that he needed to be enrolled in special education classes in school. You heard your mother explain it to people, and you recall half sentences: "Well, it's not Down's Syndrome . . ." And usually after that people were too polite or timid or confused to follow up with, "And so then?" If someone did press, you also recall, "Well, he's really highly functioning . . ." Early on, you wore your mother's confusion, her heaviness, as your own.

Instead of going there, you tap-dance a bit—which, incidentally, you are very good at—retelling your favorite moment of family therapy with your parents and siblings, as adults. You'd gone reluctantly, at the insistence of Ray, your oldest brother, who wanted to get together and "talk about how shitty things were." Sure, there was some low-grade childhood dysfunction that could be aired (along with a whole host of issues that no one was talking about, good Catholics that you are, but that kind of information doesn't generally serve a snappy, pleasing anecdote told to someone you're trying to impress). You know, stuff like that your family tradition on Thanksgiving was not having turkey (necessarily) but watching Pink Floyd's *The Wall*. Okay, that was weird, especially since you were young enough for the meat-grinder scene to be unnerving. (In those days, you were a Goody Two-shoes who prayed for homework, i.e., you never would have uttered the words, "We don't need no education.") But back to your favorite moment in family therapy: it was the very first one, before anyone had started crying or yelling or rolling his or her eyes or even laughing—which did, in fact, happen on occasion—before the therapist had even come in to say, "Welcome, everyone." In your best estimate—and you are ninety-nine percent sure that this is not mere projection—you'd guessed that everyone in the room wished he or she were somewhere else. Everyone except your mother—who, not incidentally, had played a role in many of the alleged "traumatic" incidents that would likely be discussed in this room. ("That time when I was eight and I overheard you saying that I was built like a Mack truck was so *not* cool . . . Mom.") Yep, the best moment was long before anyone placed heightened importance on events long past. Happy that her adult children were finally together, your mother's attitude was big and buoyant. As everyone else squirmed and spent an inordinate amount of time looking at the beige carpet, she winked at you from across the room, chin held high, to say, "Oh! Oh! That blue! You look so beautiful in that blue! It's really your color, you know.

Gaaaah-geous." Maybe this comment wasn't "appropriate" to the setting, but your mother is nothing if not funny—and in the context of adult family therapy, you'd gladly taken whatever lightness you could find.

Your signature stories are gaining new life with Jack, who is facing you, rapt. You are used to performing these scenes, preferring to be concerned with cues and timing as opposed to some deeper, possibly Freudian analysis. Isn't that what Elaine is for?

Jack's eyes never veer from yours. The empathy in his face makes you feel understood. What a sweet, sweet face.

Before you know it, you are launching into how things started to disintegrate with Ted after a comfortable courtship, and how eventually cheating on Ted with Ondra had opened the door to one of the most beautiful and difficult times in your life.

"I knew I was a goner when Ondra said in his broken English, 'You must look into my eyes when you hit me.'"

Jack sits back and smiles, still looking at you in *that* way. As you reveal this, you feel your chest rising. This is certainly suggestive, calling into sharp focus *you* as a sexual being. Maybe it's your tight pants—who knows?—but for some reason, you feel like it's okay, even natural, to be revealing so much. Sitting with Jack, you are reminded of being with an old friend and catching up after an extended time apart.

After a few moments of silence, you say, self-conscious, "Um, anyway . . . tell me about you."

Jack nods his head slowly, thinking. "What is it you want to know?"

"Whatever you want to tell me."

So he begins talking about his earliest memories. He paints himself as a trickster, and somehow you have no trouble believing him. The thought of young Jack inspires fondness.

A little while later, Jack asks, "Hey, do you have an iPod?" When you shake your head no, he pulls his out of his bag.

"Ooooh! How fun—I love music!" Somewhere inside you also hear a voice saying, *And romantic candlelit dinners and aimless walks on the beach.*

Jack is standing behind your chair now, overseeing the usage of the iPod. One of his hands rests on the back of your chair. "I love music, too," he says.

He shows you how to browse by artist and album, how to play songs, how to skip ahead. You find an Air album and start to play one of their songs. It's dreamy and melodic.

You declare, "Air is the best music to—"

"Clean your house to?"

Leaning against your chair now, Jack is being playful, though he is careful not to touch you. Ever so quickly, you're growing fond of his nose and how it scrunches every time he says something that amuses him. He has a silly laugh, an infectious laugh, a laugh that is clearly, clearly meant to have company.

"Noooooo," you say. "That's not what I was going to say."

You were thinking about something else, but refrain from saying it aloud, because that would be way too over the top, even for you. Sure, *Oh, Shit!* hasn't come up once, but that doesn't mean you have to sabotage this professional relationship before it has even begun.

As you flip through songs, you offer Jack the other earpiece. Now he's kneeling by your chair and you are having a good old-fashioned sing-along, bopping to nostalgic song after nostalgic song, going different places in your respective minds, but together. You're sure that if you cared enough to look around, people would be staring. Which would only add to your delight.

Every time you try to play a song, you press the wrong button. At one point, Jack grabs the iPod, presses the right button, and says with a smirk, "You have a really hard time following directions, don't you?"

Oh, you swoon. *He gets me . . .*

After twenty minutes, Jack excuses himself to the bathroom. You sit there, your hands folded under your chin, suddenly alone and wondering what in the world was the purpose of this meeting. Seduction by iPod?

When Jack returns, you say flirtatiously, "So, tell me . . ."—your shoulders are twisting in toward him—"this is your job? You just go around charming people and make them like you and—"

"This isn't my job." Jack has settled into his chair and is now looking at you with eyes that have become more intense than playful. There is no trace of a smile on his face.

For once, you are speechless. After three hours and one drink, you have talked nonstop—about Jack's favorite writers, about your love of karaoke, about everything and anything that has popped into your head, with two notable exceptions: (1) *Oh, Shit!* and (2) *So tell me, Jack, do you have a girlfriend?*

You let him pay for your beer, at his insistence.

Outside, you are walking east, in the direction of Grand Central, where Jack will get a cab and you will get the 6 train home. For someone who goes to sleep early, you haven't yawned once, even though the hour is well past your normal bedtime. The streets are wet, after a passing rain to which you have both been oblivious. The talking continues—this time about porn and how the desire to conceal such interests has resulted in the erosion of marriages all over the country. You can't say this is a topic you've ever thought a whole lot about. Ted was anti-porn, even refusing once to enter a topless club with you during a layover in Vegas, for fear of someone looking at substantive-you in an objectified way. (Oh, how this disappointed you!) Still, you nod. Everything Jack says, even the word "porn," is magically cast in a golden sheen.

When you reach the cab stand, Jack lunges toward you. He's not going to kiss you, you can tell. His forward motion is almost involuntary, and it's clear that he wants to; he's just holding back. You are grateful for the restraint, because, despite an obvious chemistry, you are determined to turn this relationship, whatever it is, into a professional one. Kissing would be, uh, bad.

"Night," you say. "Thanks again."

"Quite welcome." He kisses you on the cheek and in an almost-whisper adds, "Get home safe."

4

THERE ARE TIMES in your life that you think, and then there are times in your life that you act, without thinking. The latter times are rare, you being the somewhat neurotic overthinker that you are. But this time, this summer, you have become a doer, at least on the life front. For example, when you have an illicit sex dream about doing it with Woody Allen, you don't waste one second trying to extract a deeper meaning. Instead, you tell a handful of friends, presenting it as an inconsequential detail of your daily life. You let this dream slip to your mother, and even she can't stop making fun of you. "Woody Allen?" she said. "Cripes! That's disgusting."

You still have your day job at the health nonprofit, which is none too interesting. Many days, you belabor two-paragraph thank-you letters to wealthy donors. (Should it read, "Gratefully yours," or "Heartfelt thanks"?) While you don't think that this is the best use of your talents or time, you are pleased that the work isn't mentally taxing. You have other things to think about. Besides, the office culture is nice, as these day-job things go. For a large organization, it is decidedly friendly and positive. Determined to get a deal for *Oh, Shit!* by summer's end, you are sure you won't be here too long anyway. This thought plays over and over as you peck away on the keyboard.

After work one gray-sky evening, you head over to Williamsburg, where you will celebrate the birthday of Henry, whom you once dated for a year. Henry, with his pouty lips and shaved head, is striking. You love him for his goofy sense of humor and his earnestness, which often spills out in spite of himself.

Sometimes you and Henry reminisce about the "old days." Although the time kept passing that year, you never got serious—which was why when he invited you to Puerto Rico to be his date at the wedding of his childhood friend, you were surprised. In the spirit of "What the hell?" you went. The trip had started perfectly. He brought you to an Irish bar in San Juan to meet his brother. The name of the bar, St. Mick's, struck the two of you as ridiculously funny, mostly because someone, somewhere along the line, hadn't realized that "mick" is a derogatory term for an Irish person. Just after, you met his extremely friendly parents; Henry warned you that they were conservative, very Catholic, and would likely assume that you were a serious contender. "No problem," you said, dropping your bags in the guest room.

Since you two had to sleep in separate rooms, at night you snuck out to the kitchen, which was the room farthest from where his parents and grandmother slept, and met Henry in the china closet, where the two of you started fooling around, as you might have with your high school boyfriend. This was no ordinary china closet, though—it was filled with unused furniture and religious knickknacks, all of which were visible through the half-glass partition. But no one had cause to go there in the middle of the night. You'd assumed you were safe.

The next morning, you rose early as always and wandered out to the patio, taking a seat by the pristine aqua pool. You were admiring the vegetation—the wall of hibiscus, the line of palm trees around the yard—when Henry's grandmother pulled open the sliding glass door. Now, she didn't speak English and you didn't speak Spanish, save for a few words here and there. So for a time, you nodded and smiled. She then left for a minute, returning with a plate of fruit, toast, and orange juice. Her hand shook as she gestured toward the plate. You assumed she wanted you to eat. You said, "Gracias," and then felt your anxiety level rise, because she was settling into a chair next to you. She stared while you ate.

When you were finished, she was still looking at you, and you at her.

Wish I could say something.

Twenty minutes passed and you started to curse Henry, who you knew always slept late. You had at least another hour of this.

Just then, Henry's grandmother excused herself. When she walked inside, you were relieved. When she came back a minute later, holding a stack of magazines, you were curious.

She picked up the first one and held it for you to see: *Hola!* magazine. A Latina soap star was on the front cover, someone you'd never heard of. You nodded politely. Then she started to flip through, stopping at a picture of Princess Diana in her wedding dress. She folded the page open and pointed.

"Buena, buena," Henry's grandmother said, her voice rich with adulation.

You nodded, "Sí! Sí! Buena."

This could be fun, you thought—until Henry's grandmother

turned to her next photo, this time a picture of Monica Lewin-sky. *Uh-oh.* This was just around the time that news of her stained Gap dress had been leaked to media outlets. This game with Henry's grandmother was going nowhere good, and fast.

Henry's grandmother tapped furiously with one of her long fingers on the picture, landing near Monica's signature beret.

"Mala!" she said, her voice sounding raspier than you'd re-called. Remembering the night before, you felt your face start-ing to redden. Had she seen something? God, this was all *so* high school, only in high school you had never actually been caught fooling around, and definitely not by anyone's *grand-mother.* She continued, "Mala! Mala!" sounding like she really meant to tell you something. Normally, you could have man-aged a simple, "Entiendo . . ." Only now you are panicked. If she hadn't known about your late-night activities before, all she had to do was look at your expression, which told her every-thing she probably never wanted to know.

In an effort to cover up, you squeaked, "Sí . . . mala . . . mala . . ." and made a silent promise of no more china closet rendezvous—at least not in this house.

HENRY, OF COURSE, thought that this anecdote was funny, then and now, only he tends to focus on Nana and her stack of *Hola!* magazines, never the fact of your fooling around. You'd spoken to him just before going to Zebulon, the dimly lit music café at which you are meeting him and some friends.

You show up in a particularly industrial area of Williams-burg, just a couple blocks from the East River. The street Zebulon is on is lined with abandoned warehouses. Whoever said that parking in New York is a nightmare has never been down here.

Dressed with intention, you are wearing a flirty pink polka-dotted wrap dress and sparkly high heels. You even went so far as to smudge gray glittery shadow over your eyes. After two years of graduate school hibernation, you are ready to dress like you care again. Besides, *Oh, Shit!* is on the agenda and if one of your most embarrassing moments should come up, you at least want to look pretty.

You step into Zebulon. It's a cozy establishment with dark wood walls and illuminated circles hanging from the tin ceiling. Behind the bar, a hot French guy in a worn white T-shirt with a five o'clock shadow does his best to keep pace with orders. The place is full of people, looking so vibrant as they lift their beer mugs and brush up against one another that you have to question where they come from. Surely not the empty, run-down street just outside?

Two hours later, you are sitting with Al and Bill, two of Henry's friends from high school. You and Bill are on stools at the bar, and Al stands next to you. They are fun, these guys. You don't know them all that well, but they are the kind of people you look forward to seeing, for their good humor and general hilarity, so it hardly matters if you haven't seen them in two years.

Bill turns around, his head leaning on his palm. "Check out Henry," he says mildly.

Sure enough, Henry is standing in the middle of the room, the center of attention. Three girls form a semicircle in front of him, laughing as he lifts his shirt up to show them how he can move his slightly pudgy stomach in a wavelike fashion. He does this more than once.

Turning back to Al and Bill, you ask, "So, uh, got any embarrassing stories?" You explain the short version of why.

You are hoping that Al, the long-haired salsero with excitable eyes, will have one. His sense of humor is wacky. You have never forgotten his idea for a Halloween costume, one he came up with years ago, as you sat huddled on the dirty linoleum floor of some random person's apartment, drinking red wine out of clear plastic cups. He thought it would be really funny to dress up as a superhero—complete with tights and cape—and paint a large letter "*T*" on his chest, for "Thesaurus Man!" Although this was just an idea, Al inhabited his superhero with considerable gusto, yelling across the small kitchen, "I am Thesaurus Man! I will kill you!" then, changing his voice a hair, ". . . Or annihilate you!"

But before Al can respond, a short Korean-American woman walks up and places her hand on his shoulder. She's dressed in jeans and a white T-shirt.

"What are you guys talking about?" she asks, grinning.

Al introduces you to Susan, who is the wife of his friend Ben. Al explains to Susan that you are collecting embarrassing stories. Her eyes widen.

"Ooh! I have a great one."

"Great!" you respond.

"But first I'm going to have a cigarette," she says, reaching into her bag for a pack of Parliament Lights. Now it's your eyes that widen.

After asking if you can "bum a smoke"—is there no better way to ask for one?—you follow her outside, and the two of you sit on a bench underneath a small awning. She hands you a light and you take a drag. Ah, you love smoking. You know you shouldn't. But you do.

Susan is not shy. Before you even have a chance to come up with small talk, she begins, "Okay, this happened a very long while ago, but it still makes me turn red!"

"Really? That bad?"

"Well, it's just remembering the moment, you know?"

Turning away from her to exhale, you nod emphatically. You do know.

Susan's most embarrassing moment came when she was working in film production. She lived in Los Angeles at the time, and had landed a job as a crew member for a feature film. Every day she loved going to work, meeting new people, watching the director and actors at work—despite the long hours, this was a dream job. Then, one day, between takes, Steven Spielberg happened to walk on set. It wasn't his movie, so his appearance was a huge surprise to some fans who had been lined up to see the big-name movie stars who had been cast in the leading roles.

A crowd started shouting after Mr. Spielberg, and when he stopped to oblige one woman's request for a photograph—a hysterical request, as Susan remembers—Susan happened to be right there.

"Can you take our picture?" the woman squealed, handing the camera over to Susan.

"Of course!" Susan said, looking through the viewfinder. "Okay, this is going to be good!"

But as Mr. Spielberg and the fan stood there, smiles on their faces, waiting to hear a "click" sound, Susan fumbled with the shutter release button. Why was this happening in front of a three-time Academy Award winner whose films had grossed over eight billion dollars? Susan started to sweat. The seconds ticked on, suddenly feeling like minutes.

"Uh . . ." Susan stalled for time, now lowering the camera to look at it. It was an automatic—a simple automatic camera, made easy for everyone, except for Susan, that is—the crew member with *former* film aspirations.

After another excruciating moment, Mr. Spielberg politely asked to see the camera. He unlocked a button and handed the camera back to Susan.

"Should be fine now," he said to Susan with a nod.

After Susan successfully snapped the picture, everyone dispersed. But Susan wanted to crawl into a hole, a feeling that lasted all day.

Now, outside Zebulon, stamping her cigarette butt on the sidewalk, she groans, "Oh, the horror! To have camera problems in front of Steven Spielberg, of all people!"

"Sounds painful."

"The worst!" she says, her eyes sparkling.

"But it's kind of funny," you add. "The moment was so awful for you, but what does Steven Spielberg remember about it? Not much, I'd bet."

Your own mind trails off, ruminating on why fleeting, uncomfortable moments have such staying power, even years later. Though you've never been a big believer in regret, you appreciate the feeling in Susan's recollection, her own thoughts of, *If only that had worked out differently . . .*

You imagine Steven Spielberg picking up a copy of *Oh, Shit!* at some yard sale in five years and flipping past Susan's story.

What would that be like, to know that one's own stature contributed to someone else's feelings of inadequacy?

"Hey!" Susan says, smiling mischievously as she snaps you back to attention, literally. "So Steven Spielberg doesn't remember my most embarrassing moment. Is that supposed to make me feel better or something?"

LATER ON, YOU'VE said goodbye to Henry and company and are walking toward your car. Although you only had one beer early on in the night, you are drowsy, and the Bronx is so far. There is a row of motorcycles stacked up against one another close to your car. You are looking at them carefully when you see a tall figure walking toward you across the street. His shoulders are hunched over, hands in his pockets, even though it's not cold.

"Marco?" you ask tentatively.

"Hey, you," he says, suddenly recognizing you. "What are you doing down here?"

"Heading home. You?"

"Same. I was just down there at a party."

You remember that he only lives three blocks away. He asks you what brought you to the neighborhood and you tell him. When you mention Henry, his eyebrows raise, but he only says, "Beautiful."

Now you walk with him toward your car, making the same sort of small talk you'd made on your blind date, only this time it feels familiar, in a good way.

"You ever go to Williamsburg beach?" he asks.

You've never even heard of it. He tells you it's two blocks away, that there's a little "beach" with rocks and trees and benches. People congregate there at sunset. He goes there a lot.

"Sounds cool," you say absently, yawning, trying to figure out at exactly what time your head will hit the pillow.

"Want to check it out?"

"Now?"

Shaking his head and shrugging his shoulders at once, Marco says, "Well, I mean, not if you're tired . . ." He says this like it's the most ridiculous thing ever. Marco is European and has different ideas about staying out late.

You are tired. But you also think that summer should mean expanding your ideas about how your night unfolds— something that runs in direct opposition to calculating how long until you sleep. It is only twelve thirty.

"Okay, sounds cool."

You teeter down the street in your heels. After wearing them for five hours, the balls of your feet are sore. You are also chilly, and your teeth start to chatter.

"Mamma mia! It's not that cold," he says. When he says, "Mamma mia!" he looks at you with a tenderness so surprising that you quickly look away.

You nod your head and shiver with abandon, making loud "*Brrrrr*" noises. Marco puts an arm around you, awkwardly at first. The wool of his sweater scratches your bare shoulder. You think about it for a minute and then settle in closer. His body feels awfully good against yours.

"This is funny," you say.

"What? What's funny?"

Williamsburg beach is no beach. At the end of the street, there is an old factory building with broken windows. Opposite the factory is a brick wall. But in between the two is a surprisingly expansive view of the Manhattan skyline, the city lights twinkling against a cloudy sky. Even though the hour is past midnight, the beach is hopping. Teenage couples sit wrapped around one another on the rocks that line the water's edge. A plump middle-aged man holds his wife's hand on a bench. A lone guy eats ice cream and leans against his bike. Marco pulls you by the hand toward a bench, which is somewhat far from the water, but next to a large pillar. You presume it's a monument because there is a plaque.

Sitting down, you suddenly get an idea. It's very dark and you imagine that Marco, growing up in Italy and all, would not know a trick you learned at Brownie camp when you were ten years old: chewing BreathSavers mints in the dark and watching the sparks fly, like mini-fireworks in your mouth.

You just so happen to have a package of BreathSavers in your purse. You say, "Okay, okay, do I have a trick for you!"

He looks curious. You tell him to close his eyes and you stuff five or six mints in your mouth. When he opens his eyes, you sit there, your chin jutting toward his, chewing with openmouthed exaggeration, feeling them crush in your mouth. The more you chew, the more confused he looks. You chew harder, grinding your teeth and opening your eyes, as if that might help.

"What is this?" he says.

"A trick I learned at Brownie camp."

"They taught you how to chew with your mouth open?"

"You didn't see the sparks? Crap! You're supposed to see green sparks when I chew them."

By now Marco is miming right back to you what you looked like. "Aaaaaaarrrr, aaaaarrrr, aaaarrrr," he says, laughing.

"Must have been the wrong kind of mints . . ."

Moving his jaw in a large circular motion, Marco continues, "Aaaaaaarrrrrr, aaaaaaarrrr, aaaaaarrrrrrr . . . you are a very funny girl."

You hear two women behind you, standing near the monument. One of them says, "This must have been the first lighthouse."

Since there is no light, since the pillar is barely on water and it's a cement structure all of twenty feet tall, you and Marco look at one another, trying to figure out why they think this. Looking at his intent expression, you see something you hadn't before.

But before the word "Americans" is out of his mouth, you get a surge of energy and leap over to kiss him.

It's more glorious than you could have imagined, gentle and intense. When he places his palms on your jawline, you pull back to say, "Um, this isn't why I did the mint trick."

5

"YOU WOMEN AND your high heels—it's ridiculous."

You have met Jack seconds ago on the corner of Forty-second Street and Fifth Avenue and already he is critiquing your outfit. Yes, your new white open-toed shoes may seem a little ridiculous, but that's just because they are three days old and you're still sporting a couple of blisters. You limp to keep up and say, "Don't be a hater just because they look good."

"And *wool*? You're wearing a *wool* dress in this weather?"

Jack has a way about him, of expressing extreme incredulity at seemingly minor things. You find it endearing and enjoy being teased.

You are, indeed, wearing a wool dress. It's sleeveless and short. You are very impressed that Jack has taken note of the fabric, even if it's to chide you. He seems to know a lot more about fashion than you.

It's after work, again. You are heading for drinks, again—this time with the specific objective of talking about *Oh, Shit!*

"Here, let me help you," he says, offering an arm on which you can balance. Or try. Tugging on his sleeve, you shuffle beside him.

Lucky for you, you're headed to the outdoor café at Bryant Park. You and Jack have discovered that your respective workplaces are within walking distance from one another, approximately twenty minutes apart. You already know from the feisty email exchanges you've had this week—he's taken to using your familiar nickname and stopped signing his name every time—that the proximity could be dangerous. And fun.

When you take your seats beneath the shade of the trees, Jack suggests wine. You both fancy Sancerre and before you can blurt, "I love you!" a bottle has materialized.

Jack has already had some wine. He's come from a party to celebrate the publication of some celebrity chef's new book. As Jack tells you about his extravagant eight-course lunch, you think that his job is so much more glamorous than yours. Your monotonous afternoon in front of the computer was punctuated only twice: (1) when your high-energy, redheaded boss popped her head around the cubicle to say, "How we doin' on that thank-you letter, kiddo?" and (2) when the maternal middle-aged woman in human resources caught a glimpse of the Salon .com article you were reading about new cybersex technologies, with its headline blaring, *Single, White, with Dildo.*

The day after your last meeting at the Algonquin, you'd hastily typed up a thank-you email to Jack. In direct opposition to the belabored thank-you notes of your day job, you'd written, "Hey, I really like you!" *Click. Send.* To which Jack had responded in less than three minutes, "I really like you, too!"

Not that you need written declaration to confirm your feelings, or his. The rhythm you seem to fall into with him is so comfortable and alive that you've already started to think big. You have so much to learn! The world, as they say, is your oyster.

After only having met Jack twice, you were with your sister, up at a beach in Massachusetts. You and she had limited time, so you drove south from Boston to Nantasket Beach, which would work more for its convenience than its tranquil beauty. While on the beach, you looked around the pebble-strewn, hard-sand landscape, complete with empty fast-food bags that hadn't made it to the garbage can. There was a very large and hairy man plunked in his chair with his legs spread—you had a less-than-pleasing view. The beach was packed with people, and this was the only spot available. "God, that is brutal!" she said, giggling.

In one of those moments when you laugh at someone else's errant body hair and feel immediately guilty for it—because you know you have enough problems of your own—you'd said, "Oh, Annabelle, we're going to hell."

Never one to miss a beat, she winked. "We're already there."

"I love the agent."

Rolling her eyes, she barely looked at you and said, "Can we just say lust?"

This might not be "love," but you don't think it is lust, either. (You were half kidding with Annabelle, enjoying that the disengaged, newly single you can act like a boy-crazy eighth-grader, even if no one else approves.) When you think of Jack, you see something more pure, more heady than simple bodily desire.

Forcing the conversation to *Oh, Shit!*, you ask Jack stupid questions: "Um, so how do I write the proposal?"

You are well aware that if he weren't so taken with you, if there wasn't this chemistry, he would have no time for this. An agent meeting more than once with a fledgling writer to talk about a book idea that he hasn't seen a word of because she hasn't written anything? Suspect. Very, very suspect.

Jack clears his throat and tells you that he'll send you some samples tomorrow. He asks how you want to write it.

"How?" you say, as if it's the first time it's crossed your mind. You lift your glass to your lips and take a big sip.

"Like, are you going to write all the stories? Or will it be an in-their-own-words-type format? Are you going to get stories from diverse populations? Or will you get stories from celebrities and public figures only?"

You don't know yet. Per a suggestion from Jack, you've purchased and read one book that compiles stories from people in the public eye. The tone didn't do much for you; it felt like too many handlers had looked the stories over, making sure they were palatable for public consumption and wouldn't hurt anyone's image. *Oh, Shit!* was all about embarrassment in its plainest, unadulterated form, i.e., "Your professor overheard you calling her a bitch for giving you a bad grade? Oooh. Good one . . ."

You have one friend whose college roommate is a big movie star. When you tentatively asked her to ask the movie star if she could participate, the actress responded via email in the affirmative, although she didn't have any "good" stories off the top of her head.

"Oh, I LOVE her," Jack says when you mention this as your small piece of progress. He shifts in his seat, leaning forward. "I think she's amazing. In fact, I'm working on a movie deal with a client, and we're hoping to put the script in front of her."

"Yeah, she is really great."

He sits back, folds his arms, and crosses his legs, putting one ankle on the other knee. "If I ever came home with a magazine that had her on the front, my ex would get so jealous."

You become Sister Sell-Out, siding immediately with him, as in, "Wow, that sounds *so* unreasonable." Like you've *never* been a jealous girlfriend. You know how jealousy is—always a careful reaction of personal insecurity and tangible issues within the relationship. Long before you met Ted, for example, he had briefly dated a hot blond groupie he met at one of his band's gigs in Florida. Later, they remained friends, and whenever she sent postcards or a Christmas card with a picture of herself hamming it up with an 'N Sync member (irony, folks, irony), evidence of Ted's continued connection with his former flame annoyed you. Since it was the early days of your relationship, you chose not to admit that you were, indeed, jealous. Instead, you did one of two things: (1) kept everything bottled up inside, or (2) blamed your feelings on him, accusing him of turning to her for some kind of attention or emotional support that you weren't giving him. Yep, you know some things about being immature.

"The last three women I have been with have been crazy—you're not crazy, are you?" Jack raises one of his eyebrows.

You raise one back, and he tells you this is impressive. Like an obedient pup who likes the peanut butter treat she gets when giving her owner her paw, you raise your eyebrow at least five more times during the rest of the conversation.

You are completely crazy, yes. If this were another day, you could have given him the annotated list of why you are a raving lunatic. The first thing that pops into your head is the fact that you've been taking antidepressants for the last three years. When you decided to supplement your talk therapy with a visit to the psychopharmacologist, you were battling anxiety, feeling depressed and burdened by the darker woes of your family, which, significantly, have always seemed to escape definition.

The drugs had cleared all that up practically overnight. It would almost be a miracle if the pills hadn't also robbed you of your own feelings. You tell hardly anyone that you take these pills. When you were growing up, your father, who is a physician, barely touched aspirin. Combined with the greater stigma of battling mental health issues, this fact is never too far from your consciousness. Your anxiety is shameful, and when it really affected you, pre-antidepressants, you'd opted for the stiff-upper-lip coping mechanism. You aren't about to say, "Actually, Jack, in the interest of full disclosure, I'm on psychotropic meds." No fucking way.

Besides, you are too stuck on being categorized with his past girlfriends to answer the "crazy" question accurately. Before you can turn the conversation back to your book, he says, "I was married once."

"Really?" you say, scanning his face for age markers that would somehow make sense of this information. You're guessing that your first impression of his age—late thirties, early forties—was correct. You have a hard time believing he was married, though you're not sure why. Jack, with his high energy and generous enthusiasm, strikes you as youthful.

"Long time ago. Starter marriage," he says, reading your mind. "Lots of people have them."

"Oh, yeah . . . of course." You are trying not to look like you've made any judgments, but you have that curse: a face that never lies. Against all rational instincts, you look at him differently. He is not like you. He actually made it down the aisle with the wrong person. You overidentify here, extend the terror of your actual engagement to a real live ceremony, and it's too much. Your own chest feels the strain.

"What was her name?"

"Erika."

As he says this, you are reminded of why you love his voice so much. In the short time you have known him, you've heard him say lots of names, but never like this. His voice goes soft, especially on the *k* sound. You guess that he still loves her, which strikes you as oddly sweet and sad at once.

What happened is none of your business, so you just say, "I'm really sorry, Jack." And then add the understatement of the year: "Divorce . . . that, ah, must be tough."

Like your previous meetings and all your correspondences, time escapes quickly when you are focused on Jack. Being with him is like being in an alternate universe, one you suspect that he'd be living in anyway, with or without you. You like this about him, that he looks straitlaced but is mildly quirky, that he functions as an extreme individual, like someone else you know very well—though perhaps, by now, maybe you should know her a little better.

YOU START TO yawn, but not because you are bored or tired.

"We should get you home, huh?" he says, his voice turning soft with affection.

You nod and let Jack pick up the tab again. When you stand, you feel mildly guilty. He pauses to let you exit the café first. You turn and realize that you will still be hobbling, in these impossibly high heels, all the way back to Grand Central. Even though Jack lives downtown, he offers to walk you to the subway. You can't think of a good reason for him not to—not a reason you're willing to tell him, anyway.

By now it is dark and there is a slight chill. Strolling through your work neighborhood, after hours, you notice that the lights are out in many of the storefronts—the inexpensive shoe store, the eyeglass shop, even the cigar vendor. You walk and smile and flirt, hoping that your challenging shoe situation—and resultant limp—is charming, not annoying. But Jack is in no hurry, and you have a plan or two anyway. You are going to write the proposal, and Jack is going to look at it. Seems simple enough, you think.

When he leans forward to kiss you good night, there is no awkwardness. It's not going to be a real kiss, this you are sure of. But there is an embrace and the moment your body comes close to his is nice, even in its brevity. Just the fact that this level of thought goes into a simple goodbye should be cause for concern. But it's not. It's June. The weather has turned warm. And besides, you have another date.

Once Jack's cab is safely out of view, you dial Marco. Ever since discovering his superior kissing abilities, you've been seeing more of him. Workdays, he sends you emails on the hour, every hour. You try to impress him with your Italian, but he figures out in the first message, the one where you wrote, "*Che è la parola?*" (meaning, "What's the word?") that you've been frequenting www.freetranslation.com. One night last week, he asked you to have coffee, but your schedules were not in agreement: you had an appointment with Elaine on the Upper West Side that ended only thirty minutes before the start of the Italian lesson he was teaching on the Upper East Side. But then you found a solution.

You'd sped out of Elaine's office early to find Marco waiting for you on Broadway. He gave you a big hug and you two did exactly what two busy New Yorkers just getting to know one another might do: scheduled a cab ride through Central Park for the sole purpose of making out. It was either kiss for a half hour or . . . not. It was perfect; you asked the cabbie to take the long route and nuzzled into Marco's neck before he'd even shut the door. On the other side of the park, the cab spilled out just in front of the apartment at which Marco was teaching. When you waved goodbye to him as he was walking away, you'd giggled at the pools of sweat on his formerly dry shirt. His face was drenched, too.

"Good luck explaining that one!" you'd yelled out the window, as the cab pulled away from the curb.

"Yeah, well, I have another problem I hope I don't have to explain," he'd said, shaking his head.

Tonight, when Marco answers, you say, "I'm sorry. The meeting with the agent went longer than expected. You still up for dinner?"

You know you are misleading Marco. You think he knows this, too. But after almost six years of monogamy, you're over it, simply over it. You have no intention of settling with anyone and the longer you can postpone any mention of the m-word, you think you'll be just fine. Besides, it's not like you're going to *sleep* with Jack.

"Yeah, yeah, no problem. Uhhhhhh, you want to meet in Bryant Park? We can picnic on the grass?"

Although you have just departed from a quasi-date at Bryant Park, you say, "Sure," anyway. What's the harm? You know that you will not run into Jack. And even if you do . . .

It's going to take Marco thirty minutes to come uptown, so you offer to pick up the food. You walk back toward the park and dial Paula, your closest girlfriend from graduate school. Paula leaves tomorrow for London, where she will spend most of the summer with Fred, her boyfriend. Since breaking up with Ted, your friendships have deepened, mostly because you stopped traveling to Boston every other weekend to see him. On one of these newly free afternoons, you traveled from the Bronx to Paula's two-bedroom with high ceilings in Fort Greene, situated near the park. The bulk of the evening was spent rifling through Paula's impressive bookshelf and discussing books— all kinds of books, including memoirs, classics, and, of course, chick lit. Hours later, you looked outside and saw that several feet of snow had piled up on the streets. On the television, newscasters were calling it the "storm of the year," and Paula, ever the polite Southerner, insisted that you stay over and drive back to the Bronx in the morning. Though she was without proper winter gloves, she even offered to help you dig out your car the next morning. You'd taken her up on it, lending her a spare pair of boxing gloves from your trunk. As sentimental as she is sensitive, Paula has been known to interrupt conversations with, "Aw . . . remember the boxing gloves?" You are sad not to have her around this summer.

"Hey, girl," you say.

"Hey, how are you?"

"Great. Had a date with Jack and now am heading to meet Marco, only it's the exact same place I met Jack. Is that bad?"

"Look at you!"

You remember a specific time in the not-so-distant past when you *had* asked Paula to look at you, or, well, your trapezius. You were outside a restaurant, standing in the misty rain, asking her what the highlight of her year was, in honor of her birthday. Before she could answer, you said, "But wait! Check this out!" You'd flexed your left arm, from the shoulder down, and pointed with the right hand toward the bulging muscle just near your neck; it was compliments of the hours you spent in the boxing gym. As you did this, you expected ridicule. As in, how ridiculously vain *are* you? You were shocked when Paula was actually impressed. She's one of your most supportive friends—which is why you called her between dates.

"So, anyway, how's the packing coming?"

"Wait—two dates? Two?"

Before you respond, you are stuck. On the one hand, you think that this fact of two dates is an accomplishment to really, truly be proud of, more than the first time you figured out the rhythm on the speed bag. On the other, you feel the reverb of your Catholic upbringing and have a twinge of guilt. You are not being good.

But what the hell? you decide. Your mother did always tell you to play the field. Of course, she told you this when you were thirteen—not on the precipice of thirty. You chalk it up to being a late bloomer and say to Paula, "Yeah, it's kind of fun, isn't it?"

You decide on Thai spring rolls and sushi, which you can find at any number of delis in midtown, even at this late hour. You also run into a liquor store and buy two bottles of imported beer. You've had enough to drink tonight, and this extra alcohol will ensure that you will not rise early to write anything, or at least anything halfway decent. The man behind the checkout looks annoyed because you are being one of *those* New Yorkers, always on her cell. You mouth an apology and hand him a twenty.

You walk around the steps of the library and wait for Marco on the southwestern corner of Forty-second and Fifth. When he rides up on his bike, you say a reluctant goodbye to Paula, knowing that you will not get to speak to her so often overseas. Before she hangs up, Paula adds an earnest, "Can I just tell you? You sound great."

As you stare absently at the now-empty corner on which you'd waited for Jack just hours before, you awkwardly receive Paula's compliment with a hesitant, "Thanks . . ."

Once you're off the phone, you turn toward Marco and kiss him on the cheek.

"Beautiful, this is beautiful."

For Marco, just about everything worthwhile in life is beautiful, and you like his overuse of the word. He doesn't apply it to the standard American things one would deem aesthetically pleasing, like, say, a sunset. You have never heard him refer to any woman as being beautiful, either. (Not even you!) What is beautiful to him, and now you, through his eyes, are strange nights like these, when (1) the weather holds and (2) you have the opportunity for an impromptu picnic in a dark park with someone you barely know.

Marco walks beside you with his bike, and points to a corner of the lawn near Sixth Avenue. Once there, you sit on the grass and take off your goddamn shoes. He sits next to you and wipes the sweat from his forehead. You take the sushi and spring rolls from the bag to spread out before you. You hand him chopsticks. After rolling up his shirtsleeves, he says, "Buon appetito."

"Bone A-ppetite," you say in your best Southern accent. But your best is not very good. You are a Yankee, a real Yankee.

You are not three bites into your meal when the park ranger—park ranger in Manhattan?—approaches to tell you that the park is closing, and you'll have to leave in a few minutes.

Marco ignores him, clears his throat, and asks, "So what happened with the agent?"

You raise your eyebrows. "The agent?" Your mouth is full.

"Yeah, the guy you met with to talk about your book."

"Oh, well, nothing, really. He's helping me to brainstorm, get going, you know, that kind of thing."

Now Marco raises his eyebrows. "That's . . . nice."

"Did you bring cigarettes?"

He nods his head yes and pulls one from the pack. They are Marlboro Reds, and even though you'd prefer a Light—despite the fact that one of your friends calls Marlboro Lights "Slut Butts"—you reach over to take it.

Seven years ago you quit smoking, you thought, for good. But then this April rolled around, with its pretty blossoms and promise of a thaw. And there was another thawing, of sorts, that led you to take up this bad, bad habit again. A dear friend had been dumped by her boyfriend via text message, or at least it appeared that way for a few hours. Distraught, she came over with Paula to the apartment where you were house-sitting on the East River, and asked you to talk about your brutal breakup stories. Since you had a few (and Paula had declined, saying that she'd just had a lot of "casual sex") you launched in, failure by failure, including the one with the guy who frequented a tanning salon and also cheated on you. You recounted the time his ex-girlfriend stormed into the bedroom you'd shared with him and screamed, "Are you fucking my boyfriend?" By the time you'd gone through all your major heartbreak, your friend looked amused and you felt free. Just that morning, you had looked out across the river to the Pepsi-Cola sign, knowing that Ted lived near it, and gave the inanimate object the middle finger. You were angry because one of Ted's bandmates had unwittingly directed you to a song that Ted wrote about the aftermath of your breakup. When you listened to it online, you heard traces of old patterns that you were never okay with, but had, for worse, kept your mouth shut. That morning you were looking at the sign, thinking, *How is he reducing our relationship to this?* But that evening, after breakup stories galore, you had a moment with yourself and the East River. When heartbroken, disappointed, and angry, people do and say really, really silly things—including you. (No, on second thought, *especially* you.) You woke up the following morning feeling more generous than you had in a year. And while prancing through Central Park, head floating, you'd decided that you had too many rules in your life, one of which was not smoking. You bummed a cigarette from a stranger drinking coffee on a bench, just because you felt like it.

You smoke Marco's cigarette, and make a mental note: don't mention this to the people at the health organization. Dudley, your boxing trainer, would also be appalled. But it's just one, you reason. Okay, just one here and there.

Marco is finishing the food, and you encourage this. You don't mention that you'd also eaten with said kindly agent.

"So," you say, looking at the hovering park ranger. "I guess this means we gotta go."

"Let me ride with you back to the Bronx. You shouldn't go alone at this hour."

Of course you can go alone. It's only a forty-five-minute ride from midtown. Besides, your neighborhood is very safe. You're pretty sure that Marco is aware of these things. He lives in Brooklyn, and you know that if he goes with you, he won't make it back home before reporting to work in SoHo tomorrow.

"Yeah? You sure? My apartment is really, really far."

"It's not like two hours, right? Can't be that far."

By the time you and Marco have arrived at the Edison Avenue stop, he is asleep. You are the only two on the empty car, its long stretch of blue benches providing the same seats that nine-to-five commuters would kill for. Three empty vodka nips tumble toward the front of the car.

"Hey," you whisper, tugging on his shoulder and picking up your bag at the same time. "We're here."

Waking up, Marco spreads his hand over his face, momentarily removing his glasses.

"Jesus Christ, that was far."

"Told you."

You walk onto the platform, to your sleepy neighborhood that you liken to the 'burbs, and say, "Oh, yeah, I should warn you about my neighbors." You are thinking of the senior citizens and not Eddy.

"Mamma mia," he says, leaning down to kiss your neck. "What do I need to know?"

You stop. Bringing a new man to your home is strange. Your roommate will meet him. You'll have weird, involuntary flashes about being in that same space with Ted, the day he moved you in and gave you that look of incredulity that you used to take as a compliment—you chose *this* neighborhood, one that had no decent coffee shop but an inordinate amount of funeral homes, all tracing the same path as the elevated train. Or maybe the snapshot will be of Ondra, your Czech boyfriend, and the time he got up at 4:00 AM to get ready for your 6:00 AM flight to Denver; from the silk of your sheets, you opened your eyes and focused on his small bum and broad back as he moved to the bathroom. "Get up, *miláčku*," he called, between whistled songs. "Is time for trip!" You get so hopelessly attached.

Marco is staring at you. "Well? What do I need to know about these neighbors?"

"Ah, never mind," you say, walking down the stairs, past the all-night breakfast shop. "They're just like you. I-talian."

6

You look in every corner—is it at your job? On the street? In the elevator? At the gym? Through your email activities? You are looking, wholeheartedly, for the Perfect Embarrassing Story. In Jack's "work-related" emails, he never fails to remind you that what you really, really need are good stories. He would sound like a broken record if he weren't one hundred percent right. Besides, you need a lot more than just "good stories"— you just don't know it yet.

One Friday afternoon, you are at work when your friend Janet calls.

"I have a good one for you!" she squeals.

"Yeah?" you say, curious but not that curious. She's been calling you every week with "good ones." Janet herself is lovely and funny, and so your ambivalence about her stories is an indicator of . . . something. A yoga enthusiast, Janet tells you about taking a movement seminar a couple years back; one of the exercises was to improvise movement across the studio floor, one by one. Janet went first, confident of her skills. She didn't give a second thought to her classmates standing around the perimeter of the room, watching her. That is, she didn't give it

a second thought until a roll across the floor induced a "queef."
For the uninitiated, that's a vaginal fart. You heard this word for
the first—and you hoped last—time in the seventh grade, when
Albert Hennessy, the big kid with persistently stinky breath,
explained to you its definition, much to your horror.

"What?" you say to Janet. *How do you even spell that?* you
think.

"Yeah, it was pretty awful. Everyone standing there . . ."

"It *sounds* awful."

Your understanding of a queef is apparently subpar. You
thought it could only happen during sex, not yoga class.
(Thanks a lot, Albert.) And how, exactly, would the innocent bystanders be able to differentiate a queef from a fart?
Don't they sound the same? You ponder this point when
Janet sighs. "Yep, well . . . I don't know why I tell you these
things."

Before you can resist, you say, "Because you know I'll listen?"

This attitude of yours is not very becoming. You are the
self-selected anthropologist here. You have told your own
distasteful bodily function stories and now you want to get
squeamish?

After work, you take the subway back to the Bronx, sneaking out of the office at 4:55. No one notices. You are tired, but
you also need the gym, badly.

Dudley once told you that when you stop working out, all
the muscle you've built will turn to fat. Considering the size of
your upper body, this thought does not please you.

You arrive home and change quickly into your workout
clothes—long, baggy pants, a spacious T-shirt. Often one of
the only women working out there, you have learned to wear

loose-fitting clothing. As the white girl in this boxing gym, you are conspicuous enough.

Before leaving, the phone rings. It's Marco, who asks, "What's the word?" thinking that this American colloquialism you taught him is novel. Thinking of Janet's story, you say, "Oh, Marco, you don't want to know what today's word is—trust me."

The drive to the gym is short—only eight minutes—but it is long enough for you to hear a song you like on the radio, long enough for you to warble over the song as you drive down Westchester Avenue, and long enough for you to cease and desist when, at a red light, you notice a van driver laughing at you.

Moments later, you are pausing before the old, beat-up door, saying an extra prayer to the statue of St. Mary that sits in the small courtyard adjacent to the gym. To Dudley's dismay, this is going to be a speed workout.

"But Dudley," you plead once inside, not wanting him to be mad, as you fold your wraps around your hands, "it's better than not coming at all, right?"

Even though the heavy metal door is propped open most days, the Bronx air, which seems crisp and clean in comparison, isn't enough to cleanse the musty atmosphere. There are no windows. Inside, the small two-room gym exists on its own terms. Boxers whale on the leather heavy bags, their explosions in rhythm with one another. Summer is quiet, and this day, two boys, about fifteen, skip rope in front of mirrors patched together by duct tape. They keep their chins down. Above the cracked mirror a painted slogan reads: "It's better to sweat in the gym than bleed in the streets." All the words are black, with the exception of the word "streets," which is colored by chunky horizontal stripes of red, white, and blue. More than anywhere else you've been in the last few years, this is your home, and Dudley, your family.

Your first interaction with Dudley was over the phone, when you called last year to ask about boxing there. When you inquired about the possibility of getting a guest pass, he laughed and said, "Look, look, this ain't no Jack LaLanne. This a ghetto gym. This where the tough people work out." His voice spiked when he said the word "tough."

When you told him you were tough, he said, "Oh, yeah? Well, then you ask for me when you come down here. Name's Dudley."

Dudley is Jamaican, in his late thirties, with dark brown skin, a lean form, and well-shaved head. He's your man and you're his girl. For the entire year, he's probably the person with whom you've spent the most time. (Though you dated Ondra in the nine months following your breakup with Ted, Ondra lived in the Czech Republic, and so contact was limited to occasional packages, daily emails, and frequent text messages.) Dudley was the one who saw you through your daily workouts, as well as through your grief over ending the relationship with Ted. As your trainer, Dudley pushes you, makes you do one more round, one more sit-up, and then pays you back with good advice.

"Is it the I-talian you seein'?" he asks, wondering why you have to leave early again.

"No, it's something for my writing." For a time, your writing was about the gym, which had been the perfect marriage of heart and mind. But now you want to move more outside of yourself.

"Yeah, yeah, I know," he says. "But you know what's good for you, right? You eat good, you work out, you sleep. Ain't no time for running around with friends. The only person who really loves you anyway is your mommy. Remember that."

Somewhere in your mind, there is a file—an overflowing one—with Dudley's words of wisdom, all packed into one place. You leaf through it now and again. If you were, say, hesitant to call Ted's mother on her birthday because of the circumstances of your breakup with her son, Dudley would scoff, "You know where you goin'—be a woman." And so you call her.

Today, though, Dudley just shakes his head. "Okay, okay, you can only do an hour, that's what we'll do."

You rush through the workout, starting with the fabled jump rope, then moving to the heavy bag. You brighten when Nikolai walks in. Nikolai is a young Ukrainian boxer whom Dudley used to train, before Nikolai left him for Cioco, a jerk. Cioco isn't a jerk because he "stole" Nikolai. He's a jerk because one evening, when you were changing in the front office, he pretended to be making a call on the pay phone and snuck a peek at you in your underwear through the blinds. And you only know this because then he turned around and told everyone how "nice" you looked. You were appalled. Luis, your buddy, pulled you aside and mentioned how some stranger walked in and saw you naked. He told you the half-truth so that you would be more careful, without having to know that the man who was talking shit was someone who, most hours, pretended to be your friend, making smooching noises when he did an expert job wrapping your hands. After Luis's warning, Dudley pulled you aside and said, "Next time you need to change, tell me and I'll guard the door for you." And you said, "Thanks—

I'm mortified." And Dudley jutted his chin toward where Cioco was sitting back, hands on his paunch, and said, "Yeah, big fat man like that oughta know better." That's how you learned it was Cioco.

You don't ask Nikolai about Cioco or how his training is. Since he left Dudley, you have held the smallest bit of judgment. On a rational level, you know these things happen. People break up. But Dudley is the most solid fellow you know. Against your better instincts, you haven't fully forgiven Nikolai.

"How's school?" he asks you.

You tell him you are done and working on a book now, even though as you say this you can't quite conceive of what that book will look like or how it will even get to that point. Most people who ask polite questions expect easy answers, and you do your best to oblige them.

When you pry for an embarrassing story, he blushes. Nikolai is either eighteen or twenty-four. You don't know because there have been varying answers depending on who asks the questions. You are not the KGB and you don't really care one way or the other, but he sure does have a baby face. In fact, he reminds you of a blond Campbell's Soup kid.

"One time, when I was twelve, I puked on a roller coaster? That count?"

"Gross."

"Yes, it was." He smiles slyly.

You have encountered embarrassment in the gym, but not of the funny variety. The first time you saw two boxers spar in the ring, you were jumping rope in the back, far more interested in the verbal sparring between the trainers—Dudley and Angel, a young, handsome Puerto Rican with a good heart and loud mouth. They stood on opposite ends of the ring, each tugging on the ropes and moving their mouths faster than the punches being thrown by their boxers.

"Go back to Africa, nigger!" Angel yelled at Dudley.

"I hate you, man!" Dudley spit back.

This was venomous. Where you come from, people don't use that language. You can't even bring yourself to say or even think the entire word. Perhaps your most embarrassing moment in the gym—beating even Ron and the blame game—was then. In a place where you were always trying to downplay your difference, their name-calling made you very, very uncomfortable. You are, indeed, a white girl. You felt ashamed and held your breath just for a minute, wanting to end this awareness.

The minute the fight was over, Angel walked over to give Dudley a bear hug and said, "Hey man, I heard you bet on the black guy. What are you, racist? Why do you always get the black guys?"

You think about this moment, while staring off beyond the timer that buzzes and flashes green to signal the beginning of a three-minute round. It's not a funny ha-ha moment and therefore it's not going to end up in your book. It does, however, make you think.

Dudley says, "Eh, you! Back to work!"

But you have to go. You have your first scheduled interview for *Oh, Shit!* and you don't want to be late.

When Dudley yells, you turn and smile knowingly at Nikolai. He looks down, lips parted shyly. For the first time, you see him and his whole place in the Dudley-Nikolai divorce proceedings. He misses Dudley, too. How could he not?

You do already, and he's technically still your trainer.

Although it is the middle of the summer, you know you want to move soon, somewhere less burblike, somewhere younger and closer to the city. You're dreaming of a light-filled place in Brooklyn, preferably with a solarium for your plants and a wall-to-wall bookshelf to fill after lazy afternoons perusing used bookstores. The only trouble is, an apartment in Brooklyn won't be near this gym, a thought that inspires terrible sadness and longing, even though you haven't even started looking.

But you've already set your compass in the direction of moving—as well as writing and falling in love. There's no turning back now. Or is there?

ON YOUR WAY home after the gym, you run red lights and take illegal right-hand turns. You change quickly into your long pleated skirt and a chocolate brown tube top. Only a sliver of your belly is visible. In the interests of your demure aspirations, you grab an ivory wrap and decide to focus on the fact that your skirt falls to your ankles—and not that said skirt is see-through.

Dalton, the subject of your first formal *Oh, Shit!* interview, has found himself with an unexpectedly free Friday night because his kids are away for the weekend. He suggests that you meet at a cozy antique-shop-turned-wine-bar near his apartment.

You race down your favorite stretch of the West Side Highway; it's sunset and so your worries about being late disappear as quickly as the pinky-orange hue in the sky.

You met Dalton last year, after he did a reading at your school. Although he is a writer-writer, he is also a full-time academic, a sociology PhD whose seventeen-page résumé impressed you to the point of speechlessness. You didn't actually meet him at the reading. You met him after, when you interviewed him for a literary magazine. Due to his son's unexpected ill health, he asked if you wouldn't mind meeting at his apartment, as opposed to his office at the university where he teaches. While he played a contentious game of chess with his sniffling son, you asked questions about writing and life, glancing over, every now and then, to the rain falling outside the windows. You liked Dalton and his long answers right away. When you asked him about how he finds the time to write in addition to caring for his children and teaching, he said, "I'm like a scrap metal dealer. I like to recycle old parts."

Although you spent the entire meeting focused on him, as planned, he seemed genuinely interested in helping you with your work. When you left, he offered to read some of your pieces, especially the boxing stuff. (He had briefly boxed with his university's team.) Given your impression of him as a thoughtful writer, you wasted no time in taking him up on the offer.

A year later, you'd approached him via email and described *Oh, Shit!* briefly. He wrote back with the promise of an embarrassing story. You are sure his story will be smart. You need this. Enough of the bodily function mishaps.

You enter the wine bar and settle into a chair in the atmospheric room, with walls the color of pomegranate and flickering candles on circular tables. You dutifully pull out your notepad, then gratefully accept a menu from the waiter. Dalton enters a few minutes later, on his cell. One of his publications is making national news, and he needs to field questions from some reporter in Boston. He shakes his head in apology and you wave your hand through the air dismissively.

He takes a seat across from you and you start talking. This is easy. He's a good conversationalist, although you remember advice that an editor once gave you: *Stay away from interviewing writers! They are notoriously difficult.*

Funny, Dalton does not seem difficult to talk to, but ten minutes into the conversation you realize, *Yep, he's interviewing me, all right.* One of the pieces you'd sent him was about a "Failure Party" you once threw for your friends, asking them to join you in coming clean about all the things that maybe weren't going so right in your lives. (You'd kicked off the celebrations by hanging up a rejection letter from the University of Vancouver and some pictures of you looking especially smitten with the ex who eventually cheated on you multiple times.) Small echoes of unhappiness in childhood were buried deep in the writing. You suspect that this is why Dalton wants to know about your parents. From the limited amount of your writing he's read, Dalton knows that your mother is lively and has a gift for striking up intense conversations with strangers. (After a vacation on a mile-wide island in nowhere, Maine, where your mother bumped into two people she knew, you and your father watched in amazement at a rest stop as she came out of the ladies' room and said to a man exiting the adjacent men's room, "Oh, I will get you the name of that book—it's fantastic! You'll love it.") He also knows that, at least in comparison, your father is quieter, that he prefers solitude and tells his stories through landscape photographs. Dalton seems to sense that somewhere between these two extremes you had, at times, felt lost.

Your notebook still shut, you take note of Dalton's curiosity about your parents, and how it is likely driven by questions that are arising about the parenting of his own children. You don't know him well enough to ask. Besides, who can think clearly in the unexpected hot seat? You are supposed to ask the questions here. It's other people's embarrassment that you're chronicling, not your own. *Oh, wait,* you think. *Am I embarrassed?*

With Dalton—who is neither friend nor date—you locate a small undercurrent of anxiety. Around him, you feel like you are too much—either too loud or too lively . . . too *something.* You have been told that you were "too much" on many occasions; usually, though, this utterance comes with affection, from close friends. When you were twenty-one, you worked at a bar whose staff was filled with—surprise!—people who drank too much. Your favorite coworker was a spirited woman named Molly, who was in her late thirties, wore black cat glasses, and liked to reminisce about the old days, as much as she looked forward to the new ones. Ever the connoisseur of radio news, she came out of the back room one night, just in time for a staff meeting. She looked panicked and was gripping a family-sized bottle of Tylenol.

"You guys, I just heard that if you drink more than three drinks a day, acetaminophen is essentially toxic! We have to throw this stuff out!"

Later, on the way to a warehouse party, you walked with her to the subway.

"Hey, Mol," you said. "About that Tylenol thing . . ."

"Oh, that is so scary . . ." She shivered.

"Yeah, but did it ever occur to you to just not have three drinks per day . . . I mean, instead of throwing out the Tylenol?"

Molly cackled loudly, and at length, before answering you.

"Oh, my god—you are really too much, you know that? Tooooo much!"

With Dalton, you feel like you might be too much. You know that you cannot be anyone else, so it's not the end of the world as much as it is curious, very curious.

Good at paving over your own anxiety with babble, you are in the middle of telling some story—barely conscious of your present surroundings and company—when Dalton stops you to say, "Do you think your mother connected with strangers because she couldn't connect with you?"

You force a smile and press your palm against the wall, underneath the table, where he can't see. The air feels suddenly stuffy. You are sweating, everything coming into relief. By this point you have gulped down two glasses of wine to Dalton's one sipped martini. Your eyes don't narrow, but they feel like it. You are quick to say, "Huh. Interesting. I don't know."

What Dalton doesn't know is that you aren't thinking about your mother. You are thinking about yourself.

7

────

You are sleepy. It is daytime, some ordinary Tuesday morning, and even though the morning was once your best time of day, you can barely drag yourself off the subway to go to work. It doesn't help that you aren't stimulated by your job, or that you have been spending evenings at Marco's loft, cuddling on the couch and watching foreign movies that you never seem to watch all the way through or sneaking cigarettes out the window in his expansive corner kitchen with a panoramic view of the Manhattan skyline. It doesn't help that you haven't written a word of *Oh, Shit!* and still plan to have the proposal finished by summer's end. Nor is it ideal that, without the cushion of your student loans, you are pretty much broke and are struggling to pay Dudley his twenty-five-dollar-a-week pittance to train you at the gym. You have put a lot of imaginary faith into an unwritten, faintly conceived idea, one that only Jack seems to think will be a hit.

The only thing that gives traction to your days is your ongoing email conversation with Jack. The emails are frequent, rambling, and often funny. Both of you are particularly careful never to drop even one conversational thread, whether it be about your favorite books and why, expressions you can't seem to utter aloud but always have in your head ("Ciao for now" being yours), or proclivities toward prevarication (you both claim that lies you tell are of the inconsequential variety). Jack has a formality to his writing, even in email, that impresses you. Because he peppers his sentences with nonrestrictive clauses—who doesn't love a well-placed comma?—the effect of his phrasing is downright hypnotic.

At work, you have mastered the art of appearing busy. You are busy, of course, but hardly ever with the work at hand. When your boss comes to you with a project, you approach it in fits and starts. She's started requesting "research" on prospective donors and this piques the interest of your inner private eye. You are very good at this—you like finding quotes from a person, ones that illustrate a life or philosophy, although at times it seems like this process is completely random. What if you don't look carefully enough and miss something? You're slowly revealing to your boss—somewhat against your better instincts—that you can produce things quickly.

If you applied your enthusiasm to your job as opposed to Jack's emails, you might actually move up, at least from your status as a temporary employee. But this is not where your heart is, and naïve as it may be, you have never been very keen on playing the game just to play it.

You love books and words and *feelings*. Your mother told you from an early age that you have the Gift of Tears, simply because you cry all the time and you actually enjoy it. Only, you don't cry all the time anymore, because of the antidepressants that have been muting your emotions for the last three years. Far from the anxiety-ridden days of writing journal entries that were so fueled they seemed full of lies, you have a hard time getting back to the place of remembering why you are on these drugs in the first place. Wasn't there some rule with your insurance company that your therapy would be covered only if you were on the drugs? Is that right? If so, was the anxiety really that bad? Good God, that was some über-insurance as far as mental health was concerned. You worked hard to buy that plan independent of your job, even taking a second job to cover the additional costs, so that your mental health needs would be taken care of. Yep, this had all seemed like very serious business at the time. The insurance plan even covered the family therapy sessions. Talk about metaphor. Growing up, you never needed to play soccer to understand that it was your job—self-appointed, cosmically appointed, whatever—to be the sweeper.

Anyway, you are fine—you feel fine—and think you should go off the meds soon, only you are scared because there has been so much tumult in your life over the last couple years, with moving to New York and breaking up with Ted. When you check in with the psychiatrist, you like to talk about tapering off the meds, even though your inevitable conclusion is: "Great idea. Let's talk about it next appointment." And until that next time, you know you will never miss a dosage. Contrary to your current hunger for male attention, there are some vestiges of your "good girl" persona still kicking around.

But back to the crying (or lack thereof). That side effect of the drug sucks because even if you can't cry when someone else tells you about her most beautiful moment, or her worst, you certainly want to. And you know as well as anyone that intention is everything.

You border on the sentimental at all times and try to tell

yourself that you'll risk being corny or sappy, because you don't ever, ever want to miss out on the good stuff. You had done this for a while, missed out on all the good stuff. While you had really loved Ted, at a certain point you stayed in the relationship because it satisfied one very important definition of "safe," i.e., unchanging. That stormy night when you offered to pick him up from band rehearsal at the old warehouse so that he didn't have to ride his bike several miles home in the rain, that was when everything changed. Because he said over the phone, "No, I'm gonna ride with the guys, for solidarity," and then walked into the house drenched—and not happy about it. His refusals of your help often frustrated you, but whatever the reason, that night your feelings changed faster than his clothes dried. Or maybe it was that you were finally seeing things in a different light. You can't open the good-stuff lock if you don't have the right key.

Jack laces all his emails with flirtation. And so do you. When he recommends a book, for example, he tells you not to buy it. And so then you have to ask, "Why?" And there is buildup and back-and-forth until he writes, "You see, you, I really wanted to run out and get it for you. And no. Not as an excuse to get together. That we don't need. We'll see each other, I hope, soon enough."

You do see each other, any chance you get—brief coffee breaks, extended lunches, after-work drinks. You usually meet at one of two places: (1) the café outside your building or (2) under the "Tobacconist to the World" sign on Forty-second Street. The latter meeting spot, too, is significantly closer to your work than his. But no matter what is on his agenda, Jack has an easier time leaving his office than you do—he insists that it's no problem for him to travel a little farther. One afternoon he calls you on his way back from a lunch and says, "Let's meet at our place." And you make sounds to the administrative assistant about needing coffee and run to the sign, while he waits at the café outside your building. After some nervous minutes of wondering if you got the time wrong, looking at every dark-haired man in a suit—a varietal that overpopulates midtown—he calls, and you make a declaration that from now on your place will exactly be the "Tobacconist to the World" sign. You look forward to the kind of waiting that is expected, not endured.

This Tuesday, though, you are both actually busy. Jack often notes that he shouldn't be writing you so many emails during the workday. But you know he works well into the night most nights and commutes earlier to work than anyone you know. Besides, summer is a slower time, he assures you. Regardless of Jack's workflow, his email messages are coming with more and more frequency. He writes that he's never, ever been this intimate with a client. ("I'm your client?" you write back.) And that whatever you two have stumbled upon here, it is very special.

You know all about special, and how personal chemistry between two people is so precious, especially when there are fireworks. With Jack, you are free-spirited and bold, a little off-center and ragtag, compared to his expensive sunglasses and custom-made suit way of walking through the world. Against a backdrop of you, he is steady, offering sage advice always, never forgetting about what's important especially in the face of what's urgent. You briefly wonder how Jack is with other women. But only briefly.

Between "projects," you analyze how differently you relate to the two men in your life. Probably you should be focusing on other things, like getting your postgraduate life in order and coming up with a better life objective than the dopey "Uh, write books?"

When you think of Marco, you think of your recent visit to the gynecologist, prompted by, um, a feminine issue. You remember the physician, an older Argentine man, smiling after examining you. He said, "So, do you have a new boyfriend?" Since you are literal to a fault, you started to weigh the answer, even as your heels remained uncomfortably cupped in the icy stirrups. Well, Marco wasn't really your *boyfriend*. And, in an oddly similar way, Jack almost was. You bit your lip and sighed.

The doctor added, "Listen, we call this condition 'honeymoon cystitis.' If you haven't had sex in a while and you start having a lot of it, well, this is what happens. It's nothing to worry about."

So that would be Marco.

After, you called one of your friends to tell her the news. She wanted to know how she could catch honeymoon cystitis.

When you think of Marco, you think of sex. He is sexy, sexual, sensual—all of the above. You think it's his Italian sensibility, the impeccable attention to detail. In fact, recently you wrote him a silly text message on a whim that read, "Wanna fuck?" You were just kidding. You mean, you know, in the way that receiving something like that would be amusing. But Marco didn't write back right away. And he always wrote back within ten minutes. It was the end of the day, and you had to go pick up your car in his neighborhood, where you'd parked it the night before. You spent the entire subway ride fretting. Was that going too far? It was just a joke. By the time you reached your stop—or, actually, missed your stop and got off at the following one—your phone was ringing. Outside an Italian bakery, you stopped for a minute, to take in old memories inspired by the fresh-bread aroma. A small part of you misses your mother.

"Hello?" you answered nervously. It was Marco.

"Hey, bella, I was just wondering, I'm going to take this trip to California, to visit my grandmother. Do you want to come?"

"Your grandmother?"

"I mean, then I'm driving up the coast. That will be the fun part."

You weren't really thinking about an answer. You were thinking about his question. *My inappropriate text message inspired an invitation to meet his grandmother? You've got to be kidding me.*

Your days are too consumed with men. You are falling off track much too quickly, and yet . . . having so much fun. You don't want to kill *Oh, Shit!* before it has even begun. More than stories, you need strategy. You need a plan. On your morning commute, you jot down ideas in your notebook. Draft an email asking for stories. Try to actually *write* one such story. You call friends, make plans to gather more stories. All this busyness is well and good—but there is a problem: you are still in a state of need.

THE NEXT DAY, you manage to work an entire eight hours without too many personal emails. This small accomplishment gives you much satisfaction. Somewhere inside you are saying, *See, I'm not such a slacker.* But the truth is that Jack is on a business trip and so communications from him have taken pause, with the exception of a text message you received the night before: "At an amazing concert and thinking that you are the one who rocks." You fell asleep with a big grin on your face.

After work, you ride the 6 train home and have every intention of going to the gym. But once you are walking down Edison Avenue, your bag feels heavier than it had when you got on the train in midtown. Your eyes are tired from an all-nighter at Marco's, where you spent a few hours on his roof eating arugula with pecorino cheese and truffle oil while watching people wait for the bus at the stop across the street from his apartment. Every few minutes someone new would stop and wait. One teenage boy pressed his mouth hard against his girlfriend's as they leaned against the bus-stop shelter. There were mothers walking babies, men walking dogs. You and Marco watched, lazy with mild interest in the human scene below, set against a brick building with one lone leafy tree near the corner. When a man walking a little dog passed another man walking a big dog, there was a momentary canine standoff. You and Marco found this amusing, and he said, "Look, look. This is beautiful."

You see Eddy when you arrive at the front steps to your building. Across the way, the ladies are on their porches, and they wave big hellos. You suspect it's because they like Eddy, and not because of some goodwill for you.

"Hey, doll, what's shakin'?"

"Oh! So glad to be home . . ." You are acting as if you haven't been here in months, throwing your bag at your feet as if it carries twenty hardcover books, the ones you hope to write someday.

"Yeah, me, too. I know the feelin'—still boxin'?" Eddy finds this picture of you, with you in all your girly glory throwing punches, very odd. You nod yes.

"Just don't be ruining that face."

You assure him that your seventy-year-old sparring partner isn't exactly out for blood.

"You're too much, kid. You know that?"

Eddy tells you that he's going down to the bar for a drink, if you want to join him later. You tell one of your gentle lies and say that, while it sounds nice, you're really looking forward to a night in. Although you have been here for almost two years, you've only been to a bar in your neighborhood once, with your roommate during a snowstorm. That night you were tired of being cooped up in your room watching the snowflakes make piles on the sidewalk. While you were momentarily interested in the small, elderly Italian woman outside in her thin cotton dress and apron, gruffly directing neighbors on where to put the snow, you decided that you actually wanted to go out, storm or not. Davida suggested a bar down the street. She had never been there, either. It had a wood-paneled exterior, with a fluorescent Bud Light sign in the front tinted window. The bartender was an older woman, kindly with her squinty eyes that were painted with thick black strokes extending out toward her temples. After you were in the bar a minute, three kids ran through, yelling and skipping and screaming. You and Davida looked at one another. But before you could say, "What the hell?" they were standing up on a platform in the back of the room requesting songs on the jukebox and telling the bartender that she could be the judge of their dance contest. A few minutes later their father walked in, expressionless, and planted himself in front of a video game, back turned toward the kids. That had been your one and only time at a bar in your neighborhood, and you were sure that nothing could top it.

"All righty, doll," Eddy says. "You know where I'll be if you change your mind."

Upstairs, you see that Davida has come home early. She is stretched out on the couch. The television is on and a glass of orange soda sits on the coffee table.

"Hey, girlie, is that really you? It's been forever!" she says.

It has surely felt like forever. You don't see Davida in the mornings like you used to, because you don't wake up early anymore to write. She leaves for her job at the bank well before you even hit the snooze button on your alarm clock. Plus, you've been staying at Marco's with more and more frequency, sometimes even buying clothing for the following day at a cheap clothing store, where the $10 skirts are passable for office wear, at least at a nonprofit.

When Davida asks you about your day, you decide to take this as an opportunity to talk about Jack. Everything—your tone, your far-off expression—conveys your limitless fondness for him. Davida, never one to withhold her opinions, responds by pointing one of her long, manicured nails in your direction, saying, "Don't shit where you eat, kid."

Despite being totally grossed out by the visual her words inspire—*ew!*—you are coy, telling Davida that you would never do such a thing. You turn away to look out the window. She tries to steer you in another direction, asking, "How's Marco?"

"He's great."

She starts to look exasperated, "Well, yeah, but I mean, how's Marco as opposed to Jack?"

"Oh." You aren't exactly thinking in those terms. Oprah is on television, talking about the secret lives of middle-class suburban swingers. "Well, Marco is great . . . and so is Jack."

"Girl, you're crazy, you know that?"

Later on, you have settled into a night of television-watching with Davida. Before you moved in with her, you barely watched TV. Your two-bedroom apartment is small, and so when it's on in the living room, you can hear it from your bedroom. During graduate school, you took to forgetting about your long days with books and writing and words with bad television. Over time, dissecting reality television shows with Davida started to take on an air of precious quality time.

"Hey, Davida," you say. You are sitting on the oversized chair, your bare legs flung across the arm. "Can I write that story about Papi?"

"Oh, lordy, does that qualify as embarrassing?"

"Well, kind of." You think for a minute, fingering the edge of the chair's cotton slipcover. "It's certainly a good story."

A few months earlier, Davida had made a trip to Delaware, where her parents live. When she arrived that afternoon, her father came running out to greet her in the driveway. Immediately she knew something was wrong. Her father is laid back; the sight of him rushing was unusual.

"Davida, Papi died. Your mother's a wreck."

Davida's chest became heavy. Papi was her maternal grandfather, and was young and healthy.

"What?" She almost didn't believe him. But when she ran into her parents' house, she found her mother sitting at the kitchen table, folded over with her cheek pressed against the wooden surface, in tears.

"Your uncle Victor just called" was all her mother said.

Davida is nothing if not efficient. Instead of asking questions, she approached her mother, touched her gently, and said, "I guess we should make some phone calls."

Her family is large, and calling everyone was no small task. Davida pulled out her mother's address book, sat down at the table, and picked up the phone.

"I'm sorry to tell you this, but . . . Papi died today. We're gathering here. Why don't you come over?"

"Papi has passed away. Come over to the house."

"Yes, it's good to hear your voice, too, but unfortunately I'm not calling with good news—Papi has died. Everyone's gathering here."

Within a half hour, the house started to fill with Davida's aunts, uncles, and cousins. One by one, they walked in, shaking their heads in disbelief. The scene turned chaotic quickly. The sound of loud sobs rang through the house. Aunts were speaking over one another. Some voiced regrets that they hadn't spent more time with him. Others could only focus on, "But he seemed so healthy . . ."

Davida managed to get in touch with her social worker sister, who was, at that very moment, at work driving a van full of troubled youths back to their residence program. When Davida told her the news, her sister burst into tears. When she got to the home, she walked into her boss's office and said, crying, "My grandfather died. I'll be out for a couple days."

The only person that Davida hadn't reached was her cousin Jennifer. Jennifer was getting her wisdom teeth taken out, someone remembered. Davida left more than one message on her cell.

After an hour or so, the doorbell rang. Must be Jennifer, everyone assumed. But when Davida opened the front door, standing on her parents' front steps was none other than Papi. Holding a cake.

"Papi?"

Her grandfather stood there, flushed cheeks, saying, "Davida! What a surprise! I didn't expect you to be here."

At this point, everyone in the house rushed to the door. One of her aunts fell to her knees and screamed, "Papiiiiiii! You are aliiive! Papi's alive!"

Papi looked incredibly confused. All of his children were there, tugging on his shoulders, fighting to hug him first, then fighting to hug him the longest.

"We thought we'd never see you again," one of Davida's uncles wailed, tears in his eyes.

"This is a miracle!" another yelled. "What a miracle!"

Davida stood there, dumbfounded. Her mother stepped forward to explain that Uncle Victor had, that morning, delivered the news that he had died.

"Huh?" Papi said. "No, no, Popi died. Not me."

Popi was a more distant relative, a second cousin by marriage. The news of his death was sad, but, for Davida's family, not as devastating as the erroneous news of Papi's demise.

Everyone was quiet for a minute. Someone muttered, "Jesus Christ . . ."

"Well, while we're all here, maybe we should have lunch?" Davida suggested.

Her sister sat there shaking her head. "Are you kidding me? Now I have to go back and tell my boss I was mistaken about my grandfather dying!"

The doorbell rang again. This time it was Jennifer. Her mouth was full of bloody cotton, her cheeks swollen with Novocain.

Jennifer's mother was sitting next to Papi now, on the couch.

"Look!" she shrieked, pointing directly at Papi's face. "Look! Papi's alive!"

Jennifer's brow furrowed, and even though the surgery had impaired her speech, she managed a, "No thi-it!"

AT THE PROSPECT of including this story in *Oh, Shit!*, Davida pauses.

"Hmmm, it's really a different kind of embarrassment . . . Oh, lordy . . . go ahead."

After the Papi/Popi mix-up, Davida's mother had asked her if she'd told you about it. Davida had said, "Of course."

Davida's mother was chagrined. "Oh, she'll think we're a crazy family."

True enough. This type of craziness is, well, crazy. But from all those years you spent working in bars, you've heard plenty of people insist that their families are crazy. Whenever people make this admission, no matter what the mood of the conversation, for a split second their eyes turn downward. You've seen it a million times, a subtle expression that momentarily reveals, well, shame for not being just like everyone else—or at least what everyone else appears to be, i.e., normal.

"I'll just try it out, see if it works, Davida," you say.

Winking from her perch across the room, curled up in the corner of the couch, Davida says, "All right, kid. Knock yourself out."

You need to "knock yourself out." When you are in the right groove, attentions focused on the right things, your work ethic is good. You think of your devotion to boxing, the stretches of waking at 4:30 AM to write, the drive even to get into graduate school in the first place. Eight years ago, after your first therapy appointment, which was prompted by the cheating faux-tanner, you had an *aha* moment: you had some, uh, issues. Wanting desperately to unearth how you'd gotten there in the first place, you asked Dr. Nick, "Are you free this weekend? I could use a marathon session to just"—you'd swatted your hand from side to side—"get this stuff out of the way."

You were only half joking.

But now you can't find that motivated path. It's somehow eluding you, and so you grasp at straws and force yourself to look at almost every story, scene, or vignette through the lens of embarrassment. There's only one problem, you're beginning to realize: the topic of embarrassment, as presented to you, by you, is straight-up boring—with a capital B. If you meet someone at a party and have a stilted or dull conversation, though, you'd never think, *Oh, God. This person is so boring.* Believing that everyone is inherently interesting—and all the better if they are interesting in nonobvious ways—you'd think, *What am I not seeing?* And so when it comes to your compilation of embarrassing stories, you are realizing that it's time to extend that same logic to the topic of chagrin. While you enjoy the act of collecting the stories, the stories themselves don't seem to be revealing any deeper meaning about human existence—at least not that you are able to see.

8

WHEN YOUR INNER world is unsettled, you look outside for order. Control freaks know this practice well: when nothing of consequence seems in place, they do things like monitor food intake carefully, passing up BBQ ribs with a self-referential, third-person statement of, for example, "No, thanks—ribs aren't a Gabrielle food." They are overly clean, never allowing dust to settle even for a second in that hard-to-reach area behind the toilet bowl. They do not do well with delayed flights, lost wallets, or canceled plans.

You, on the other hand, have a string of lost credit cards, which would be impressively long if you could even count that high. The number of times you've said, *Oh! I need to clean the bathroom!* is exponentially higher than the number of times you actually *have* cleaned the bathroom. You like to eat a little bit of everything and use the third person only as a referent to those who are not in the room.

While you do not consider yourself to be controlling of your external environment, you're starting to think that a more directed way of living could be in order. You've been apartment-hunting in Brooklyn, to no avail, although you have told Davida that you plan to move out by the summer's end. You run through the list of places you can see yourself living, the jobs you can see yourself doing, and all of these things expand far beyond New York and the health organization. Or even "writing books" for that matter. You are free, head in the clouds; on most days, that feels like a very good thing.

This day, you are driving to Brooklyn, with a fantasy of your afternoon already vivid in your mind. You see trees. You see grass. There is a blanket. Jack is there, and you have the blessing of an open blue sky. The purported purpose of the meeting is to sign an agreement with his agency, as an official declaration of your professional relationship, although none of this feels very worklike. Your creative imaginings continue, all the way down the Brooklyn-Queens Expressway, drowning out the Saturday afternoon traffic.

The reason you are signing an agreement is because last week you'd continued to use the phrase "If we work together . . ." when referencing anything to do with *Oh, Shit!* Finally, Jack had written you an email: "Do we need to sign an agreement? I would hate it if you worked with anyone else on this."

Of course, you, too, would hate to work with anyone else. Even though you are a little light on the actual work side of things, Jack has smarts, verve, energy, and, best of all, enthusiasm for you. One day, sitting underneath the shade of the magical trees in Bryant Park, he told you that all you needed was an arc for your stories. You are flattered by the genuine interest he seems to take.

Your careful language of "if" is a combination of your philosophy background and your grandmother, who became a widower at age fifty, when her husband died suddenly of a heart attack. Both Nana and your schooling have taught you never, ever to take anything for granted. Sometimes, unfortunately, this also means overquestioning situations—because, in the end, how does one really know?

Today a signed agreement will be sufficient evidence for you. Before meeting, Jack had suggested (via email) that he bring wine. You picked up the office phone and called him immediately, in a huff: "This is a *work* meeting. We are not drinking wine at a work meeting."

Ever polite, Jack deferred to your wishes. Then you called Dan and happened to mention nixing the wine. From across the country, he called you out, "Oh, for god's sakes! Would you stop being such a stick-in-the-mud?"

Okay, okay, you thought. But you did say no to drinking wine. Instead of grabbing a bottle of Sauvignon Blanc and admitting you'd had some help in changing your mind, you bought a bottle of Moët. There, *not* wine.

It had also been your full intention to bring peanut butter sandwiches. You don't remember how it came up, probably as a result of something to do with your budget, but Jack was excited about the prospect of peanut butter sandwiches. Driving down the expressway, you realized that you'd forgotten them. Well, forgotten even to make them in the first place. You would not have given this a second thought if Jack had not been so exuberant about extra-crunchy on white bread. Jack's enthusiasm extends further than your work; in fact, it makes frequent appearances after most things you say, do, or even imply.

Forty-five minutes late, you drive by your meeting spot at the corner of Fifth Avenue and Carroll in Park Slope and see him standing there, on this bright sunny day, with his phone in its familiar spot: on his ear. The light is green and you need to park, so you roll down your window and yell, "Hey, Jack!" as you speed by him. Standing there in jeans with his free arm up, he shakes his head and yells back, "Where are you going?"

You find a parking spot on Fourth, right by the McDonald's, when you realize that you have yummy champagne but no glasses out of which to enjoy the bubbles. You go into McDonald's to ask for two cups when you come up with a solution to the forgotten peanut butter sandwiches: hamburgers and french fries. You love the idea—something really, really nice with something really, really not nice. So you.

A few minutes later, you are lugging your big bag—now with the champagne and the fast food—up to the corner, where he is still waiting.

"Hey," you say. "I'm so sorry I'm late." You lean in to give him a kiss on the cheek. He kisses you back. "Yeah, what took you so long?" You can tell from his half smile that he is happier to see you than he is annoyed.

"Just . . . stuff. But I have a surprise that will make up for it."

You walk with him toward Prospect Park, up picturesque streets with brownstones and well-maintained gardens. Hydrangeas are in abundance. *This is where I want to live,* you think. Jack remarks on your outfit. You are wearing a sheer top with black cotton pants. Referring to the skin showing beneath the gauzy shirt, he says, "I can count the number of times I've seen you covering your belly—even at work. Three."

That's a slight exaggeration, but you get the point. Even when you are working in midtown, you bare your midriff most days. The office is heavily, erratically air-conditioned and so you often wear an oversized blanket sweater inside, safely covering your belly button.

"I told you," you say with a smile. "I'm lookin' to get fired." This is a line you borrow from a disgruntled employee at an ice-cream parlor who once gave you an extra scoop of mint chocolate chip gratis.

"You can't get fired. You need a job."

Jack's ever-present voice of reason sometimes misses your steady stream of wisecracks. Bit by bit, Jack has become more comfortable with you, and likes to give his two cents, even when the situation at hand has nothing to do with him, or sometimes even when it has nothing to do with you. Case in point: your friend calls you, upset because her boyfriend of three years admitted that he had been taking her for granted. You mention this to Jack and he, not knowing either your friend or her boyfriend, says, "She needs to dump him—once that starts to happen, it's really the end. Trust me." Jack is authoritative about everything—the economy, the environment, relationships. In this odd time of transition, you cling to firm opinions, even if they are not yours.

By the time you and Jack are approaching the park, your conversation has already taken several turns. You learn what Jack is doing later that evening (attending a party in the neighborhood). You tell him what you are doing (picking up a "friend" at JFK, although you don't refer to your friend by his name, i.e., Marco). Neither of you have ever spent significant time in this park, although you'd both like to. As always, there seems to be a lot on which you two agree.

There is a steady paved-road loop around the perimeter of Prospect Park, threading the outskirts and providing a path by which many bike, run, and walk. At certain hours, this road is open to through traffic, although today you notice only a random police car or DPW truck driving by. The air is fresh, fresher than it should be for July. Beyond the road, you see a clearing, a vast patch of green, dotted with sunbathers, Frisbee players, and lounging families. On the farthest side of this patch, where the lawn slopes up to meet another stretch of the road, you see one large tree and two upright chairs. They are empty.

"Look!" You are jumping like a child, at the risk of dumping the secret french fries all over the bag. "Those are for us!"

"No way," Jack says, even though there is a big smile on his face. "No way those are free. That would be too perfect."

Alana, your college roommate, likes to tell the story about the time you two were studying abroad in Italy and decided that your spring break should be spent in Spain. Another friend made reservations at a four-star hotel in Marbella, right on the southern coast. Although you were broke and your main source of money was your father via Western Union every time you ran out (which was embarrassingly too often), you shrugged your shoulders and said, *All right*—refusing to believe that this trip wasn't going to work out exactly right. But the facts of things not being all right became very clear when you pulled up to the palm-tree-lined driveway leading to the hotel. Alana kept checking in with you, because she knew you hadn't been to Western Union yet. "Are you sure it's going to be okay?" she asked more than once. You just waved your hand and said, "Oh, yeah. Absolutely. I'll just make it to Western Union." But after a quick check-in, you discovered that Western Union was closed. You and Alana strolled down the boardwalk, taking in the ocean vistas and letting the sea air sweep away your money issues. You stopped for drinks at a waterfront café, where a large Russian man introduced himself and insisted on buying you margaritas. That worked for you. He had taken a particular interest in Alana, commenting repeatedly on the fact that she was platinum blond and Jewish. When he took out his wallet to make a point about how meaningless money is and went to take his lighter to a wad of American currency, you had let your mind wander to the cool blue ocean. Still, you managed to point your index finger toward the cloudless sky just in time to say, "Um, I'll take that." And so he gave the bills to you, which amounted exactly to one night's stay at the hotel you couldn't actually afford. Alana cites this story as evidence of the fact that things always have a way of working out—especially for you, thanks to your progressive outlook. A hair older now, you think the story makes you sound like a complete bimbo, but Alana's version is never far from your mind.

Somewhere inside you make a mental note, one of the first with Jack, even though you have now known him for two months. You do not appreciate his naysayer comment about the chairs, and remind yourself that you'd like to be around people who live in a world where this scenario would be not only plausible, but *likely*. Your internal voice doesn't make too much noise, though. There is too much you like about Jack to dwell on something so small.

As you two approach the chairs, it appears that they are, indeed, free. You both sit down, settling into your seats as the late afternoon sun relaxes on your faces. When Jack is seated, his legs splayed out, you pull out the champagne first.

"Very nice!" he says.

"I figured since I already dismissed the wine idea . . ."

Then you pull out the McDonald's bag and begin to divvy the fries from the burgers, pulling out every packet of ketchup you can find.

"Why is this so perfect?" Jack says, shaking his head. "This is so perfect."

You don't take too much credit for his pleasure. Your choices had been whimsical. Besides, with Jack you seem incapable of doing the wrong thing. This does not make you in the least bit nervous (although maybe it should); instead, you love the attention, and especially the way he seems to always see your best, brightest you, one that is free-spirited, optimistic, and quick-witted. You have forsaken the other, darker sides of your best you in favor of Jack. You feel much too much . . . joy . . . when you are with him to give it a second thought.

You open the bottle and toast, "To *Oh, Shit!*"

"To *Oh, Shit!*" Jack seconds.

While the pretense of your meeting is to sign the agreement, you could just as well be on a romantic date, thanking the gods of fate who carried you and Jack out of your regular routines to finally meet. But, as usual here, the lines are happily blurred—so blurred that before you know it, the entire bottle is empty, the folded hamburger wrappers smeared with leftover ketchup, and only one minute burnt fry is left in the hollowed-out paper bag. Jack has spent a good portion of the afternoon talking about his family. It began with his question of what to buy his brother for a birthday gift—you had zero suggestions—and turned many a rambling corner, as your talks always do. While you relate to his desire to navigate tricky family dynamics and still keep closeness with loved ones, there is something about his delivery, his keen attention to the immediate family, that makes you pause—

well, as much as one can pause after having drunk one-half a bottle of champagne. If you had to locate your uneasiness, you couldn't. You just know something bothers you.

Maybe it is the place you go when he tells you about a pact that he has made with his sister. They are very close, and if one doesn't like the other's choice in significant other, then that spells g-o-o-d-b-y-e for the potential partner. Sometimes they even spy—*wait, did you hear that correctly?*—on one another's dates. You tell yourself that you are bothered because you would never turn to any of your siblings for this kind of guidance. You tell yourself that you are bothered because it reminds you of Ted and his sister, their unusual closeness, how you and he and she shared every last detail of her dating life before she'd met her sweetest beau; in the end, the closeness of Ted and his sister had not worked in your favor, because even though she had become one of your dearest friends, she never forgave you for breaking her little brother's heart, and maybe hers, too.

What you are decidedly not telling yourself is that somewhere you are scared, terrified of being judged by strangers. Mostly, you like yourself and your occasional verve. Your ability to laugh, almost always. Your thick hair and muscular body. The very things that seem to make you *you*. But you aren't all of these wonderful things all the time, and the one thing you do not love is the pain. Like a tiny crocus making its way through new soil, it pops up on this sunniest afternoon to say: Don't you forget about me.

You've wandered down from your perfect chairs, on your almost perfect afternoon. You are tipsy. Jack is tipsy. You had intended to spend a couple hours with him in the park, and then return to the café on Fifth Avenue to write, before picking Marco up from his flight home from California. But you don't do well with alcohol. This is why, for the majority of your graduate school career, you mostly avoided booze. For many reasons, you are no Hemingway or Bukowski.

"C'mon," he says. "Let's get oysters at Blue Ribbon."

You have only been there once, with Paula, after class one night. It was snowy and you ordered bone marrow, steak tartare, and the matzo ball soup. Part of you wants to leave, and write—you know, that thing you've only been claiming to do for the last two months. But the other part of you is steadily under Jack's spell. You will follow him anywhere, and it's not just because you've had too much to drink. In fact, you will have more to drink.

"Can we see the wine list, please?" Jack asks the bartender, once you have acquiesced and are standing inside the restaurant, at the bar.

The three hours you spent at the park were decidedly not focused on your writing. In one of your afternoon coffee breaks earlier that week, Jack promised to reveal a new idea he has about your writing, something he sees that could have great potential. In this steady stream of babble you two have continued to spill on one another, has he taken some piddly detail or trait and unearthed something valuable? When you begged him to tell you that very minute what the idea was, he said, "All in good time."

Since you are agreeing to work with him on *Oh, Shit!* at least, you decide to flip through the agreement first before asking again about the idea, which he has promised to share.

"What's this?" you ask, pointing to a clause about foreign rights.

"Are you going to make me explain all of this?" he says.

You raise one eyebrow, and he sighs, before leaning in close to walk you through the agreement, section by section.

When you are done, you take a pen, garnered from the bartender, and sign away. There is light flooding through the bar, and people are drifting in and out, in this odd in-between-meals hour.

Now you are sitting on a stool at the very end of the bar, far from the windows and close to the spot on the bar where the waitresses pick up their drink orders and carry them away to waiting diners.

"So!" you say. "Tell me about this idea."

You think it is bound to be such a great idea that you will become rich immediately just by its mere utterance into the ether. There is no map for greatness, at least that you can see yourself. Better to let someone else figure it out. And even better that this someone else is handsome. You are already planning the vacation you will take with your easily earned dollars, flying to the Maldives, situated in the clearest Indian Ocean, where you will be supine all week long on a hammock with a book. (And what a coincidence! Jack has always wanted to go to the Maldives, too.) No all-inclusive Florida vacation for you.

"You are so impatient," Jack chides. He is shaking his head and leaning in closer to you, lifting his glass to his lips. "Impossibly so."

With this last comment, he takes an index finger and dabs your nose. The implication here is that he finds you cute. The you that recites one of Mary Oliver's lines ("We are, none of us, cute")—that you has disappeared. Instead, you flirt right back with Jack for a few moments, before clearing your throat.

"No. Really. Now is as good a time as any, isn't it?"

"Well, okay," Jack says. He is sitting upright now, his back grazing the wooden back of the chair. "Maybe it's just me, but I think you are really, really funny. Like, hilariously funny. I've said it before: all you need is the right arc."

This was his big idea, the one he made you wait for? No doubt you *do* need an arc. This resonates well enough. But his announcement of you being "funny," like it's a brilliant discovery? Even *his* brilliant discovery?

For a few minutes you sip your wine and nod your head in agreement. (You hear that women are more likely to do this than their male counterparts.) Maybe you say, "Uh-huh" or "Interesting" or "That's a thought . . ."

You excuse yourself to the bathroom and Jack politely stands while you leave the bar area. While in the unisex stall, you stand there and think for a minute. You do not have to go the bathroom and are, in fact, buying yourself some time to figure out how to express an honest reaction. You think for a few more minutes, your dizzy head leaning against the dark red wall. It comes to you.

"Jack," you say, before pulling out your seat to scoot in close to him again at the bar. You are standing there, purposely waiting for him to notice that you won't sit until you've said what you need to. "Listen, I need to tell you something . . ."

He looks alarmed, maybe even nervous, his green eyes scanning the room. "Yeah?"

Standing straight-backed, you say, ". . . I . . . am funny."

You just stand there looking at him, poker-faced.

"Uhhhh, yeah, okay. Of course."

You are not good at actually keeping the poker face and turn to say, "Gotcha! . . ." Then add, as you take your stool, "But I know I'm funny, trust me—it's not 'just you.' "

You don't know how Jack takes this. You don't know if he thinks you're a weirdo for having to announce that you are a funny girl. (Probably.) He doesn't know that all throughout college this had been one of your biggest insecurities: that you had no sense of humor. Nor do you suspect that Jack fully understands why you, indeed, find your very response to him hilarious in and of itself.

After two more glasses of wine, it is almost ten o'clock. You need to leave to pick up Marco, but you should absolutely not drive your boat of a vehicle to the airport. Jack tries to get you to skip the airport and join him at the party. After Blue Ribbon, you walk with him to get coffee. As you are pouring the milk in your cup, he says, "So what's the name of your friend?"

Jack usually refrains from these kinds of direct questions. On Monday mornings, after you have spent the entire weekend at Marco's loft, you tell Jack all about what you did—rode your bike down the Brighton Beach boardwalk, went to see an open-air movie in Williamsburg—but make sure never, ever to use "we."

"The name of my friend?" you repeat, although you heard him just fine.

"Yes," he asks, eyes peering into yours.

"Marco." The milk overflows the coffee cup and you reach for napkins.

"Marco," he says, helping you mop up the counter.

"Yes, Marco—he's Italian."

"Italian-Italian or Italian-American?"

"Ah . . . the former."

"And how do you know Marco?"

"He's the business partner of a friend's boyfriend."

This is all you say about Marco, and Jack asks no more. This question, this simple question, opens up a new world of dialogue with Jack, one that relates to your dating life in its present form. This makes you very uncomfortable.

After Jack tries again to get you to cancel your plans, you tell him, somewhat firmly, that the airport is not far, that, yes, you've had a lot to drink, but that it was spread out over some time and you'll be fine to drive. You say this with confidence, even though it's not true. You are not fine, although you are willing to make yourself both feel and seem that way.

Despite his questioning of your sobriety, Jack gets in your car with you when you offer him a ride to the party. It's several blocks away, and you want to take him there, in part because you'd hate for him to ride the bus or grab a taxi, and in part because you love to be with him and want him by your side as long as possible.

When you pull up in front of the house, Jack says, "When are we going to fight?"

He means boxing.

"Please," you say jokingly. "I'd knock you out in a heartbeat."

"I know." He sounds out of breath.

The car is dark and you see Jack's face all lit up by the streetlights. His eyes are caught in the shadows, and you are focused on his lips, those luscious lips.

To break the silence, Jack leans over and punches you in the shoulder, hard. Strangely enough, this is the second time in two months, since the second grade, that you have been playfully punched. The other time was by Marco, before you kissed him.

After a lengthy pause, Jack gives you a quick peck on the cheek before jumping out of the car. With Jack outside, the charge drains out of your car, your heartbeat beginning to slow. He tells you to be safe. You drive away, confused.

You have missed Marco and his warmth, but haven't given him much thought during the last six hours with Jack. You are going to pick Marco up at the airport, like you are his girlfriend or something. When you told him you couldn't make the trip to California, Marco understood and asked to borrow your sleeping bag. Before giving it to him, you folded the most flattering photo of yourself that you could find—a black-and-white profile shot of you walking with a self-satisfied smile through the cobblestone streets near Montmartre—and placed the picture by the opening of the bag before rolling it back up. When Marco camped, he would find you, in image only, near the place meant for his pillow.

On the way to the airport, you get a text message from Jack: "As always, had a wonderful time." Despite having had too many glasses of wine, you manage to write him back, when your car is stopped at a red light: "Me, too. Thank you."

When your car is waiting in line at the arrivals terminal, you get another message from Jack: "Drive safe, okay?" You write him back to tell him that you are safe; you have arrived. Marco is standing on the curb with his bags; you toss your phone in the back seat. You get out to greet him and your extended kiss causes honking horns. Marco always feels so good. *Shit.* Onlookers smile at you, as if to say, "Ah, young love!" They have no idea.

When you pull back from the hug, you hand Marco the keys and say with a burp, "If you don't mind, dear . . ."

Once in the car, he tells you all about his trip. Marco's grandfather has become jealous in his old age, much to the dismay of his wife, who now has to answer the probing questions of her once-gentle husband, even when she's just going to the grocery store to buy a stick of butter. This personality development was the focus of the time Marco spent with his family. His aunt even urged Marco to join them on a trip to the doctor's office, for an appointment his grandfather had made. But, never much of a joiner, Marco had declined. Later, he was relieved, when he learned that the reason for the big family outing was because Marco's grandfather was hell-bent on getting a prescription for Viagra.

Your hours with Jack are distant now, in the company of Marco. You don't even stop to think how much of a yo-yo you are becoming, ever enjoying the pendulum swing between one man and then another. Your states of being are colored by a sense of "with" and not "without."

In the passenger-side mirror, you watch the road as it curves behind you, opening up to a small two-lane highway. You see the white lights of the cars moving in the opposite direction, and the red lights of those in front of you. Any stray thoughts of how long you can keep this up are quieted when Marco reaches over to press your hair down at the nape of your neck.

That night, you are back in his bedroom, this place where you feel so comfortable. You are in bed, listening to the *Amélie* sound track—both of you slowly headed for sleeping and dreaming.

"This one is my favorite song," you murmur, brushing your lips against Marco's neck. You make satisfied "Mmmm . . ."

noises for no particular reason, and feel your stomach filling out against his, then falling in with an inhale.

Also half asleep, Marco puts on his glasses and walks across the room to the computer, the source of the music. He squints his eyes and looks at the screen. It takes you a minute to figure that he wants to know the name of this song, the one that is your favorite. He makes no announcement of his intentions, just moves quietly and steadily, as the glow of the computer screen lights up his face. Even though this registers, the sweetness of the moment is, most unfortunately, lost on you. You are too occupied scanning through the snapshots of your day, so varied and colorful, to see what's right in front of you.

9

THE SMILE IS already on your face, even before you open your eyes. Today is the day you have been waiting for.

After work, you are heading to the Vineyard with Marco, but more important, most important, you have a lunch meeting with Phillip Lopate, a talented essayist, novelist, and critic whose essays you adore so unabashedly it is actually embarrassing. You met him three months prior, when Mr. Lopate did a residency at your school. His visit involved a master class, craft talk, a reading, and an evening dinner reception. Normally, with such visits, you'd attend one or two of the events, never missing the free dinner, even if it was the type provided by campus food services and was, more or less, what you'd get in the cafeteria. (Ever the graduate student, you often brought empty Tupperware in which to collect the leftovers.) But with Mr. Lopate, you had attended every event, even arriving early to get a good seat at three out of the four activities. You'd read a great deal of his nonfiction work, yet none of his fiction. You were enamored with the turns his musings took, usually beginning with some sort of question and continuing on through perfectly smart attempts at finding an answer—or five. With his personal narratives in particular, his writing always seems to surprise the reader in you.

At the postreading dinner, you'd walked into the same graduate studies building where you would later meet Jack. Dinner was stretched out on a long folding table against the far wall, and you helped yourself to a large plate of pasta and marinara sauce. You saw him, his tall, white-haired self, sitting somewhat awkwardly in a tweed jacket against the arm of a sofa in the middle of the room. Students and faculty were wading through the room, settling into seats and sipping soda from paper cups. Wasting no time, you took a seat next to Mr. Lopate and, as the expression goes, began to chew his ear off.

You were effusive in expression of like, extreme *like*, of his work. You pandered some, asking him about writing about his family and siblings. You wanted to know because, like Mr. Lopate, you, too, are one of four children—and you, too, were the favorite of both your mother and your father. (Note: you know, knew, by this time, that it is not true about being the golden child, but sometimes you say things that aren't true because [1] they sound good; [2] you think that the other person might respond well; or—*sigh!*—[3] they just come flying out of your mouth before you can take them back.) You couldn't tell if he was semi-amused by you or just relieved to be distracted from the fact that he was the guest of honor. Probably the latter.

"How do your siblings feel about you writing these things?"

With a wry smile, he'd said, "I tell them that they can write their own books!"

Although he might be kidding and has already gone on to give you a straight answer about what it means to write honestly from your own perspective in the inevitable face of disagreement from others, you have filed the "Write your own books!" line away. You promise yourself to remember this. And use it, should the need ever arise.

You started to notice that your colleagues were beginning to give you dirty looks. You knew that you were not being collegial in hogging Mr. Lopate's time, but reasoned that anyone else could have invaded Mr. Lopate's personal space if she wanted to. You're not special. But before long, Mr. Lopate had looked at you with his kindly eyes and said, "Well, dear, I should mingle. That's why they bring me to these things."

You were not as self-conscious as you should have been, jumping up to say, "Of course! Thank you so much for coming!" But as you jumped up, you forgot about the plate of uneaten pasta—and dumped it unceremoniously on his lap.

"Mr. Lopate!" you said. "I am so sorry!" You ran to get a napkin, but he had waved you off. "Don't worry—it's fine."

Later, when the dinner was over, you went to say goodbye to Mr. Lopate and apologize again, when he said, "See? I've already forgotten about it."

Two months later, you were in the office of your advisor, who happened to be a friend of Mr. Lopate's. Your advisor suggested that you send a nonfiction piece you'd written about an aging boxer and his faded glory to Mr. Lopate.

"Phillip loves weird sports stories," he said.

Before your advisor was even finished, you'd excused yourself from his office and run all the way across campus—a notable feat, since you don't run many places and have, in general, chosen "I'll be late" over "I'll look really stupid sprinting." You'd emailed him your "weird sports story," opening with, "Dear Mr.

Lopate, I saw you speak this semester. You might remember me? I spilled marinara sauce all over you . . ."

He'd been kind enough to respond that, yes, he did remember you, and that he really liked your story. As a fledgling writer, you took this one a looooong way. Clearly, you were in need of encouragement, and for it to come from someone whose work you admire, well, this pleased you. You paused before sharing the "news" with your graduate school friends, because (1) that may appear boastful and (2) most important, it simply isn't news in the real world. You also paused before telling your nonwriting friends, because they may not have ever heard of a Mr. Phillip Lopate, and his stature was part of the delight. Instead, you settled on telling your mother, who you knew would be excited, regardless of whether or not she'd ever heard of him. When you read the email aloud, you saw something that you missed the first time: "I'd be happy to get together and talk writing with you over lunch sometime."

"What? Oh—that is wonderful!" she'd said.

You realized that your mother might have shown as much excitement if you'd just told her that you went to Century 21 and, according to your sales receipt, saved more than one hundred dollars on underwear. (And if you actually had saved one hundred dollars on underwear and told your mother this, you can bet that she'd be calling you later with a delayed reaction of, "I was thinking about it, and, ah, just how much underwear do you need anyway?") Still, you were glad that her response was positive. In these postgraduate days, in which you spend many an hour dreaming of your all-day writing times and there's no book deal in sight, you'll take what you can get. And besides, it was generous of Mr. Lopate to offer. Either the marinara sauce hadn't stained, or he doesn't pay much attention to things like that.

This morning you are lugging your weekend bag to your car, practically skipping on down the road. The sun is shining, and the part of your brain that houses both nervous and excited feelings is flashing. You are dressed for the occasion, wearing a flower-print skirt and a matching blue sweater. Normally you don't match so well. But this purchase had come from a shopping excursion with your mother, the talented shopper. In the store, you'd run into the mother of a childhood friend. Your mother chatted with her while you rifled through the racks of discount clothing. When you went into the dressing room with your mother, she sat in an empty changing area and said of the friend's mother, "Oh, she's really hoping her daughter gets a boyfriend. It's been a while, see." You just said, "Uh-huh," and were very, very glad that you did not say what was really on your mind (*Maybe she's a lesbian, Mom?*) because less than a moment later, the friend's mother had walked out of the stall next to yours. There was an awkward pause before she told you how flattering the skirt was. In other words, this outfit is symbolically perfect for soliciting an *Oh, Shit!* story.

You are speeding down the interstate and thinking of later on, when you and Marco will have settled into Vivian and Ellis's vacation house. The morning traffic doesn't bother you one bit, not even as you crawl along and surmise that this morning, once again, you will be late. You don't care because tonight you will cook fresh lobster and drink a delicious bottle of rosé champagne. Your head is filling up with decadent scenarios— hearty clam chowder for an afternoon snack, diving into the warm waves on the south side of the island, looking up at the stars with Marco, from your sleeping bags, because you are planning on sleeping out in the fresh island air. When your thoughts skip to lunch with Phillip, your circuits can't handle it. How good can one day be?

Thud.

Fudge! you curse, as you absorb the shock of your car rear-ending the car in front of you. This is so not part of the plan. *Mother-fudger!* you add for good measure.

After exchanging insurance information with the driver, a middle-aged woman, you are on your way again. You feel terrible the entire way in, thinking of her face as she stood there in a state of disbelief. She had been very nice about the whole incident. But still . . .

When you arrive at the office, Jack calls you. As always, he sounds breathless.

"Can I see you before you have lunch with Phillip? I have something for you."

Doesn't he know by now that you will see him any ol' time he asks?

Twenty minutes later you are sitting with Jack at an outdoor table at the café. The air is balmy and you have a tall, unsipped iced tea in front of you. When you approached the table, Jack had taken a long look at your legs in the skirt before standing to kiss you. Sometimes he does things like this for effect, to let you know that he's paying attention. But today you can tell that he's surprised at how nice you can actually look when you give your appearance a little TLC.

You are sitting across from one another, looking intently, the way you have come to do. Although he is looking more tired than normal and keeps complaining of getting little or no sleep, you think that he is beautiful, just beautiful. It's his eyes, especially, that you are taken with, in part for their intensity and in part for their clarity. They are the prettiest green.

Earlier in the week, when you'd told him that you were meeting with Phillip Lopate, he said, "How on earth did you get an appointment with Lopate? Oh, wait, I know. You charmed your way in." Jack is always finding ways to flatter you, and you are always struggling to feel comfortable with the fact that you like the flattery. A lot.

More and more, he tells you how physically attractive he finds you. When you try and deflect his compliments, say, by calling attention to the fresh coffee stain on your white shirt or your unruly wavy hair or the adolescent-worthy pimple on your chin, he just shakes his head, and even once said, "C'mon. You know how I feel about your noggin."

"Here," Jack says, pulling something out of his pocket. You love presents. You especially love presents that come with a card attached, one that has your name scrawled across the front. Jack hasn't written a card, but this hardly matters. He doesn't always rise when you leave the table, either, but in your best, most rational moments you do remember that you are not the Queen of England.

He presents you with one rectangular-shaped blue magnet. There is a picture of a bunny, with the words, "Oops! I pooped on your things!" below the image. This magnet makes you slightly uncomfortable, mostly because you know he knows—well, by now—the story of you in Melody's car.

"Oh, thanks," you say, your voice rising a bit.

Then, he hands you another magnet, the same size, which reads, "Well-behaved women rarely make history."

You smirk. "Jack? What do you think of me?"

"But it's true!"

The last magnet he gives you is your favorite. There is a graphic of a little girl with curlicue hair in a pretty pink pinafore. This one reads, "I'm happy—don't ruin it!"

Your eyes get wide when you read it. Jack adds, "That one is absolutely you."

The talk moves from magnets to motives. Jack gives you a lecture, one that seems slightly rehearsed, about how to approach Phillip for a story to go in *Oh, Shit!* He begins with your least favorite words,

"Now, what you need to do . . ."

You are listening, or trying to. You take the occasional sip of your beverage and try extra hard to keep Jack's gaze the whole time he's speaking. It's not really your thing, being told what to do. But Jack is the professional here. Your luck with Mr. Lopate hasn't been stellar so far; but today you are feeling well, living in the anticipation of what will be. You are confident. You know how to talk to people. Lunch will be no problem. Besides, you are better when you don't rehearse anyway.

Jack must see this in your expression, because he stops himself. "Well . . . you know what to do. You'll be great."

You smile and say thank you, thinking how the bonus visit with Jack has been the nicest surprise of your day so far—which, in all truthfulness, isn't so hard, considering you rearended someone on your way to work.

An hour later, you are sitting with Mr. Lopate in the dining room of an old midtown culinary institution. You have ordered another iced tea and are picking at your cold crab salad while Mr. Lopate talks. A native New Yorker, he has a very distinct accent, soft around the edges. You notice that he's wearing tweed again, even though it's an impossibly warm summer day. In visage only, Mr. Lopate reminds you of pictures you'd seen of your paternal grandfather when he was younger. But Mr. Lopate strikes you as a gentle soul, something you would never say of your grandfather, who was a very live-out-loud kind of person. You have memories of Papa showing you his brand-new candy-red shotgun or sipping a glass of a royal blue liqueur on the rocks at the Italian restaurant he frequented every Sunday. Colorful, the man was colorful. He stocked his basement full of the latest, greatest toys for his grandchildren's visits, and once bought two cars in the same exact color (red, of course) . . . just because. As your father once said—and you detected pride in this statement—"Papa was never apologetic about having fun."

Over lunch, when Mr. Lopate asks you to describe the embarrassment project, you launch into your idea. You want to make it sound smarter than it actually is. You don't want to tell him that, so far, your prize stories are all embarrassments of the bodily function variety. Of this, you are actually embarrassed. You stammer and can feel the tone of your voice jerking higher, like a kite on a windy day.

"Well." You take a big sigh. "Honestly, it's really the beginning."

When you mention that you may collect the stories and print them as a straight transcript, with only careful edits here and there, Mr. Lopate suggests, "You could bring the same eye to these stories that you brought to the story about the boxer."

You nod, but cannot fathom making stories about excrement either meditative or atmospheric.

When you ask him for an embarrassing story, he thinks about it for a few minutes before answering.

"Well, years ago I read a girlfriend's journal and she'd written how great I thought I was."

When you ask him if he'd be willing to include something like this in your book, he tells you he thinks he already wrote up something about it. He'll look for it and forward it to you.

Mr. Lopate then opines that you will have a hard time collecting the stories that are truly embarrassing, because those are the ones no one wants to talk about.

"Coming out of a bathroom with toilet paper on your shoe is a lot less damaging than, say, someone who wakes up after forty years of marriage and realizes that she no longer loves her husband."

This is true. You will have a hard time getting people to really share, as much as strangers open up to you about the most bizarre things, such as the guy who once told you he was mortified when, asked at a comedy show to name an animal that started with the letter A, in front of the whole audience he screamed out, "Orangutan!" Still, to ask about the more substantive embarrassments is akin to asking someone what part of their personage they would most like to conceal. The answers are bound to be filtered. In the case of replies to the standard job interview question "What is your biggest weakness?" potential candidates rarely ever answer with honesty. No one says, "I get easily bored and have a proclivity to web-surfing." Usually, it's the trite, "Oh, I'm a workaholic," or "My perfectionism really gets me down." People like to find ways to cast themselves as hero or coming out on top. You should know: you're a perpetrator.

To Phillip, you make halfhearted murmurs about how you want *Oh, Shit!* to run the gamut, being sometimes light, sometimes tender, and sometimes dark. But you cannot exactly figure out how to do this. Instead you hear yourself saying with false assuredness, "Like everything else, embarrassment exists on a continuum, and I want to cover the whole spectrum, from the lighter, more surface embarrassing moments to the ones that are rooted more deeply in shame." Forget writing. You should have gone into sales.

Mr. Lopate has provided you with the kind of questions you need to be asking, and now you want to buy him lunch.

When the bill arrives, you press your palm firm against the vinyl holder. "Oh, *Phillip*," you say, using the first name you are suddenly so comfortable with. "Please let me get this—you've been so generous with your time. I insist!"

He concedes and says a polite, "Thank you."

You sit there—stomach full, mind active—and enjoy the glow of a perfectly lovely lunch. Maybe even for a minute you refrain from saying anything at all. The silence hangs comfortably, until you notice the waiter hovering. He's standing there, hesitating, looking at you like he wants to whisper, but can't.

"Um, do you have another card? This one didn't go through." His tone is lowered, one of apology.

You, in fact, do not have another card. Your chest freezes and you lose your calm breath, as you try to scan your bank account's activity of recent days. *Fuck!* you think. *Fuck!* In your rush out of the house this morning, you must have forgotten to tell Davida to wait until tomorrow to cash your rent check. She works at a bank, and your rent checks always clear instantly.

"Uh . . ."

Without hesitating, Phillip pulls his wallet out of his coat, throws a card down on the table, and says, "This could be a good hustle for you, dear."

You only wish this gaffe were intentional. Your eyebrows are all scrunched up. Your day had been going so well. Well, sort of. And here you have a perfect *Oh, Shit!* moment, only it is happening *to* you.

As you and Phillip walk toward the exit, you say, "Oddly enough, I don't feel all that embarrassed." This is true. Your humiliation could be much, much deeper than it actually is. After talking with Phillip about the more complex versions of this feeling, what's a little glitch with your finances?

"You shouldn't," he says matter-of-factly.

"Well, this means that you'll just have to let me treat next time. I owe you one."

Before the uselessness of your bank card was highlighted, there was no guarantee of a next time or even pretense of a next time. And now you have an excuse to meet with Phillip Lopate again. Even if a future meeting were as brief as ten minutes, you'd take it. Inside, you are smiling a very, very big smile. Outside, you are trying not to let it show. But you know how that goes, and so before you two part on the street corner, taxis whizzing by, Phillip says with concern, "Do check your balance, though."

YOU DO NOT check your balance. You don't need to. If your card didn't cover a seventy-dollar lunch, then what's the point?

Back at your cubicle, you overhear your baby-faced, twenty-something office mate apologizing to her father. She has a Long

Island drawl: "Dad, I am sorry I called you a fucking asshole yesterday. I had too many jelly beans and you know how sugar affects me . . ."

After smiling to yourself, you call Jack.

"How was it?" Even though Jack has become increasingly busy over the summer—he's now juggling several projects at the finish-line stage—he manages to make time for you, even when you're calling or writing to tell him ridiculous things. Last week, for example, you were looking at the website of a photographer in Los Angeles, related to a work task. In this photographer's portfolio was a photo of James Woods. You re-membered an interview with the actor that you read several years ago. When asked about why he always dates women sig-nificantly younger than he, Woods said something to the effect of, "Well, when you're picking out a dog, you want a puppy, right?" After seeing Woods's photo, you shot off an email to Jack immediately, relaying this quote. In two minutes, Jack had written back, "You sure do have a lot of interesting stuff in that head of yours."

"Lunch was perfect, Jack!" Phillip is somewhere under-ground, taking the subway back to his house; no need to feign regret anymore. And you are focusing on the fact that you will—with any luck—have the opportunity to meet with him again—and this time it will be your treat. For certain. *Turn-ing lemons into le-mon-ade . . .* you think, far too happy with yourself, considering that the virtual stranger you invited out to lunch ended up paying.

First, you tell Jack about the flow of conversation, how you'd discussed the topic at a theoretical level and ran through differ-ent ways to bring life to your idea.

"Good, good."

Then you mention that Phillip said he does have an embarrassing story, of sorts, and that it was of the meatier kind you were hoping to start collecting.

"That's great," Jack says. You picture him in the office you've never seen, phone on his ear and multitasking, definitely writing an email to a client and nodding to his assistant, who probably needs to tell him something ASAP. You envision Jack gripping a pencil in his mouth, for a reason you have yet to determine. There is a stack of writing samples and proposals to the left of his computer, none of which are yours.

"But wait, wait, the best part is that my card got declined!"

"What?"

When you explain the circumstances and how it had played out in the bustling restaurant, Jack says, his voice sounding far-off like it sometimes does, "Wow . . . that couldn't have gone more perfectly."

When you hear the distance in his voice, you have yet to take it personally. In fact, this tone carries a mutation of his general enthusiasm, like you have just wowed him into near-speechlessness.

"Only you . . ." Jack continues.

Five minutes after you put the phone back on its base, an email from Jack pops up in your inbox: "I may not be your sugar daddy yet, but will you please let me give you a loan? You shouldn't travel with no money."

Although Jack is, of course, right, you are hardly focused on his offer. Instead, your reply is one little word: "Yet?????"

"Yes, 'yet.' Don't make me say it again," he writes back. "Let me help you."

You find this curious. You have never imagined yourself with a sugar daddy; in fact, the notion offends you. You have friends who would warm very quickly to the idea—and truth be told, you might even be one of them, if presented with the right opportunity—but you have always fancied yourself of the sugar mama variety. You are a self-sufficient woman and independent, too. Or at least that's what you aspire to be.

No, thanks, Jack.

He is satisfied with your actual response that you are traveling to the Vineyard with a "friend," and this friend can cover you (not that Marco even knows this. . .).

With his "yet-ness," Jack is becoming bolder, more transparent. He wants you. Jack wants you. And unfortunately for Marco, you want Jack, too. This is something you will probably have to stop denying. Probably sooner rather than later.

Hours later, you are in the car with Marco, headed north. The color of the sky is late-day sunny and the clear weather forecast is just one of the reasons that you are both very excited. You are with a million other cars, most of which are also headed to weekend getaways. You have told Marco all about Vivian and Ellis—or, well, at least one of their most embarrassing moments. When Vivian, who is somewhat shy, met Ellis's aunt for the first time, she'd taken her dog, a regal yet slightly awkward Doberman. Ellis's aunt had taken one look at the dog and then said to Vivian, "Wow, bet that dog takes a big shit." Vivian had suppressed any reaction, keeping her mouth pressed in an even, unintelligible line. Ellis's mother had started to squirm. To fill the awkward moment of silence, Ellis's aunt thought that the best follow-up to her socially inappropriate comment was to follow with another, as in, "So, Vivian, tell me, how's the sex with Ellis?" Within seconds, Ellis's mother was shuttling her sister back to the mental hospital, hoping that this brief yet potent exposure to Ellis's erratic family wouldn't scare dear Vivian away.

Marco picks up the three magnets that you've thrown in the console. The Friday afternoon traffic is heavy, as expected. But you don't mind, and Marco doesn't seem to, either.

"These are funny," he says. You can't tell if his meaning of funny in this context means: (1) laughter-inducing or (2) peculiar. If you have any sense of Marco, he means the latter.

"Oh, they're from the agent," you say, your eyes steadying on the long line of cars inching up the FDR in front of you.

Marco is low-key. You don't suspect that he has ever had even one dramatic fight. For the most part, he is even. One night, you'd sat in his kitchen telling him that you thought Maria was upset, possibly with you, because her boyfriend wasn't taking time off from their business to spend a weekend away with her, like Marco was with you. You were sitting on chairs next to one another, eating white rice with chopped tomatoes and olive oil. He turned toward you and pulled your face in close to his: "There is one world I care about, and that is the one that you and I are in."

This was music to your ears. You'd grown up keeping close the idea that you could save other people, i.e., family members, from themselves. But all this did was limit your own sense of possibility, making you useless to everyone—never mind delusional.

You like that Marco has never met your family, that he only knows you as you—not someone's daughter/sister/cousin/ niece. He has taken to calling you "Milly," after you googled one of his Italian words you didn't understand. When you plugged in "abbraccio"—which means hug—the website of Milly d'Abbraccio came up. Ms. d'Abbraccio is an Italian porn star, whose gigantic boobs are the focal point of all images on her site, even outshining her big bottle-blondness. You like being called Milly, especially because Marco gives extra emphasis on the opening "emmmm" sound. It is not the name you have grown up with, and therefore is free of all past associations.

"Your agent gave you these?"

You feel stupid when Marco says "your agent." Although you are glad that this is a professional lead, you feel like a liar when you refer to the agent as "yours." (In general, the "my" article is one you are only comfortable with when referring to things you truly own, such as your arm or perhaps a handbag.) To your family and friends, you don't call Jack by his given name. Instead, you insert a cold, distancing article in front of his job title. "The agent" moniker makes him seem like a character, and not a living, breathing person with whom you want to share every little thought that rolls through your head, no matter how inconsequential it may be. *Must tell Jack this,* you have come to think more often than not.

"Uh-huh," you say to Marco. Your relationship with Jack is just too bizarre to stay the way it is. Last week, you both counted and you'd sent hundreds of emails to one another, even though you met less than sixty days ago.

"Interesting," says Marco, placing them back to their position in the console. "Very, very interesting, my dear."

At this point, you do not know that the rest of your weekend will be rife with inconveniences. Your car will break down less than one hour outside the city. You and Marco will get to the

Vineyard precisely twenty-four hours late, after spending the night at a seedy motel in Norwalk, while you wait for an assessment of the $1,000-plus repairs that your car needs. You will find a dead fly on the bed in the motel, and spend most of the night worrying that someone could barge right into your room since the door doesn't lock, and you hope it's not the guy from the parking lot, whom you heard refer to his wife as "bitch" in a decidedly sober manner. You and Marco will start to kiss, until you both admit that the room, with its dead-air cigarette stench and makeshift paint bucket turned trash can, has stripped the hubba-hubba right out of you. When you go back to pick your car up a week later, you will stay at your aunt and uncle's house, where Uncle Bill will accidentally walk into the room in which you are staying and see you completely naked. No, you don't know that any of these mild annoyances are about to befall you; somehow, you are betrothed to this idea of living in a positive, if fantasy-based, existence.

Leaving the city, you look forward, out to the sky, where the treetops meet the clouds. In the face of traffic, you take a deep breath and remind yourself that you have no control, that you and Marco may miss the early ferry. That's okay. You are determined to focus on all that shines, as if it is gleaming for you and only you. You've ignored Marco's indirect questioning about Jack and the magnets. Why worry about details?

Bump.

Mother of god, you've done it again, gotten carried away in thought while driving and rear-ended another car. For someone who'd never even tapped another car's bumper while parallel parking, you sure are making up for lost time in this very short span of nine hours.

"Milly, you okay?" Marco asks, reaching across to press his hand against your chest.

Thankfully, this is not as extensive as this morning's rear-ending, in which the other car's back bumper had been damaged.

You are staring through the windshield in shock, preserving your breath in case the situation requires a good, agitated scream. For better or worse, your feelings of frustration are buried deep.

A heavy man with slicked-back salt-and-pepper hair slams the car door as he gets out to look at the damage. You are gritting your teeth, praying for good news.

When he sees that everything is intact, he turns to you. You have said, "I'm sorry!" one hundred times over, but he doesn't seem to hear you.

"Watch it!" he yells gruffly, pointing an index finger in your direction. You shrink from his offensive. "What are you, lady? Completely out to lunch?"

10

AUGUST IS FULL of last-ditch efforts to cling to summer. You schedule more time at the beach with Marco, cuddling on beach blankets and reading until sunset. You throw any bit of conservative behaviors aside, even opting not to use your trusted 45 SPF suntan lotion. *Why not enjoy what I have now?* you reason. With your accumulating bills and desire to move, you are aware that stress could be imminent. You try, most days, to forget about all the variables in your life, still emailing Jack every day, all day. The talk at your coffee breaks with him turns from silly banter to grand promises.

"I want to give you the life that you deserve," he says one afternoon, at the café on Forty-second Street. You look at his face with such adoration—those open eyes, the prominent nose— that you can't imagine not having been immediately smitten with him from the first time you saw him. "You are going to have an amazing career."

Although this smacks of the sugar-daddy talk, you hear it in a way you hadn't before. And that's because part of you needs him to be right.

"Oh, please, Jack," you brush him off, and take a sip of your iced tea, looking out to the cars streaming around the corner from the traffic jam on Lexington Avenue. You pretend you aren't taken with his promises, but this is just posturing. Your head goes to an imaginary house on the beach, the one you've always wanted. You don't know if it's on the East Coast or the West Coast, but you do know it's secluded, and that it's a perch or nest or even womb from which you will produce lots and lots of work. Of course, there is a hammock in the yard and you will take afternoon naps there and tend to the irises and peonies you've planted by the back patio. You will make a rule: no cut flowers in your house, unless they are from one of your backyard plants.

"It's true. You are going to do some really great things," Jack continues.

Although there has been talk of turning *Oh, Shit!* into a musical (Jack's idea), you cannot envision it, past an impressive horn section. (You'd like to handpick that tuba yourself.) When you press Jack, he tells you not to worry, that everything will come in time. He holds these ideas, promises of huge success, and tells you to wait.

And waiting is exactly what you are doing—and not because you want to. Life, it seems, has handed you no other options.

AFTER WORK THAT day, you head up to Annabelle's in Boston on the Chinatown bus, which runs from Chinatown in New York to Chinatown in Boston. The bus line used to be a small operation, yet now it has blossomed from the first time you took it with Ted, crammed up in a small van with several other passengers. You have to take the bus this time because you had visited Annabelle the weekend before and, once again, your car broke down. Your coworkers gave you long, pitiful looks when you mentioned the continuing saga of your automobile troubles. Although you are tired from another week spent hanging out with Marco at night, you force yourself to bring a notebook and tape recorder, in case some good stories appear. These days, you don't know the meaning of rest.

When you arrive at Annabelle's, she is upset. You open a bottle of red wine and sit out on her second-story porch, which is lit with white Christmas lights, smoking cigarettes and catching up on one another's week. The guy she had been dating—and very into—turned an abrupt, mean corner, breaking her heart. You look at her pretty face, strained with worry, and tell her if you bump into the guy, you'll give him a one-two punch. You know you will not, as does she, but in times like these, the most appropriate thing to say is often inappropriate. You just want to make her feel better.

When either of you is upset, especially if it has to do with romance, you take great pains to comfort the other and let her know you're there for her. All strains of sibling rivalry, jealousy, and competition—which, thanks to shame, you will never even admit exist—are erased. During one particular rough patch, while Annabelle was living in Los Angeles and breaking up with her fiancé, you flew out four times in twelve months, so that the two of you could do fun things like eat Hot Dog on a Stick, have sushi in a place with a strobe light and dancing waiters, and drink beers and meet boys after a day at the beach. Even in hard times, Annabelle is really good at making the mundane appealing. And a part of you loves feeling useful. (Not to mention that when she needs you, she calls you more.) In times like these, you are most fiercely sisters. Growing up, Annabelle was your mother, older sister, and protective brother all rolled up into one, acting as the chaperone on your school field trips, teaching your Sunday school class, and taking you to get your driver's license. If you had a disagreement with a friend and wanted someone in your corner, Annabelle was the one you went to. She was also the first to tell you that you were being rude if you had a friend over and didn't offer her something to drink. Certain echoes of these mothering times still pervade your relationship, only you are not a child anymore. You bristle if you hear judgment in Annabelle's voice.

Annabelle takes a long drag of her cigarette and then lets it out. She is curled up on a wicker chair, and you are sitting likewise, on the matching love seat. Her cat comes out to rub his back against the legs of her chair.

"I mean . . ." she says, looking far off, past the rows of Victorian houses on her street. You imagine your presence almost unnecessary. Her voice is incredulous, and again, you are at a loss for words. When you broke up with Ted, Annabelle managed to say all the right things, including, "What do you want? Karaoke? Dancing? I'm there." Now you only want to make her feel like everything is going to be okay. Only . . .

She continues, "No one's ever called me a whore before . . ." She puts down her cigarette and sighs. "Well, except for Mom."

She says this so matter-of-factly that it's all you can do to suppress a laugh. You barely talk about the moodier aspects of your mother's personality, except with Annabelle, because with her you never have to explain. You remember the time well, even though you were only nine or ten years old. It wasn't the least bit funny then. To the best of your recollection, your mother didn't call her a "whore"—she suggested that Annabelle was acting like a "slut." The reasons were preposterous and had everything to do with your mother's fears about your sister's innocence. When she was in high school, Annabelle had been spending the evening at her boyfriend's house, with his whole family, including his grandmother, who, incidentally, was very fond of dirty jokes. (This was the year you learned about euphemisms.) Your mother called, only to find out that everyone was in the hot tub, which set her off. Soon you were in the front seat as your mother drove over to Annabelle's boyfriend's house. Your mother ignored the speed limit and drove clutching the steering wheel, her face revealing panic. You remember sitting next to her in the dark, wishing that there were more streetlights on the back-country road.

After a long sigh, you consider reminding Annabelle that your mother actually said "slut" and that this distinction is somewhat better because "whore" implies payment.

Instead, you say, " 'Except for *Mom*?' " Chuckling. " 'Except for *Mom*?' "

She looks at you with her heavy blue eyes, trying to find amusement where there is none. After a halfhearted laugh, she looks away, glum.

You sit back against the chair and look out to the row of two-family houses across the way, watching as the smoke from your exhale floats across the porch. Even though the smoke from Annabelle's cigarette will cross to meet yours, even though she is sitting less than five feet away from you, you note, as neutrally as you can, that your perspective heightens a distinct separation between you two, one that is neither good nor bad.

THE NEXT AFTERNOON is wide open, as summer days are wont to be. You reluctantly set out for an errand you really don't want to run. While you are in Boston, now that you've picked up your newly repaired car, you also need to pick up your bike. It's been at Ted's old apartment for over a year. He doesn't live there anymore, having moved to New York less than three weeks after you broke up. But the old, rickety three-speed on which you used to zip around the Boston streets has been hanging out on the back patio of the house for months. You called his landlords, Pat and Babette, who are a couple, and told them you'd be by to remove it from their property. Pat and Babette are young and cool and you were friendly with them even before Ted had moved into their downstairs apartment. As you drive up the hill, this familiar street, your chest starts to clench. It wasn't that this place had so many memories for you and Ted; he'd moved there only after you'd moved to New York, and your nights and weekends there had been limited. By this time you are beginning to feel the distance, and so you don't expect that seeing his old yellow house will be too traumatic.

But when you park your car outside of the side entrance, near the back patio, you stop. Today is August 6. Exactly one year ago, to the day, you are returning to where you'd ended one of the most important relationships of your life, walking into Ted's bedroom after a long waitressing shift, after a long summer of fighting and falling in love with someone else, after a long, drawn-out conversation between the two of you that never seemed to arrive anywhere, always debating the merits of staying together or moving on—not that either of you could even imagine what that would entail—after all this, you walked into his bedroom in your greasy jeans and sweaty black T-shirt to say not much more than, "I think we should break up."

He'd looked at you then, from where he was stretched out

on his bed reading a book. His eyes said, "I hate you." This was the man who never let you go in his sleep; every night you spent in his bed, you could expect to wake up with his arms wrapped tight around you, with warm kisses on your shoulders or cheeks. This man, the one you adored right back, this was the man you were dumping.

Why you didn't remember this very significant anniversary before you'd scheduled the bike pickup was beyond you. Sometimes you have a way of looking miles above, around, and beyond the very, very obvious.

When you ring the bell to Pat and Babette's apartment, you hear, "Helloooooo! Come in!" Babette's voice, with her strong Australian accent, is so dainty.

As you walk up the stairs and into their kitchen, you are flooded with memories of cocktail parties and lively debate. You'd buried your backside against their stove many times, with one arm across your chest and the other holding a drink, often offering your two cents about city politics or some local band's bassist. (What is it about those bassists?) Many times in this kitchen, you'd had something to say. The fact that this was once very significant to you is palpable now.

"Would you like a beer?" Babette asks, after a warm hello hug. She settles quickly back on the couch, draping a blanket over her folded-up legs. A strange man wearing glasses is sitting across from her, also drinking a beer. His shaggy brown hair is unkempt, flying in at least four directions. The top four buttons on his wrinkled shirt are undone. Either his chair sinks low or he's well over six feet tall.

"Um, this is Luke, Pat's good friend," Babette says, the corners of her tiny mouth turning upward. "He's just arrived from Africa, and I suspect that Pat's forgotten, since he's, um, out."

"Hi, Luke," you say, taking a seat next to his. "Long flight?"

"Oh, was it ever!" His voice is raspy and loud, each of these qualities so strong that you can't decide if the end result is appealing or appalling. "But I'm here now. On va-ca-tion, having a few beers."

You notice a few empty bottles near his feet.

Going further on the theory that Pat forgot about Luke's arrival, Babette says, "Well, it's really too bad, because Pat and I are going to see Coldplay tonight."

"Oh, it's fine, Babette. I'm easy—totally happy to just hang out on my own. I might head down to Harvard Square and get a pint." Turning to you, he adds, "That's the neighborhood I grew up in—can't wait to see all the old haunts!"

You spend the next few minutes catching up—you tell Babette about your life in New York, sans all the sordid romantic activity. You have this feeling that people who knew you with Ted have a hard time imagining otherwise. Maybe it's just you.

"Well, I should get going," you say, standing. Slightly uncomfortable with everything that hasn't been said, i.e., that you've spent the greater part of the last year adjusting to life without Ted, you finished your beer in record time.

"Hey, can you drop me at Harvard Square?" Luke asks, throwing one hand in the air. His hand, like everything about Luke, is big. You've known him all of five minutes and already pegged him as one of the lucky few who know how to live large.

"Sure, no problem." You have plans to head to a barbeque cohosted by your friend Lyniah. Lyniah, a former-coworker-turned-friend, has been saying how much she hasn't been looking forward to the party, and the only reason you were invited is because you are visiting from out of town. You wouldn't get the chance to see her otherwise.

"Listen, Luke, I'm going to a party. You're welcome to come. I mean, I won't know anyone except for my friend, and she keeps telling me it's not going to be very much fun, but, hey, if you have nothing else going on, you're more than welcome."

Next thing you know, you've given Babette a perfunctory kiss on the cheek, loaded your bike into the trunk with Luke's help, and are driving away from Ted's old house, Luke sitting in your front seat.

Before the barbeque, you have two objectives: (1) buying Luke clove cigarettes from the newsstand in Harvard Square; and (2) buying champagne to celebrate the new chapter in Lyniah's new professional life. She's just told you that she's quitting her job at the dysfunctional women's center nonprofit, where you used to work, too. You'd had three primary reasons for leaving: (1) your boss scheduled four-hour meetings on the patio outside so that she could chain-smoke; (2) said boss also liked to schedule meetings at the bar across the street so she could scarf down one of their fantastic chili dogs and then talk about how she wished she could lose weight; and (3) said boss, a white woman, made mandatory the "Examining White Privilege" weekly support group, which really bummed you out, mostly for its heavy secretiveness. Although the goal of this group was purportedly to make the center a more racially inclusive place, the lone person of color on staff—Lyniah, who is African-American—knew nothing about what was actually going on behind those closed doors. Maybe that was a blessing after all, since it was not uncommon to hear statements during the meeting such as, "Actually, you might not know this about me, but I'm actually black. I mean, my whole family, the people I really care about, are black, so . . ." In your mind, the group worked in direct opposition to its intended purpose. You were glad to quit. Given your personal experience there, the occasion of Lyniah's resignation is a happy one indeed.

"I wanna buy the champagne," Luke says. "I'm the guest. I'm buying the champagne."

Although Pat and Babette's neighborhood is populated with spacious Victorians, the ones behind Harvard Square are even more well kept, as distinguished by their prim lawns, carefully tended flower gardens, and chipless paint jobs.

Rolling down his window, Luke sticks his arm out and splays his fingers to catch the late-day air.

"Oh, see that house?" he says. "That's where creepy Old Lady Johnson lived. My brother and I used to torture her cats."

The newsstand happens to be in the busiest intersection of Harvard Square. Luke opens the door before you've completely pulled over and says, "Be back in a minute! Don't leave. Heh, heh."

A minute later, with his clove cigarettes in hand, Luke yells (or at least it sounds like he's yelling), "Man! I love this place. Shit, it's changed so much. Mind if I turn the radio on?"

"Be my guest."

He changes the stations until you hear the opening chords of Elton John's "Tiny Dancer."

"Wait! I love that song."

"No way! Me, too."

By now the air is pouring through the windows and you are both puffing away on your sweet brown cigarettes, with the volume on the radio turned way up, singing *"count the head-lights on the highway"* in chorus. Even though you're navigating a tricky roundabout, you manage to sway your head from side to side with the words.

The sun settles on an invisible horizon. Despite passing the restaurant where Ted had proposed, you are completely free of worry, sadness, and any sort of general concern. You love when life takes these sudden turns.

You reach the liquor store before the song is over and so you pull into a parking spot with the car still idling, sitting there with Luke, making sure you belt out every last word of "Tiny Dancer," because that's just the kind of people you are.

LUKE LOVES LYNIAH immediately, and is now very happy that he insisted on buying her the bottle of champagne. Upon meeting her, Luke had given her a big bear hug, which was an amusing sight given their difference in height. Her face was jammed up practically into his armpit, her eyes looking out at you, slightly panicked.

Now you are sitting on folding chairs in a small back alley, drinking lots of beer. White lights lace a chain-link fence, and flickering candles are scattered everywhere. Contrary to Lyniah's misgivings, the party is quite fun, with an eclectic mix of guests—some students, some young professionals, some bohemian types, and . . . Luke. He is, by far, the loudest person at the party. He slaps his knee. He whacks your back when you say something he finds funny. Luke is the least self-conscious person you've ever met. You have already asked him for an embarrassing story and his response came faster than most: "Me? Nah. I never get embarrassed. I have no shame."

You don't believe him, not at first. Later, you and Luke have befriended Kyle, a young black artist. The three of you are talking about failures in love when Lyniah walks by. Forget love. Luke is on to lust, his eyes trailing off in her direction.

"I love African women," he says.

You and Kyle look at one another. Did he really just say that?

"Oh, man," Kyle says. "Luke, dude . . ."

When Lyniah walks by again, Luke pulls her arm. She's holding a plate of food wrapped in tinfoil.

"You are so beautiful," Luke says. "I love African women."

Although Lyniah is black, she grew up in Texas. You start to point this out to Luke: "She's not Africa—"

But before you can finish, Lyniah, who has warmed to Luke considerably over the course of the evening, interrupts you to say in one breath, "*SomepeoplesayIlookWestAfrican*." Then she moves along to the kitchen.

"Wow, you were right, Luke," you say, remembering his comment about having no shame.

He whips his head in your direction and bellows, "What? Right about what?"

Sitting back on your folding chair, marveling at the coziness in this tiny outdoor space, you say, more to yourself than anyone else, "Everything. You're right about everything."

11

YOU ARE PRACTICALLY homeless. Although Davida hasn't found a replacement for you—she keeps joking she hopes you'll change your mind—you have less than three weeks to figure out in which borough you'll begin your autumn. Money is still tight. After rear-ending that woman a few weeks ago, your insurance company became hip to the fact that you don't actually live in a small Massachusetts suburb anymore, a case you possibly could have made while still a student. But now you're practically a fraud—or just lazy—and your auto insurance rates tripled overnight. You're still scraping by on your temp wages, and the prospect of asking to borrow money from your parents again doesn't feel like an option. You are sure they would help if you asked—they have never denied you. But the truth is that you are twenty-nine and it's about time for you to have a growing savings account or a Roth IRA. Only you don't.

You found an ad on craigslist that looked promising: an apartment share in Park Slope/Windsor Terrace. You don't know much about Park Slope, other than what you learned on your hours-long nondate date with Jack, and that's enough to give you an optimistic feeling. As you are driving to look at the place, Marco calls.

"Milly, want to have dinner later?"

"Sure, just after I check this place out. Shouldn't be too long."

Traffic is tough on the BQE. You are moving ten miles an hour just after crossing the Triboro Bridge, looking perhaps a little too closely at the sign above the truck's bumper in front of you: "How's my driving? Please call 1-800-566-4322." Does anyone actually call those numbers? You wonder if the driver doesn't feel a little helpless, like a mini-pinscher whose owner made him wear a sweater, even though it's seventy degrees out.

When you realize that you're going to be late for the appointment, you call the contact listed on the ad. Serdar seemed nice enough from his email communications and you are looking forward to meeting him. As much as you loathe the actuality of impending joblessness when the temp gig is up and homelessness, you like the aura of possibility it casts on your future. You have no idea where you will land in three weeks, and so most times you find a twinge of excitement perusing job and apartment listings. Not only do you want to start fresh, you need to.

When you call Serdar to tell him that you are going to be late, he answers on the fifth ring.

"Hi, hi."

Is it you, or should you have brought someone with you? You hear no voices in the background, even though the ad had indicated it would be an open house.

"Serdar, I emailed you about seeing your place," you say, feeling uncertain. "I'm running a little late."

Although he says this is no problem, you are now slightly concerned. He sounds nice enough, yes. But it had taken him a long pause to respond.

You dial Marco back: "Can you come with me?"

When you pull up in front of Marco's building, he is leaning against the heavy industrial door.

"Mil-ly," he says, sounding so I-talian, with an upward emphasis on the first syllable. Always one to take his time, Marco is sauntering toward your car. He leans into the driver's-side window to give you a kiss on the lips.

"Hurry, babe! I'm late already."

As he walks around the front of your car—still moseying—you look at his delicate face, his thick mass of curly hair, his lanky frame, and think, *What am I going to do?* Marco is darling, fun, and easy to be with. He always has something smart to say. He's very considerate and treats you well. He's sexy as all hell. Your only problem with Marco is that he's not Jack.

Jack, Jack, Jack, you think, sighing. *Where is he?*

The night before, Jack had mentioned that he needed to buy a baby gift for one of his clients. You suggested some early childhood books from your absolute favorite line in children's literature. You love these books so much, and Jack is so busy, that you offered to make the selection for him and place an online order. Pleased, Jack had thanked you over and over, telling you that the idea was so brilliant he couldn't imagine that he hadn't thought of it himself. (Of course, this was written in an email with an e–smiley face—☺—at the end of the sentence.) In return, Jack had offered to help you reshape your résumé, adding in an email, "I'll have it ready in two days. I wouldn't do this for anyone else, just so you know. But I'll do it for you."

Marco hears you sigh.

"What is it, Milly?" he says, touching your face. "Tell me."

"Nothing," you say as you look in your rearview to pull away from the curb. "I'm just . . . I hope this place works out."

Safety concerns aside, inviting Marco was a good idea. Once you get off the exit, he holds the directions and tells you when to turn left, when to turn right. You are far from the area where you'd been with Jack. Over here, there are rows of two-story brick apartments. You note more chain-link fences and white plaster fountains than greenery.

"Wait," Marco says. "I think this is on the park. Beautiful."

Sure enough, you take a left onto Prospect Park Southwest, which is where you'd been with Marco last week, picnicking under a big shady tree and making a long list of celebrities you thought might be inclined to share an *Oh, Shit!* moment. (Number one was Cameron Diaz.) That day, you'd mentioned to Marco how great it would be to live on the park.

Today is lucky. You pull in front of the apartment building and there is a spot. But it's not an apartment building: your potential new apartment is a pretty gray brownstone, with large bay windows and an actual stoop. You start to imagine the stoop sales you might have, how you might set up a nice reading nook in front of the window.

"Wow, Milly—this is beautiful."

Once out of the car, you skip over to Marco's side, jumping up and down as you grab his hand while crossing the street. "Yes! I could live here!"

After you ring the doorbell, you wait. You ring it again. Under the glare of the streetlight, Marco puts his arms around your waist and begins to kiss you, deeply.

While you and Marco are still smooching, a man in his early thirties answers the door. He is paternal-looking, with a full goatee, brown skin, and heavyish frame. He's wearing brown cords.

"Hello. I am Serdar," he says, extending his hand, looking at the two of you with mild amusement. He has a warm face, with open brown eyes and a ready smile. His voice is heavily accented, and you have already guessed from his last name that he is Turkish.

You introduce yourself, then Marco. When Serdar doesn't hear Marco's name, he asks you to repeat it. Marco responds instead, giving a proper rolled *r* to the pronunciation of his name.

"Ah, you are Italian?" Serdar asks as he welcomes you into the foyer. While they talk, you take a look around: there are two doors, both framed in well-preserved dark wood. Serdar points to the left door and says, "This is where the landlord lives, but he's never here."

You nod and follow him through the door on the right, up the dark stairs, with Marco following. You look at the carpeted steps and think, *Okay, so I can vacuum.*

The cramped second floor has three bedrooms, an office, and a large bathroom. None of these bedrooms are for rent, Serdar explains. He lives with his girlfriend, Nisa, in the large front bedroom with bay windows. Another friend, an Albanian, lives in the back bedroom, next to the office that Serdar uses. The third bedroom, just next to the one Serdar shares with Nisa, is really more small than cozy. He mentions that the Albanian's sister, Sophie, will be there. Looking into the bedroom, you remember when you lived in a room this small. It was on a side street in Cambridge, and though there was barely room for your bed, you loved the wrapped-up feeling you got whenever you settled under the covers to read. You read somewhere that humans feel protected in small spaces. Sure, there was no room to dance if you felt like it, but you didn't have to worry about filling up empty space.

Serdar explains that Sophie will take this room when she comes back from a trip to Vienna.

When you ask how Serdar found the roommates, he explains that the four of them lived together for a time in Istanbul, where they were studying at a university. Now all four of them are doctoral candidates at NYU, all in different departments.

"We are all poor graduate students," he explains.

Even though you have a lot of experience in this area—once adding honey, balsamic vinegar, and even mustard to your rice and beans because you couldn't stand the thought of eating another poor man's flavorless meal—you say nothing. You nod your head as Serdar leads you up to the third floor.

Let there be light, you think. Despite the number of other desperate, cash-strapped young women examining every corner, also hoping to call this place home, you look beyond the clusters, beyond the small talk, barely hearing a self-satisfied, "I used to work for *Who Wants to Be a Millionaire?* but now I'm with Martha Stewart," beyond the unframed, oversized red World Social Forum posting hanging on the hallway, eyes skipping all the minor details of dust balls in the corner and a wicker chair with broken straw fanning off one of its arms—all because you are overcome by the feeling of space.

Space. This is what you feel, like you are outside, standing on the beach, vast sky overhead, not caring whether it's rain-ing or sunny because you are free, open to whatever it is this landscape has to offer. You have already begun to plan your morning writing sessions, how you will hunker down on the couch with a cup of coffee, your computer, and the blanket of trees outside the window. You need this.

Marco says something that doesn't register. You feel his hand on your shoulder. He is pointing to a stained-glass skylight just over by the living room. On the third floor, the living room owns the bay windows. There is a wide-open area of light hardwood floor, filled only with a couch, two chairs, and a decaying wicker coffee table; dusty issues of the *New Yorker* are suspended off its bottom shelf, because that is broken, too.

Opposite the bay windows, sliding wooden doors lead into the dining room. A family-sized table practically fills the whole space, with six mismatched chairs lining its perimeter. *How "flea market,"* you think.

You like walking through this space—with its stark walls and plethora of windows, you imagine everything and nothing at once. When you get to the bedroom in question, you see west-facing windows, through which the sun likely spills. You like this. The room is approximately the same size as your room at Davida's. You wander through it, not looking too closely at anything. Even when you see that there is a white cabinet built into the wall with real live bookshelves, it registers briefly and second to your gut feeling that this is the place where you will flourish.

With the prospective roommates you are being shy, and silently feel relief that you haven't told any completely inane associative stories, like your Beavis and Butt-head moment in Turkey, when you and your brother spent the greater part of your day in Istanbul being amused by the Turkish language's bent toward phonetic spellings (*taksi, milyonair,* and *turtel*) and having a speed postcard-writing contest (images of Kemal Atatürk accompanied by text that read, "Know who this guy is? Founder of the Turkish Republic. That's right. I'm in Istanbul."). Even you know that sometimes certain things are better left unsaid.

Marco takes a seat across from you, crosses his legs, and begins to talk about Europe. Somewhere in the back of your mind you think, *Glad I brought a European.* Marco makes conversation with Serdar and Nisa, who is a somewhat quiet redhead with freckles and pie-shaped cheeks. You notice an interesting phenomenon: the less you say, the more Marco speaks. It's a technique you learned in oral history class: when one becomes comfortable with silences, one creates space.

Serdar encourages you to sign a notebook, to write your name, contact information, and one identifying characteristic. Concise has never been your thing and so you write that you like to box, write, run, and make people laugh.

When you get up to leave, Marco stands, too, clearing his throat.

You turn to your potential roommates: "So, I'm interested. When will you decide, Serdar?"

"Soon. We need to decide very soon."

Marco gives a nod, extends his hand to your hosts, and you both slink down the stairs, waving goodbye.

Later, you are having dinner at a sidewalk café that Marco had heard was good. The cuisine is so-called Italian, but you swear that someone put a stick of butter in your fennel salad. Conversation is quiet tonight; mostly, you are tired and ready for some stability. You feel your phone vibrate in your pocket. Even though you know it's rude, you clear your throat and sneak a look at who is calling you, keeping your phone tucked in your lap, below the table. But no one's calling you. Instead, there is a text message from Jack, which reads, "Is it so crazy that I want to see you tomorrow?"

Crazy? Yes. Unpleasantly so? Far from it.

You are flush, and it's more than your hot cheeks. You are flush with men, flush with possibility, and you can imagine no place you'd rather be—until you notice Marco's face, his eyes looking concerned. Clearing his throat, he knows something is changing. Your stomach feels queasy.

Patting your belly, you say, "Who puts butter in fennel salad? It's so good all by itself."

When he shrugs and lifts a forkful of grilled pizza to his mouth, you put your own fork down in exasperation, look down at the sidewalk, and murmur, "Nothing like ruining a perfectly wonderful thing."

"You can't take that place," Jacks says.

Serdar emailed you this morning, less than twelve hours after you looked at the place, to tell you that the room was yours if you wanted it. You are thrilled. You don't want to over-analyze: your main objective is to cross off "finding a home" from your to-do list.

"Why not?" you counter, taking a sip of your buttery Sancerre. Feeling a gentle buzz rise to your head, you realize that this sure has been a summer of plenty for you. Now that you're drinking with regularity, excessive alcohol consumption has come to settle on your hips. Since you have essentially abandoned your gym already—boxing only twice last week—your body, like your life, is in flux. "Why the hell not, Jack?"

"Because, because, because . . ."

Jack is leaning over the table, his head coming as close to yours as it can, still keeping within the unspoken rules of your nondate dates (Rule #1: Thou shalt not actually kiss). This time you are not at your usual Bryant Park restaurant or the sushi place on Forty-ninth. Jack has insisted he take you to Nobu, since you love sushi and he loves sushi.

"Because you should always look at other places, to make sure that you are getting the best possible apartment. It's common sense."

You're sitting in a row of tables for two arranged by the window. You see lots of patrons with well-coiffed hair and shiny makeup. In the bathroom, you'd taken note of how every woman seemed to be clad in black and had at least two shopping bags on her arm. This is so not your scene.

At your table, the lights are dim, and with all the wine you've had, you only see the glow of Jack's eyes, how they grow more intense when he talks about something he cares about. He cares about a lot. You adore this quality in a man.

"But Jack, I'm taking it. I had a good feeling when I saw it last night."

"Well, that's good. But it doesn't mean you shouldn't see what else is out there."

He could very well be talking about your attachment to him, if only he weren't taking the great lengths to impress you that you take to impress him. You have all but decided that Jack is the one for you—this fact became clear to you when it took you forty-five minutes to decide what to wear on this date. (You finally chose your favorite Nanette Lepore butterfly skirt, the one with the ruffled slit right up the front center seam; to you, this skirt says, "Celebrate!") You don't want to end things with Marco—who likes to end a perfectly swell thing? However, you have given yourself already to Jack, in ways that you don't see possible with Marco, or at least you've stopped wondering if they were possible with Marco. Sure, you have never crossed any physical boundaries with Jack. But he is the one you turn to when you have questions, when you need to think an idea through, when you want, simply enough, to be seen.

"Do you think our relationship is strange?" you ask, knowing that this is a rhetorical, masturbatory question. But lately with you and Jack, it seems that your favorite topic of conversation is, well, you—as in second person plural.

"Um, yeah . . ." his tone flip. Jack is lifting his glass to his lips. Although his head is angling down, his eyes look up at you, more serious than you've seen them.

"Just curious," you say, winking.

Food comes soon after and you feast on rock shrimp tempura in a rich spicy cream sauce, maybe the tastiest you've ever had. Sushi follows and for the next two hours, you drink and talk and eat and talk more.

By now Jack knows everything about you—at least your narrative. There's not a story that you haven't told him, whether it be about Ted or playing field hockey in high school or your trip to Tanzania. Jack is your champion. You know that you are still processing everything that happened with Ted, that you're not fully over the end of that relationship. Sometimes you vent to Jack, telling him every last thing that bothered you about Ted, even the most minor details, i.e., he didn't like capellini or his concern with the impressions he made on others. Jack indulges you, always listening. He soothes you with a nod of the head, and tells you how happy he is that you're no longer in a relationship that, by the end, had come to feel rather constricted. You are so happy to have found such a sympathetic friend.

You think you know as much about Jack. You know about his professional ambitions, how hard he works to please his clients, colleagues, friends, and family. You see how earnestly he tries to do the right thing. You know about his relationship with his wife, and how his dedication to his work was eventually problematic. But when he talks about meeting her on an afternoon ferry to Bainbridge Island and being instantly blown away by their connection, Jack says, "It was like we hit the jackpot." When he says this, his expression fades into memories. The mood is oddly comfortable; you sit quiet until your Jack returns to you. You know how hard their breakup was, intuiting how much his wife's absence has marked him, even if he doesn't ever say too much.

When you and Jack talk about your exes, the subtext has become, *That will never happen to . . . us.*

After dinner and nearly four glasses of wine—you couldn't finish the last glass—you and Jack are walking down a sidewalk in Tribeca. The streets are dark and there are very few cars driving by. Although it is August, you feel a chill. You hold on to Jack's arm for stability, looking up to warehouses, the exteriors of which appear like slate-colored sheets. Once again, your shoe choice sucks. (This time it's high, high black stiletto slip-ons.) It's late but you don't want to go. With Jack, you never want to go. But you can't drink more. You also can't go home with him. Jack is not impulsive, this you know. Any turning point of this relationship will be well planned. Or at least thought out. So Jack hails a cab for the two of you. He insists on paying for your cab to the Bronx, which runs about fifty bucks. You'll drop Jack off on the way.

Once you get into the cab, you realize that you are very, very drunk. Your stomach feels full, too full, like you've just eaten ten butter-drenched lobsters. While you normally love lobster, you are sated to the point of remembering that lobsters are bottom-feeders—*yuck!*—and besides, you didn't even eat lobster. You slump down low, your back sliding against the vinyl seat. Your legs are curled up, the slit in your skirt revealing your favorite mole with a brown gradation that is planted on your upper left thigh. Jack joins you in the back. For the next fifteen minutes, you two sit shoulder to shoulder. This new experience excites you. Your hair is matted against the seat, and you turn your head all the way toward his, so your chin rests on your shoulder. Your hand rests in the small space between you. His is carefully on his lap, but the gesture of his palm is open. You both sigh.

From your low vantage, you see buildings and storefronts as the driver whizzes by them all.

"Jack, look!" You are pointing to the stars, the ones that might as well be imaginary for all the light pollution in Manhattan.

"What?"

"Nothing—just the stars . . . if we could see them. How great would that be?"

"This is crazy . . ." he says, looking into your eyes. "I feel like we just won the lottery." His tone has gone soft.

Ignoring any and all warnings in your head, i.e., *um, the "lot-tery" comment sounds maybe too familiar?*, you shimmy over closer to him by a millimeter. You barely notice his breathless voice—it's his body, his being, that matter to you now. You are close, closer than you've ever been. The cab pulls over to let him out.

After Jack jumps out onto the sidewalk, he leans in and gives you a kiss on the cheek.

"Good night."

"Night, darlin'."

In less than forty-five minutes, you are lying in your bed in the dark, blinds open. Since you fell asleep in the cab, it was a miracle you even made it home. No cabbies in Manhattan have ever known how to get to your distant Bronx address. But you are home, and now you are holding your phone to your ear. Last winter, you hosted a group of teenagers who were in town to attend a social justice conference in Morningside Heights. After the conference, you'd rented a movie and gotten Chinese takeout, but through it all, one of the girls, a fifteen-year-old named Beba, stayed on her phone. The next morning, she'd made a joke that she had woken up with her hand cupped to her ear, like she'd been talking on her cell phone even in her sleep. Beba's phone addiction was cute.

You have no comments on your own Jack addiction. It's just too consuming and wonderful to even think twice about. And so here you are, after spending the whole workday with Jack (via email) and then your whole night, too (face-to-face), you are home in your bed, but you are not alone. Jack stays up with you, on the other line. You are saying everything you haven't yet had the chance to, going over your long list of favorite songs and telling him the words your mother said to you the day after you lost your virginity, i.e., "Now, honey, I know it's nice to hug and maybe even kiss, but just don't use your tongue, okay?" Inside is a well you hadn't known existed; the water keeps rising, not falling. Who even knew you had this much to say?

There is so much time, so much time passing, and all you want is to be still for a moment. You sigh. You hear Jack sigh, and try to picture where he sleeps at night. What kind of alarm clock does he have? Is his comforter light-colored? Are his walls beige? Whose photographs are framed on his nightstand? You don't ask, only imagine—knowing that it doesn't really matter because tomorrow he will text you first thing, probably before 7 AM, to comment on what a beautiful morning it is, what a beautiful night it was.

12

―――――

LAST SPRING, WHEN driving to school, you'd heard a morning radio jockey suggest a new state motto for New Jersey: *New Jersey . . . Who Farted?* This made you giggle at the time and if Jack had been in your life, he's the one you would have called. But he wasn't, and so you probably kept that gem to yourself.

You are in New Jersey—sans the scent of flatulence—spending the night with your second cousin and her family. Everyone has gone to sleep, and you are on the pullout in the basement, talking to none other than . . . Jack. Although Heather is only a handful of years older than you, she is in a different phase of life: married, with three delightful children, the oldest of whom is already thirteen. Despite disparaging stereotypes, you rather like New Jersey. Heather and her family live in a very green suburb, with lots of space and yards. When you drive down the main street toward her house, marked with solid yellow lines that motorists actually observe, you are reminded of where you grew up—the large Victorians, the clusters of families gathered outside of church on Sundays. You'd visited here one Halloween, just after you and Ted broke up. You were filled with regrets. Being with Heather and her family, you remembered, perhaps too clearly, exactly what it was you thought you'd have with Ted: children, stability, a forward-moving, creative, created life. After that trip, you returned to your apartment on Edison Avenue, pulled out the most miserable chick-folk songs you owned, lit some candles, and cried on your overstuffed couch for a good hour. You didn't even care if Davida heard you wailing. Usually crying released your worries, but this time you were inconsolable. You fancy yourself self-sufficient and so you knew it was bad when the only thought running over and over in your head was not, *I lost so much!* but rather, *I want my mommy.* Even though you were twenty-eight, you decided that there was no time like the present to lean heavily on your parents. So you pulled yourself together and called them. Whenever you've expressed doubts or feelings about being down, their voices on the other end of the line always sounded incredulous to you, as in, "This is not the daughter we know . . ." But this time you'd had no choice. Without missing a beat, they offered to clear their schedules and meet you the following day, at a seafood restaurant halfway between your house in New York and their place in Massachusetts. You took them up on it, gladly.

This time, New Jersey doesn't inspire melancholy. Heather made a pizza from scratch and served you a margarita upon entering. At dinner, you marveled at how engaged and astute Heather's children are. As you sat at the kitchen table and sipped, Karen, her ten-year-old daughter, crawled around the table to take the seat closest to yours. She asked you questions and told you about her new haircut, her Halloween costumes, her new friends at school. The last time you were here, you stayed well into the afternoon, watching the kids until Heather's husband finished running an errand. From outside, you heard the phone ringing, but when you went to answer it, you overheard Karen whispering into the phone, "Dad, don't come home yet. I want her to stay longer."

Over dinner, the topic of your most embarrassing stories project came up, as it does. With fall imminent, you've tried to give this project more focus lately, although your attention is always coming up short. Once, you were going to have drinks with Jack and so you decided to write up the story about Melody and your accident in her car—so you could at least say that you tried. It took all day, in your sweltering apartment, to write three meaningless pages. They were terrible. Usually you are not the type to deprecate your own writing efforts. But really, with this—a story you're obviously better at telling aloud than writing—there was nothing more you could surmise than, *This stinks.*

But over dinner you didn't mention your flailing to Heather, or anyone else, for that matter. Jack knows, and gently reminds you every now and then, that he can't sell a book that hasn't been written. (Okay, sometimes not so gently . . .) Instead, you told them about the concept: "It should really be cathartic," blah, blah, blah . . . Heather's husband Brad said, "Oh, I have a good one!" He went into the living room and pulled down a framed picture of Heather, Brad, their two sons, and one daughter, posing on a picturesque beach backdrop, with reeds swaying in the background. A planned photograph; they were all wearing khaki bottoms with white tops, a color scheme that accentuated the family's blondness against an orange-washed sunset.

"Beautiful picture," you admired.

"Yeah, but look here . . ." Brad said, pointing to their youngest son Nathan, who was only five at the time. "Look at his shorts."

Sure enough, there was a small wet spot near his zipper seam.

"Ha!" Rob, the oldest son, yelled out. "That was so funny!"

"Yes, but the best part is that here we have this framed picture, and it was on our mantel for two years until Rob pointed it out," Brad added.

Under your guidelines, an *Oh, Shit!* story has to come from the person who was actually embarrassed—and you didn't plan on grilling your eight-year-old second cousin to get a good story. You are desperate, but not that desperate. When Nathan entered the room, poking around with a half grin, Rob said, "Hey! Remember this?"

Shrugging, Nathan looked at the picture, blinked his wispy blond lashes a few times, and said with a knowing, amused half smile, "Yeah? So what?"

"Is that the spirit or what?" you tell Jack over the phone, relaying Nathan's response, which to you spells the budding of unshakable confidence. You don't know where this kid will be in fifteen years, but you hope it's in your corner. A defining characteristic of embarrassment is that, when it happens, the person on the hot seat just wishes that the ground would open up and swallow him whole. In this instance, Nathan of the Solid Self-Esteem does not qualify.

You, on the other hand, are somewhat embarrassed, lying down here in the dark, hoping that Heather and Brad don't hear you whispering to someone who's not even your boyfriend. When your phone reception dies, you creep up the stairs to get the cordless from the kitchen. On your way back, your chest is tight with anxiety, as if Heather and Brad are your parents and you are breaking the no-phone-after-ten rule.

What am I, sixteen? you think. It's two o'clock in the morning, and you've already been talking to Jack for two hours. You hope the kids don't hear you. You are definitely not an adequate role model for responsible behavior.

But this doesn't stop you from calling Jack back on the cordless. Once you are settled beneath the covers, you dial him again. It's funny, because Jack is spending the night at his cousin's apartment on the Upper West Side and also feeling self-conscious about staying on the phone this late.

"Hi, there," you say when Jack picks up. "Now, where were we?"

Already you have told him millions of stories, tonight and all the other nights.

"Jack," you say. "Why do I feel like I'm about to jump off a cliff?"

There is silence for a minute. You can hear him breathing, before taking in a gulp of air.

"I'll catch you—I promise."

Indeed, you can't really be concerned with how you're going to land. It's too late. You see no other options in your life but to pursue Jack.

"Hey," you say timidly. "Is it me or do you feel like we've already had sex?"

Jack scoffs. "Well, with all those emails, we've been mentally screwing each other for months now."

You smile, even though you have slight disdain for the word "screw" as a synonym for sex. (It just doesn't make any sense, at least none that you can figure.) In the dark, you smile because he's right. You have, in fact, been "screwing" him for a long, long time. Just by being his quirky, inquisitive self, Jack has answered some question you hadn't even known you needed to ask.

"Look, I'm sure you know this, but I've been seeing someone."

"Marco."

"Yep."

"I know."

"Yeah, and it's all been very . . . casual, but still, I didn't want to tell you."

Over the summer, the thought of making Jack jealous or even having him imagine you spending weekends away with another man was too much. You hear, have heard, the vulnerability in his voice. It reminds you, faintly, of your own.

"Jack," you continue. "What are you doing tomorrow night?"

"Having dinner with you."

ON YOUR WAY back to New York the following morning, you wait a few exits on the Jersey Turnpike before calling Marco to ask if you can stop by his loft. You two had planned on having dinner in his neighborhood later that night.

"Sure, Milly. I'll be here."

As you inch your way toward the Holland Tunnel, you feel sadness. In starting something with Jack—really starting something—you are about to lose Marco. It is only fair to Marco. Despite your aversion to the *M*-word, you aren't exactly the type of girl who is comfortable sleeping with two people at once.

By the time the tunnel spits you out into the chaos of Chinatown, you aren't any more ready to tell Marco goodbye. He is fun-loving and easy. His niceness fits. And yet, here you are about to dump him, without so much as a conversation as to . . . why.

Because you are filled with dread the entire way to Williamsburg, the ride feels like it's taking hours. When you finally pull up in front of Marco's building, you sigh before looking up to the rooftop upon which you two had shared so many fun times.

This is going to be fine. This is going to be fine.

After you ring the doorbell, Marco comes down to let you in. Just out of the shower, he is toweling his hair dry.

"Milly!" he says, kissing you on the cheek with a big *mw-ahh* sound. You wish he weren't so happy to see you, that his bare skin didn't feel so cool and fresh. Why is that always the way? When you get to his bedroom, he asks, "Where should we eat tonight?"

You sit on the chair at his desk and look around. You see the Strand book bag that he'd bought for a friend two months ago. There was a time when this bag made you suspicious. Who was he buying book bags for? But now the bag is just a reminder of all things kind and considerate, everything you're about to give up. You look toward his blue bedspread, still wrinkled up from his sleep the night before. The window across from his bed affords the room lots of light. You spent many mornings looking out that window, your head nestled on Marco's shoulder.

By the time Marco turns around, waiting for your answer, you have started to cry. The tears fall hard, much harder than you're prepared for. Within moments, snot runs down your nose and you're reaching around blindly for a tissue. The fact that you were on the phone with Jack until four and have had less than five hours' sleep doesn't help the situation. Your eyes are already bloodshot.

"Milly? What is it? What is it, my dear?" His voice sounds so concerned. He takes your head and pulls you closer to his chest, his hand patting down the back of your hair. "What is it?"

You stay there for a minute, sobbing even harder.

"Marco," you manage, pulling away, "I can't do this anymore."

"Whoa," he says, backing up toward his couch. He looks like you just punched him in the stomach.

"I'm sorry. I know. I—"

"I'm just really surprised." He's looking down at the carpet now, and you struggle to catch his gaze. If you say anything else, you must look him in the eye.

"I know," you say, only you can't finish because now you are crying harder than before.

"Why?" he asks.

"Okay, whew." Deep breath. "There's, ah, someone else."

Marco blinks for what feels like forever, then puts his glasses on.

"Okay," he finally says, sighing. "I mean, I guess one of us had to make a decision at some point or another . . ."

You think that he's being remarkably calm, and you are suddenly having pangs of self-doubt—self-hatred, even. You are so unworthy.

"Honestly, Marco, there's no good reason for me to break up

with you. You are wonderful . . ." Again, the tears flow. "It's just that . . . I think I met my . . . soul mate."

When you were with Ted, you'd both scoffed at the idea of there being "The One" (a minor or telling detail?). If you were you watching you now, you'd be making fun of that person. Soul mate? Who are you? But you are not watching you. You *are* you, and all you have is this belief that you have spoken the truth, as best you know it.

"It's just that . . . I hadn't really experienced passion like this in a while . . ."

This stops you. How can you just move so easily from one man to the next, even if your intentions with Marco had been to play it safe all along? You did, but you didn't. People are not disposable, especially not this person. Actions always have consequences—why have you been ignoring this fact?

You say nothing, and Marco says, "So, who is it?"

"Um, it's Jack," you say, sheepish. "The agent."

He smiles—an odd smile, but a smile nonetheless. "I thought so . . . Well, I wish you the best of luck, my dear."

"Yeah, I figure if this goes sour, I can always get another agent," you joke.

He obliges you with a halfhearted laugh. "You're a smart girl. You know what you're doing . . ."

Funny, you don't feel very smart at this moment. You are alive and sensitive to even something as minor as a muted breeze coming through the small crack of open window, yes. But smart? Not exactly, because, to you, this indicates being in some sort of control.

Marco suggests coffee. You like this idea, normalizing an

otherwise unpleasant situation. You walk to Fabiane, where they have the best croissants, find a table, and talk about all the things you'd normally talk about—weather, what you did last night, life's purpose. When you see a woman smoking, you lean over to ask if you can have one. Moments later you are puffing away, wishing that you didn't have to make such a hard move. The choice itself seems simple enough. The way it is going, you only have one choice. Jack, Jack, Jack. But you are sentimental and soft and have never been fond of goodbyes. Words between two people never seem to live up to the larger moment of finality. Marco sips his espresso and shakes his head.

When Marco walks you back to your car, you look down the now-familiar street, seeing previous versions of you with him. You start to cry again. He can't say goodbye, not here, in front of the building where you'd had so much fun. If it weren't for Jack, who knows how long this would have lasted? But you have crossed Marco off the list and are turning the corner, after which this relationship will no longer be an option.

"Well," you say, not knowing what to say. "Uh . . ."

Instead of saying anything, Marco grabs your face and kisses you, softly. He opens his mouth, and you don't argue. The kiss goes on, passionate. Knowing that you're going to see Jack tonight, this doesn't feel exactly right. *Remember me*, he seems to be saying.

You get into your car and roll the window down. Marco leans in. "If you are ever in need of love, Milly, you know where to find me."

You pull away from the curb heavy with nostalgia—who knew that you could have created so much in only a few months? But every storefront you pass, you shake your head and click your tongue. *No more Williamsburg,* you think—at least not like it was . . . Even the annoying traffic light on Metropolitan Avenue, just before the BQE, is tinted by your fond-memory lens. You recall the story of when a second cousin turned four. She sobbed and sobbed, and when her mother asked her why, she said, "Because three was just so gooooooood, Mom!" This is exactly how you feel.

As you drive back to the Bronx, over the Triboro and down the Bruckner, you are still sad. This makes two breakups in one year (with Ondra being the first). And even though your heart may have been broken just as much as theirs, both part- ing conversations went pretty well, considering the uncom- fortable drama inherent in making changes. In fact, Ondra had expressed the same sentiment as Marco, only he had said, "Wherever you are in the world, always know that there is someone here who loves you." Although your heart is heavy, you feel lucky—blessed, even. It is a good sign, you tell yourself, that the days of histrionic breaks are over, that you've chosen to spend your time with good men, men you feel safe with, men who are smart enough to let you go.

YOU DRIVE DOWN the West Side Highway to pick up Jack at his brother's apartment. You are on your favorite stretch, where the full view of the Hudson is imminent. You take a small plea- sure in this and try to steady your breath.

When you had arrived home from Marco's, Davida took one look at your blotchy red face and said, "Oh, God—what happened to you?" You told her a little, but couldn't bring yourself to give her a play-by-play. Your bed was calling. After a long nap, you woke up with a heavy head, but your heart was considerably lighter. You waited all of three minutes, opening your eyes slowly, surveying the familiar scene outside your window, before rolling over to pick up the phone on your nightstand.

"Jack, when can I come get you?"

"Is now too soon?"

So here you are, rounding the corner exit on Seventy-ninth Street. You used to come this route every week to see Elaine, only she's been on vacation for what feels like forever. You could use your therapist right about now, someone to sit with you and your jumbled feelings, someone to listen, or, in Elaine's case, someone who would be sure to tell you to take things slowly. But since your school health insurance ends on August 31, you're not sure if you can afford to see her anymore. Your mind flips through snapshots of all the memorable times you raced here, hoping not to be late to your weekly appointment, even though you almost always were. You drove here in the rain, battled crabby cabdrivers in the snow, felt a glow of hopefulness as you parallel-parked into a spot on West End Avenue. You met Elaine after Ted and during Ondra. You told her about your parents and your siblings and how you were happy to be living in a different state from your immediate family. She has never been averse to your metaphors.

When you pull up to the corner, you dial Jack.

"I'm here," you announce. A few minutes later, you see him standing on the curb, impatiently waiting for cars to pass. He gets in your car and you put it in park. For less than a moment you just look at one another, in anticipation of what you've already been anticipating for quite some time.

"Hi," he says. You have Jack in the flesh, not over email, not over the phone, but right here in person, in this very small space of your front seat. "You look beautiful."

You'd taken extra care getting ready. You dried and straightened your hair, fixing a long, light blue patterned scarf like a headband, its ties floating down from the back of your neck. You put on skinny capris and a short-sleeved white shirt. The only thing you didn't do was apply lipstick, and that's because you have an agenda.

Before you can thank Jack, you see his body stiffen. He's holding his breath close. For a minute you imagine Jack as an awkward teenager who is asking his crush to the prom and is afraid of being turned down. You see this, and want nothing more than to just hold him, remind him that you have already said "Yes."

You don't see Jack in this light very often. Usually he is the picture of professional cool, someone who calculates his words and acts with sure strategy, doing his best to keep everyone happy and never making an offensive move. Even his "Is it so crazy that I want to see you?" text message had an air of deliberateness.

You are not about to tell Jack that you broke up with Marco by telling him that Jack was your "soul mate" but you do want more, more than what's been expressed in your lengthy emails, phone conversations, and even heretofore nondate dates. If this is greedy, it doesn't stop you from wanting.

You have a big grin and Jack has a big grin and neither of you can believe that this is about to happen. Lights from the street twinkle. Your bodies are distinct and for the moment it is perfect. Everything in this world, as you want it right now, belongs to you.

Jack darts over the console and presses his lips to yours. His kisses are sometimes sure, sometimes unsure. His breath is sweet. His skin against yours makes you want to fall down. Every nerve ending in your body tingles. You concentrate on the feeling of his breath on your cheeks, as your chest lights up with anticipation.

"Hi," Jack says, moving his lips toward your cheek.

"Hi," you say back, breathing just as heavy as Jack.

After a few more minutes of making out, you say, "Where should we go?" You haven't eaten a thing since the homemade scones that had been a family effort at Heather's this morning. Was that only this morning?

You want to go somewhere cozy, comfortable, where you can bleed softly into Jack, not someplace where you need to be upright and formal. Jack suggests an Italian place in the East Village. You look in the rearview before pulling out. As you drive, he puts his hand on your shoulder, squeezing it intermittently. Miraculously, there is no rear-ending.

At the restaurant, you are seated next to Jack at a corner table with rustic touches of dark wood and flickering candles. If you ever struggled with decorum, its meaning has really escaped you now. You inch closer to Jack, Jack inches closer to you. Your thighs are touching, and you can't help but continue to kiss and kiss and kiss (although it's not of the French variety—you are not this far gone). Your head rolls perfectly into his neck, and so you kiss that, too.

The scents of rosemary and garlic emanate from the kitchen. Never have there been better, cleaner scents. You are oblivious to your fellow diners, some of whom must have noticed the electricity. From your years of working in restaurants, you have

many memories of watching other couples in similarly tight em-
braces, in the good ol' can't-keep-their-hands-off-one-another
fashion. If any of your coworkers ever made a snide mention of
an overly affectionate couple groping one another at Table Four,
you'd joke in a fake Hungarian accent, "Oh, don't be jealous,
dah-ling. There's love out there for you, too, somewhere."

You are a crazy person. Your head floats with images and
dreams and sensations that you swear you've never—never!—
felt before.

"I feel like I'm on Ecstasy," you whisper to him.

"I know, I know . . . This is crazy . . ."

You don't talk much, spending the bulk of your dinner staring into his eyes, an image that is oh-so-cliché for good reason.
You can't worry about cliché or coolness. Sometimes you just
have to let yourself go—this is something that you haven't been
very good with in the past.

You experimented with Ecstasy in your early twenties, when
it was still permissible to do things like that without the Catholic guilt oppressing your what-ever attitude. The last time, you
were in Italy, where you studied abroad. You were in a club with
friends, dancing, when Todd, one of your group, pulled you
aside to tell you that he heard someone in the back was selling
X. So you went with Todd, back to the little room with bright
overhead lights and red banquettes. Two girls sat side by side,
one of them screaming in a panic, "What was that shit? I can't
see anymore—I'm fucking blind!" The other girl was lounging
in repose, her bare feet dangling over her blind girlfriend's legs.
She looked so blissful and calm, sounding like the pitch-perfect
stereotype of a stoned college girl: "Man, this is, like, great. This
is soooooooooooooooooo great." One look at her and you said,

"I'll have one of those." An hour later, you headed to the small club owned by Darko, your Macedonian boyfriend. By the time you reached Darko's, you were blitzed, eyes moonshiny and skin tingling. Darko took one look at you, smiled, and propped you on a stool behind the bar. You took ice cubes from the bin and traced wet lines along your bare arms and décolleté. In your chemical-induced oblivion, you were breaking all sorts of social decorum rules—and not giving a fuck. And this is exactly how you feel at dinner with Jack.

You lean in toward his ear and whisper, "Isn't our waitress just beautiful?"

She is a full-figured blonde, with a slicked-back ponytail, an open, shiny face, and bright green eyes with shimmer on the lids. When she comes to ask you how dinner is or if you need anything else, you just stare at her, smiling.

"Yes," Jack whispers back. "She is. She really, really is."

After Jack pays the bill, you say, "Wait, let's tell her how gorgeous she is."

"Okay," he says. "But it should come from me. It'll mean more coming from a man."

Jack, your new love Jack, is so wrong—soooooo wrong. Of course it will mean more coming from a woman. The stereotype of jealous, catty women doesn't even touch the grand scope of female behavior. When one woman compliments another's beauty, that prized attribute, it means more because it's—usually—just for the sake of noticing. When it comes from a man, even if he is with another woman, there is always the question of sex. But you are too happy, too dizzy, to argue your point. Do you smell apple blossoms? *Another time,* you think dreamily, as you defer to Jack's lead.

As you stand to walk toward the door, Jack holds out his arm for you to lean on. This time you are not wearing impossible heels. You have on flats, and so the arm is there for you just because. You like this and give him yet another smooch.

When you pass the waitress, you say a bright, bubbly, "Thank you!" and Jack adds, in his most formal, charming tone—God, his voice is amazing—"We just wanted to tell you how exquisite you are."

The waitress looks surprised—flattered, but surprised. You have to hand it to him. You would have said "pretty" or "beautiful," but not "exquisite." How good he is, this Jack, with words.

"Oh," she says, gesturing her hands all around. "Oh, thank you. And you, too—with your happy"—her hands flutter wildly—"love table!"

As if on cue, Jack looks at you and you at him. You kiss again, not because you're trying to embarrass her or anyone else, just because you can't help it. You don't think about potential consequences, like making the waitstaff barf.

Outside on the street, you kiss more. You can't seem to walk ten steps without stopping for a little smoochy-smooch.

You are leaning up against your car, Jack on top of you. He pulls back to clear his throat and make a very Jack-type announcement (if he were twenty-five years younger, you'd swear he rehearsed these lines in front of a mirror): "I don't think we should have sex tonight."

You spend longer and longer kissing, until the time feels right to go. As you drop Jack off at his apartment, he turns to you to say, "This . . . is crazy. I've never felt this way before."

"Me neither," you respond, smiling that silly smile that feels like it's here to stay.

Driving back up to the Bronx, you notice a bright full moon in the nearly black sky. Oh, the sky is so open. Under this moon, billions of lives are being lived, at this very moment. You look in your rearview, at the sparkling Manhattan skyline that has never once failed to give you a thrill, for its geometric intricacies, but also for the sense that there's just so . . . much . . . going . . . on at once. Who wouldn't be attracted to that landscape of possibility? So many lives there are, and so often, you're spending your day just sitting there staring at your own belly button, wondering if your boss has noticed you took an extra fifteen minutes for lunch. This moon—is it new?—reminds you that you are very happy to be living the life you are.

Looking at the empty highway before you, only one car a quarter of a mile ahead, you think, *I don't even care what happens tomorrow.*

13

BEGINNINGS ARE FRESH: fresh as in new, but also fresh as in "dope" or "the bomb." They are, even if you wouldn't be caught dead actually uttering any of these words aloud. Beginnings are the "Praise be to God!" feeling you have when you open the stall of a public restroom and find a newly cleaned toilet, the water still sudsy and blue, the seat still up. You once knew a woman who said that when she walks into public bathrooms in this state, she feels like a queen being crowned on her brand-new throne. She says lots of funny things, that one. Once, you were with her on a group vacation to a beach destination. When the proposition of skinny-dipping came up, you'd hesitated, because of your spanking-new Brazilian wax and how embarrassing that might be once you stripped down, not having one single hair on your nether region. She took one look at your wincing face and intuitively cracked, "What are we—a bunch of preschoolers?"

But back to beginnings: they are clean slates, where nothing has been messed up, where lofty ideas retain every inch of their initial sheen, and where everything is still possible, luminously so.

In one week, you and Jack have submitted to coupledom. You have seen each other with more regularity, if that is possible. You meet at the café outside your building on sunny days, just like you used to, only now you sit on his lap. One afternoon, you are giggling together when a waiter comes out with two chocolates, which you hadn't ordered. When you look up from your bubble, both of you surprised, the waiter points inside, to where you can see the entire staff standing behind the counter, clapping. They are not the only ones who notice your smitten state. When you accompany Jack to look for sunglasses he lost the night before, you cozy up to one another in the back seat of a cab. You are on top of Jack like a complete lovesick fool, and Jack is nuzzling into your neck. This whole week, you haven't stopped giggling.

"Hey," the driver says. "Save some for later, if you know what I mean. It's like eating rich chocolates . . ."

Strangers pass you on the street, giving extended glances. When you stop in a movie theater lobby to hug one another, a staff person walks by and says, "Hey, hey, this is a family place," even though there is nothing remotely lewd about your embrace.

When you took him to a party at your friend's lake house, the two of you acted like there was no one else on earth—a fact that did not make you two very popular guests. At one point, after you and he had split a bottle of wine, you started dancing in the empty living room. You were wearing only your bathing suits and when you fell into one another on the couch, your friend had come in to ask you to "tone it down" because there were teenagers around.

Your physical chemistry—mostly kissing so far—has not disappointed you, as you feared it might, given your already established intellectual compatibility. Could you really be this lucky?

You forward one of Jack's syrupy emails to Dan, because you want some kind of witness to this blossomed romance. Dan doesn't write back, "Oh, good for you." Or, "Sounds like you're having fun." Instead he writes a one-liner, stating that Jack seems "bottomish." You delete Dan's email immediately. His reaction does not indicate the unquestioning seal of approval for which you had, apparently, been looking.

At work, Alison, an older—than you—woman with a romantic streak, says with a faint patois accent, "Oh, look at you! Invite me to your wedding, okay?"

One afternoon, you are in Bryant Park, again sitting on Jack's lap beneath the shroud of trees. You are, once again, giggling and kissing one another's neck, when he feels his phone buzz. His sister sent him a text message that reads, "You keep sitting on your phone and calling me. Stop it!" You are both mortified for a moment. Oh, no, the sister you haven't met, but know that your viability with Jack depends on whether or not she likes you, the one who could be spying on you this very minute—now she's overheard your silly whispering? You don't even remember what you or Jack had been saying, but you're sure you wouldn't have said it if you knew you had an audience. When Jack calls her later, she says she only heard "the two of you giggling like idiots."

Approval. It's something you secretly want, crave, but deep down are not sure you deserve. Anything that complicates your bliss, you banish.

After boxing one evening, you head back to your apartment to fix dinner. You are munching on a bag of pretzels, chewing with your mouth open, when Dan calls. All summer he's been busy working full-time and preparing for his return to school, and so you haven't been talking with quite as much regularity as normal. The times you have talked, though, you've been so consumed with Jack that it barely crosses your mind to ask Dan how he's doing with any transitions of his own.

"How's my girlfriend?"

It's been one week since things with you and Jack have taken off, one short week, and already you are beginning to forget what your life was like prelovesickness. Hell, not only have you forgotten, you haven't much cared.

"Gooood," you say.

"Yeah?"

You go on and on. Jack said this. Jack did that. Jack and I are playing hooky and going to the beach tomorrow. Me and Jack . . . Jack, Jack, Jack, Jack, Jack.

Your water is warming, but you can't seem to find the cover, even after looking underneath the counter, in your messy pots and pans drawer.

"So, I think—I think that he's someone I might want to have children with . . ."

There is a long pause. Dan is your best friend, the one to whom you can say anything and—most important—the one from whom you can hear anything. (Once he even got you to submit to a belly-button-shaving. It was unfortunate, especially when the repairmen walked into his apartment to fix the air conditioner and saw you holding your T-shirt up while Dan bent down on his knees and worked his electric shaver around your midsection.) You inhale the silence and go to a blindingly light vision of yourself in a bright kitchen with Jack and a brood of adorable children, pouring pancake batter on the griddle in kiddie-pleasing shapes. You will be a stay-at-home mom, in part because it sounds good and in part because Jack wants this, too. He made a point to see where you stood on the matter on your second real date-date.

"Um, can I just say something?"

Dan's tone is serious, the tenor deep. You know this voice. It might as well be your very own voice of reason, like the time he pointed out that perhaps dating someone who doesn't speak English might not exactly provide the kind of firm foundation for communication that you'd been hoping for. ("But we use a dictionary?" was your feeble response.) This voice, as much as it sometimes brings your fantasies to an end, is a valued one.

"Uh-huh," you say, talking with your mouth full of pretzels.

"Well . . ." Dan pauses again. You can hear him taking a deep breath. "Well, it's just that maybe you should slow down a little."

"Uh-huh." There is a bright, fuzzy center of your happiness, lodged somewhere in the heart of your stomach. And it's not because you're eating pretzels. Dan's voice barely touches it. "I'm all for you being happy and being happy with Jack, but come on, it's been, like, one week."

A hint of amusement invades Dan's caution. You almost, almost know that if it were any other day, if you were any other you than the current lovesick one, you might have actually laughed at yourself *with* him.

Instead, all you say is, "Yeah, I know. You're right." But you don't really mean it. You mean, you know Dan is right. But your words, your body, your being are all vibrating at frequencies beyond rational thought. Who the hell cares about "right"?

Something happens, though, when you tell Dan you agree with him. You start to question the rocket pace with which you and Jack have opted for takeoff. The pace feels out of your control—delightfully so, most hours. Yet now, with Dan, you are uneasy. He has located the tiny point of doubt. In theory, yes, you should move a little slower, or a lot slower. But your heart is already with Jack, and so what's the point, really? Only one sailboat is floating across your horizon.

You don't dare tell Dan that you've had other fantasies about Jack, beyond the kids-and-family variety. Even more precious, more pressing than imagined children is your actual writing. One afternoon, you were sitting on your couch, talking to Jack on the phone (of course). You were rambling about something, he was rambling about something, and then an idea moved from blurry to sharp focus. You were exploring ideas of coupledom and the looming influences of money when he said it first: "You know, I could see us writing something together."

Funny, you were just thinking the same thing—only you were too shy to say it. This is very much your equivalent of saying, "I love you," only you have never even entertained the idea of having a writing partner before this moment. But these bursting feelings of goodness and love know no bounds. Not even your writing is sacred.

You would almost be nauseated with yourself and your desire to mesh everything with the being of someone you'd only known for three months, if only you had a little perspective. But this is not your lot. Self-sickening far beyond you, you take the ideas and dreams about Jack and keep them as quiet as possible from the outside world. No one would understand anyway.

"Dan?" you say. "Water's boiling. Gotta run."

THE NEXT MORNING is glorious, glorious, glorious. You called in to work and faked a groggy, tired voice to say that you had a stomach virus. You suspect that the assistant knew you were lying, especially since you were a hundred percent fine the day before, as demonstrated by your rosy cheeks, wide-open eyes, and permanent grin. But when one calls in ill to work, when does the person on the other line ever say, "Yeah, right!"? You almost wish she had.

A pink flowery beach bag is packed in the back seat, just inches from your rainbow-striped wide-brimmed hat. Underneath your tank top, the straps of your gold bikini are visible. The thought of showing Jack this piece of heretofore unseen apparel brings you pleasure. You and he are speeding down the Long Island Expressway, on your way to Fire Island. You are driving and he is not. His hands are bony like his knees, and when he touches your shoulder, you feel the slight oil on his fingers rubbing against your bare shoulder.

"My parents want to know when they can meet you."

"Yeah?" you say. "Well, I'd love to meet them. When are they in town next?"

Jack is clearly lovesick, too. "Mmm . . . not soon enough."

You hand Jack the printed directions to Bay Shore, Long Island, where you will catch the ferry. You don't know much about your destination, but have heard from friends that the towns are quaint and the beaches are pretty.

On the ride, pauses between you and Jack are longer, con-versation less driven by getting everything in. Your time to-gether almost always has limitations on it. He needs to get back to work. You need to get to bed. But here you have hours and hours. You hope, silently, that this is only the beginning.

Now that your living arrangements are settled—you move in one week to Serdar's—you need to figure out your work situ-ation. You yak about possibilities and Jack offers suggestions, concrete ones, about where you should be looking and what, exactly, it is you need right now.

"All you need is some stability and a good paycheck, while you figure the rest out. Look at the New York Public Library's website. We know people there, and maybe I could help."

Since you have neither stability nor a good paycheck, this seems like sound advice to you. You are grateful. Although Jack had offered a few weeks ago to redo your résumé and get it to you within twenty-fours hours, he hadn't. You asked him about it a week later, because you wanted to send it out to some po-tential employers. Even though you had been hesitant to ask—he was doing you the favor—you'd prefer to do it yourself if he hadn't gotten around to it. But Jack snapped at you, for the first time, saying, "You are so impatient!" You filed the response away, almost admiring his quickness to deflect. Almost.

Once you reach the ferry station, you are taken with the water views, the boats, the vista of outdoors that you don't so much get from your Edison Avenue apartment building.

"Wow," you say. Last year, when driving through Columbus, Ohio, in a rental car with your entire family, your mother, from behind the wheel, had remarked, "You ever notice that we say 'Wow' a lot in this family? Everything's a 'wow.'" Even though she'd said that last "wow" somewhat snidely, moments later she was looking for German Village, where there was rumored to be an Oktoberfest happening. But you were driving through a burned-out industrial area, without so much as a deli in sight. Your mother pulled the car over when she saw a businessman on the sidewalk. "Mom, he's on his phone!" you yelled from the back seat. Never one to be restrained, she rolled down the window, leaned right over your father, who was used to this sort of thing, and said, "Excuse me, sir? Where's Germantown?" When the man shrugged his shoulders, she responded with more than a little exasperation, "I'm looking for dancing . . . fun . . . wieners!" What else was there to say? Wow.

Half an hour later, you and Jack are sitting on the top deck of a small ferry, on your way to the island. While you peer over the railing, looking down at the ripples of dark water, Jack leans back onto the bench, with his arm around your waist and a smile on his face.

Once the boat docks, you and Jack meander through "town," which seems to consist of one market. You don't see any sand beaches, only a rocky shoreline, punctuated with wooden docks that have faded to gray. The trees are green, shrouding the wooden pathway that cuts across the island. When you look in the direction of the path, you see a small strip of ocean, idyllically framed by the curvature of tree branches on either side. The shape reminds you of a heart.

After a five-minute walk, you find yourselves on an empty beach, with white sand and high tide water. You plop down your bag, spread out a blanket, and take off your extra clothing, which includes your bikini top; although seminude sunbathing had not been your intention, it just seems like the right thing to do.

Only after your top is strewn in the sand do you realize that Jack has never seen you naked. *Oops,* you think, as he inches closer from behind to kiss you on the cheek and fold his arms around your neck. He did already know that you have small breasts— and that you are self-conscious about this. To reassure you, he'd once said, "The smaller the breasts, the prettier the face."

A few moments later, Jack's shoulders hunch up as he walks toward the water to take its temperature. You wonder if he thinks he should be more muscular; even though his chest is as ghastly white as your ass, you love everything about his body. When he comes back, you lean into him on the blanket. If you are a cat, Jack is your patient owner, stroking your back.

Moments pass too quickly, so that even seconds after you make mental notes—what you're talking about, how he touches you—you have forgotten everything but the blindingly bright sun in your eyes. You invite it in, this light. You throw out your mental notebook, the secret tally sheet you keep because deep down there is a part of you that really doesn't want to be screwed ever again and so you draw meaningless lines in two columns: (1) What I Do for Others and (2) What Others Do for Me. This has never been a generous place. Still, you remember the words of Ted, who had tried to make you feel better when you were disappointed because someone you loved and were counting on to keep her promise didn't: "Your life has been marked by all the things you haven't gotten. Of course you're keeping track."

ON THE FERRY ride back, you and Jack share his iPod headphones again, this time choosing a more nostalgic Crowded House song. Flipping through songs, you are creating a sound track to what may be one of the most ridiculous times in your life. Beneath the cloud-covered moon, you wonder again about feeling memories of the present in the present. This just isn't possible. But it seems to be. The image of you and Jack under the moonlight is already fading into sepia tones.

Before heading back to the city, you and Jack decide that an ice cream from Friendly's is exactly what you need. So you stop and order one hot fudge sundae, and then share it on a bench near the old parking lot.

You take out the iPod again and shuffle through the songs. You feed one another plastic spoonfuls of gooey fudge and vanilla ice cream, while keeping your heads close enough to enjoy the music.

"Ooh! Ooh! I love that song!" you screech when you find the Cure's "Close to Me." He makes fun of you being so excited, tapping your nose with his finger more than once. You love the deep sound of his laughter. You wonder, if you knew him just a little better, if he wouldn't be snorting right now.

This goes on and on, until the sundae is gone and you notice the cars in the lot have dwindled, leaving behind random oily puddles in their wake. When it occurs to you to check the time, you realize that you have been sitting in this decrepit parking lot for more than an hour. It's later than you thought, and you both have to get up early the next morning.

If you weren't so dazzled by your day, the light, your dreaming, this sound track, and especially Jack—Jack, Jack, Jack—you might have paused a minute to think, *What the hell is wrong with me?*

PART II

Autobiography is only to be trusted when it reveals something disgraceful. A man who gives a good account of himself is probably lying, since any life when viewed from the inside is simply a series of defeats.

—GEORGE ORWELL, "BENEFIT OF CLERGY: SOME NOTES ON SALVADOR DALÍ," 1944

14

OKAY. SEPTEMBER IS almost here. Time to work. Time to get some things in order. Even you are bored of hearing yourself go down the list of all that could be more stable in your life right now. At least tomorrow you are moving, you tell yourself, as you scan your mostly packed room on your way to work. You had planned to hire movers, but when you ring Jack on your way to work and tell him how much they are charging, he says, "Cancel them. I'll get a van and we can do it."

"Really?" you'd asked. "You'd do that?"

"With pleasure," Jack says, already in his office even though it's before eight. "Oh, I have to take this call. Talk soon. Big kiss!"

Then he stops himself. " 'Big kiss.' Jesus. Who am I?"

"You're asking me?" you say with a giggle, before hanging up the phone.

In the meantime, you have pared your belongings. You've already gotten rid of many possessions that were infected with memories of Ted. Although you'd cleared out the nostalgia impulsively—an impressive collection of handmade cards with watercolor images you weren't entirely sorry not to have to pack, the weighty, hardbound dictionary he bought for you, and customized with ink drawings of his likeness and your likeness all across the pages, for example across the "beautiful" entry. Really, you loved it when he gave it to you—could there have been a more perfect gift, a thousand pages of definitions?—but in a regrettably rash moment of "This part of my life will be over *now!*" you chucked it in the garbage.

At work, you scurry in and say your morning hellos to all the people in your row of cubicles. As always, the air feels slightly stale. Sometimes the light makes you think of department stores and shopping for bathing suits. You see something you like, head into the dressing room, and then frown at the sight of your hips in the glare of the overhead bulbs. And this is what you sometimes think of on Monday mornings, when you settle into your secondhand swivel chair, trying to put the weekend's relaxation out of your mind so that you can actually do some work.

Instead of pulling up the proposal you are working on, you open your personal email account. Jack has already sent a "Mornin' Darling" message, and for a moment your anxiety is quelled. All is right in the world. But you did not open your personal email to write to Jack (although you will, and do). You are all about intention today. Last night, you drafted an email with the subject line "Calling All Embarrassing Stories." Your deadline of having the proposal finished by September isn't going to happen, since that's tomorrow. But you plan on sending this email to everyone in your contacts, and asking them to forward to everyone in their contacts. You've explained *Oh, Shit!* in one page, asking people to respond if they'd be willing to have their most embarrassing moment catalogued—anonymously, of course. You used a couple examples, including the story of a woman who attempted to cheat on her fiancé by posting an online personals ad, but the first person who responded was her ex-boyfriend—whom she'd just seen the week before; the ex-boyfriend had written, "Didn't you just tell me you were getting married?" In sending out this email, you have high, high hopes. You have a large circle of fun-loving, don't-take-themselves-too-seriously friends and acquaintances. Stories should just start to roll in once you send the email.

In Jack's email, he approves of the "Calling All Embarrassing Stories" email. You were waiting to send it, in case there was something you were missing or in case he had constructive thoughts on describing the project.

"Looks good," he wrote.

You pause for a minute. Are you being too hasty in sending this out within twelve hours of writing it? Maybe Jack will have more ideas later, when you can actually talk about it, when he's not juggling his five thousand projects. Lately, before meetings, he's been making remarks about difficult women. You write him frequent pep talks, advising him before meetings not to call anyone "stupid," not even in his head. Besides, so-called "difficult" women tend to be interesting. Even though you're sure he was just venting and that you're telling him things he already knows, he writes back, marveling at how you always know how to say the right thing. With the summer ending, his compliment makes you nervous. Jack always seems to be able to say the right thing—but you? No way. In fact, with other friends and family, you are known for saying the exact wrong thing, like, "Oh, your boyfriend dumped you? Good. Now I can tell you that our nickname for him was 'Yucky'—good riddance to that guy." Or, "Yeah, get used to that crappy heartbroken feeling. It's going to last awhile." Those who love you know you mean well. You hope.

The truth is, you don't really have time to waste. You pull out the long list of people to whom you'd like to send the *Oh, Shit!* email. You did your thinking on the subway ride home the night before, making notes of those you'd need to call versus those you could just email. There are exactly one hundred people on the list, and you are sure that you will think of more as time goes on. You just need to start somewhere. Anywhere.

Click. Send.

I'm off! you think, settling back into your chair with a sigh. A memory of Ted's familiar voice creeps in, ". . . *like a herd of turtles.*"

THE DAY IS almost over. Jack and you have agreed to meet outside your building at five. He sent an email and you agreed it was perfect timing, although you were surprised he could make it so early. He made a crack about meeting close to the 6 train so you could get to boxing on time. "Wouldn't want you to be late for the gym . . ."

You are readying yourself to leave work, proofreading the funding proposal for work that you managed to finish today, in spite of the many responses to your first *Oh, Shit!* email.

You heard from Betsey, the older woman from last semester's workshop. A kindly woman, she wrote, "Thank you for thinking of me." She suggested you look into *Daily News* archives, because they used to publish this sort of thing in a weekly column.

You heard from Lilli, your friend and former coworker who lives in Massachusetts and wrote a few bits about her sister-in-law's most embarrassing moments, and none of her own, because she's "too smart" for those. (An e-wink followed this statement.) Her sister-in-law's were: First, when she went to buy shoes at a store and the male cashier asked her for her phone number. "I have a boyfriend!" she replied, indignantly. "It's . . . for our database," the humorless clerk replied. Second, when her father asked her to get gas for the lawn mower, she didn't, telling him when he got home that she couldn't lift the mower into her car. And third, when Lilli asked her to go outside and heat up her car, her sister-in-law came back in a few minutes later and said, "I can't tell if the heat's on or not. It's too dark out." With this last one, you reread it three times. You decide that someday Lilli will find it very funny that your initial response was, "Wha'? Well, if it was dark, then how was she supposed to know?"

You heard from Tee Jay Pusher, your first kiss. From his home in North Carolina he wrote, not to tell you an embarrassing story, but just to say hi and that he loves email. You'd written back immediately, asking him if the time you kissed in the seventh grade, in the bushes behind your elementary school, would count as one of his most embarrassing moments. "Huh?" he wrote back. "Do you mean that classic line of yours?" Before meeting up with him that day, you were terrified. It was your first kiss, completely planned and scripted, and you were too shy to tell any of your friends, or to ask even what might happen during one's first kiss. The following week, you'd read in *Young Miss* that practicing on one's own wrist was a perfectly acceptable way to get ready for your first smooch. Although you wouldn't have spent a millisecond sucking on your own arm, this small bit of guidance might have made you at least feel better. But you had no advice, just your raw nerves as you walked into the tall bushes, where Tee Jay was already standing. Tee Jay had a twelve-year-old tall-boy swagger that made you very, very nervous. He acted experienced, something you weren't. He acted like he knew everything, which was exactly what you wanted to act like, only now, here in the bushes, Tee Jay was about to find out that you didn't know one very critical, possibly life-threatening thing: how to make out. When he leaned in toward you, he wasted no time inserting his tongue in your mouth. *Yech!* you thought. *This is what it's all about?* After enduring five minutes or so, you pulled back and said you were going to be late for dinner. You couldn't run through the playground fast enough. When you got home, you paced in a circle on the lavender carpet in your bedroom. A creepy feeling had settled and you felt like puking. Instead, you picked up the phone, called Tee Jay, and said, "Look, I have this sick feeling in my stomach, and, ah, it's *you*. We can't go out anymore."

Years later, when you and Tee Jay were both in the wedding party of your friends, he said to you, "That was hands-down the worst way anyone's ever dumped me!" He was laughing, of course, which is why now you think it would be okay to include this story in your collection. He must have been embarrassed. But after he writes back about the "classic line," you sit there and think for a minute, adding up all your own ill feelings of shame. *Oh, wait. I guess that would be one of my embarrassing moments, not his . . .*

Well, the replies so far are a start. None of these stories are quite what you're looking for. It seems that email might not be the best way to capture them. You can't read anyone's body language as they are retelling the stories, nor can you see their faces, looking for traces of what lies underneath just a funny old story.

You head downstairs to meet Jack. You don't want to be late anymore.

Once outside, you lean against the building, taking for granted all its Art Deco touches and special place in the history of New York architecture. When it was built in the twenties, it had been the tallest skyscraper. But to you this office is just a place to pass your time. You look down at your phone and see that Jack is five minutes late. You sigh and take in all the passing cabs. Commuters gather in clusters on the corner, waiting for the light to change. Everyone, every single person on this curb, has a different look, and yet—you are all waiting, more or less, for the same thing.

Earlier in the day, Jack mentioned that he needed to get "this surgery." You were alarmed, of course, but he quickly reassured you that it was "nothing," and that he'd rather tell you about it in person. So here you are, in person, hoping that he comes soon. You haven't seen Jack in one whole day. Feels like forever.

When you look at your phone again, you see that he is now fifteen minutes late, not very Jack-like behavior. You call him, and get no answer. Again, not very Jack-like. You text him, thinking that maybe he's on a call. No answer. Do you have the wrong location? You thought the email had been very clear about where and when to meet. In fact, it was. So where is he?

Another twenty minutes pass. By now an uneasy feeling has settled in your stomach. You could just leave, explain later that there was a mix-up. But the thought of touching Jack is what pushed you through the last half of your day, and you are not about to give up now.

Your hands are shaky as you pick up your phone to check the time once again. Since you met in May, Jack has always responded to you right away, no matter what business he had at hand. Now you're wondering if this waiting is a sign of things to come?

Your head is turned in the other direction. You are tired of looking down the street toward the block he should have come down a while ago. The intersection is even busier than when you first started waiting. So many people, going so many places. It's the same scene as the morning, minus all the cardboard cups of coffee.

"Hey!" Jack says, grabbing your shoulder. You turn around and all of your anxieties are quieted. He looks as good as you remember—clear eyes, adorable smile. As he leans in to kiss you, you say, "Where were you? We said five."

"Oh, we did?" he says, looking away. "I didn't think we decided on a time and then I got stuck on this call . . ."

"But it was in the email," you say, although perhaps you should just let it go.

"Oh, was it? I'm sorry."

And that's all you needed to hear to move on to the business of being with Jack like you want to be with Jack, engrossed, enveloped, enraptured. Ignoring.

"I know this little park over here. We can go sit for a few minutes," he suggests. "Wouldn't want you to be late for the gym!"

"Ha, ha." Your exaggerated flat tone indicates that you don't really find his "teasing" to be all that funny.

Almost skipping in your girly polka-dotted dress and white

open-toed pumps, you are compelled to link your arm with Jack's.

"Those heels again, huh?"

Everything that Jack says seems to have an intended import. Before you crossed the line with Jack, you would have been paying careful attention to each and every word he uttered. Now, though, you are blinded by visions of hearts, flowers, stuffed animals, primary-color helium balloons—all things saccharine. Instead of responding to his crack about your shoes, you plant one on his cheek. "Mwah!"

Sure enough, there is a small courtyard with a small pond at its center, shaded by trees. Despite its location in bustling midtown, the courtyard is quiet. Along the far west wall, there are tables arranged in an even row. You point to one of them and take a seat. Jack sits next to you and before you can ask him about his day, how the call went, he stares at you, silencing any polite questions. You kiss him. If you had seen this vision of yourself, and PDA gone wild, you would have scoffed, "No way!" But it's "Yes way!" as you climb out of your chair and onto his lap.

"Come here, you," he says, shaking his head. "It's so great to see you."

You are too delighted with this "happy hour" to say anything other than your favorite phrase, "I know."

After a few minutes, you pull back to say, "Wait, so tell me about this surgery. Is everything okay?"

His neck shrinks into his button-down, mostly because with you on top of him, he has nowhere to pull back to. He clears his throat and shakes his head.

"Oh. That."

"Yes, that."

"Well, it's not serious, just something that needs to be taken care of."

"Like what?" You are impatient. If you were not lovesick, you might have said, "Quit the stalling and spit it out!" Your mother tells a story of being in a hair salon with your brother David when he was small. He was trying to tell a story and he kept stopping. Finally, the hairdresser said, "Spit it out!" and so he did—gathered the saliva in his mouth and spit it on the floor.

"Like what?" Jack says, imitating you in a higher-than-normal voice.

When you say nothing, he says, "Okay, well, I've got a deviated septum and I'm trying to schedule corrective surgery, like, soon."

"Deviated septum? You snore?"

"Not *all* people with deviated septums snore," he says, playful.

You lean back and look at his nose—his beautiful Roman nose. You can't imagine him with a petite button nose, or even a skinny nose.

"How long has this been an issue?"

"A while. Sometimes I have trouble breathing when I sleep. It seems to be getting worse, so . . . I just want to clear it up."

"Well, they better not mess with that gorgeous nose of yours. Please tell me that there won't be any cosmetic changes."

He sighs and looks away, "Yeah, of course not. Just tweaking the cartilage, that's all."

A moment later he adds, "And these damn doctors keep dicking me around—I'm supposed to have a firm date by now." When you eye him suspiciously, he adds, "Hopefully in the next few weeks. We'll see."

This subject suddenly seems like a touchy one. You decide to veer off in another direction. "Got some good stories today."

"Yeah? Anything you can use?"

"Not really, but it's a start."

Jack shifts you on his lap, encircling his hands around your waist. He nods his head and looks you in the eye, not in the I'm-mad-about-you way, but in the you-need-to-listen way.

This stance always makes you nervous. Your own father has never, would never, talk to you in this authoritative way. In fact, when you were nineteen and told him over brunch on spring break that you'd been having some problems with your appetite—as in, there was a complete loss for a few weeks—he listened to you, like he always does, stopping to look you in the eye and wait before saying anything. That morning, he tried to chip away at your hopelessness: "We are many different things in our lives, many different people. This isn't going to define you forever." Of course, he then followed up soon after with more practical concerns, about consulting a nutritionist to help with a meal plan and perhaps going to see a therapist. But never in your life has he told you that you had to do anything, not even finish all the food on your plate or drink your milk. So you feel strange when you look at Jack, clearing his throat, readying for lecture. Jack acts like the father you never had. Only trouble is, you never really wanted that father. Or did you?

Jack is changing gears—his face holds the expression of someone who feels like he absolutely *has* to tell you something, and he expects you not to like it.

"What you need are great stories—not just good stories. They have to be great."

This makes you uneasy. You don't know much about where you are going with this, but you would, of course, also like these stories to be "great." Only, Jack's emphasis makes you feel like you're out of the loop as to what a great story might be. Does he take you for a fool? You tell stories all the time, good ones, mediocre ones, and on occasion even great ones.

Instead of announcing this to Jack, you just nod. No need to be defensive, especially since you are nervous about getting people to open up. It hasn't been easy so far.

Again, you change the subject. "Jack, what do you think you need to work on, you know, in life?"

Jack's face barely belies surprise, but you see it, for a second. Usually, when you catch him off guard, he uses a long "Ahhhhhhhhhh" to buy himself some time to come up with what are always well-thought-out answers. His forehead wrinkles.

"Well, I'd say I need to spend more time with my family and less at work."

"That's a good thing to work on."

"What about you?"

"Ummmmm . . . I guess that I'm impatient?" You are thinking of your need to sell the proposal, even though you are barely sure what you want the book to be about.

"Well, actually," Jack says, "I've been meaning to talk to you about something."

Now what? This time you sit up. An interracial couple walks by, holding hands and smiling in your direction, as everyone seems to do these days.

"I've been thinking boxing is getting in the way of your life, and if you try to do it when you move to Brooklyn, it's really going to take up a lot of time. You have other things to focus on."

You are not in the ring, but you do feel like you've just tried unsuccessfully to defend yourself against a very solid uppercut. You love boxing. And once again, no one tells you what to do. Um, right?

"I'm not really sure what to say about that."

"Look, I know you love it. You'll do what you want to. I'm just saying that it could make your life better. You don't have to listen to me." He's looking at you nervously now.

Although Jack hasn't explicitly said, "I want you to stop boxing," the way he brought it up concerns you. *I've been thinking...*

But you don't go to the full-blown infuriated place, which would be something like, *You've "been thinking about it"? Give me a break. You barely know me.*

The trouble is, though, that you want Jack to know you, and so you do what you have to, to keep up the illusion that he already does. Desperately—so desperately that you're willing to suspend any and all sound judgments, as in, *Who does he think he is?* All your wishes of stability are wrapped up in him. And so you don't challenge this, his persuasive suggestion of what's best for you. You are queasy, because you also think he might actually be right. A week or two of driving two hours in traffic each way to the Bronx and then back to Brooklyn and you would have made your own decision about saying goodbye to the gym and your beloved Dudley. But now, if you make that decision, it will forever be associated with Jack. Even if you do it for yourself, you struggle with the feeling that you will have done it because he told you to.

You think back to your initial decision to start taking antidepressants, when you'd been with Ted for three years. You'd been ruminating for a while, in between bouts of worrying that took up most of your waking hours; when you realized that insurance would pay for your therapy only if you were medicated, that had tipped the scales. Still, as you look back now, you wonder if Ted's approval hadn't played a larger role. That first week on meds, you'd battled a persistently runny nose and dizzy head with thoughts that an anxiety-free life might make it easier to focus on your boyfriend.

"Are you okay?" Jack asks. You slide off his lap, moving back to your own seat, and shake your head.

"Yeah . . . but something"—sigh—"about this conversation is very unsettling." Big sigh. "I'd like to talk about it, but not now." Sigh. "I can't find the words . . ."

"You?" he teases. "You can't find the words?"

When you don't smile, he says in a serious voice, "Look, I'm just thinking about what's best for you."

"Uh-huh." You nod, looking away toward the street. "I get that."

For the next fifteen minutes, you put that uneasy feeling aside and hold his hand, tell him stories, and listen to what his face seems to be saying. That he loves you.

You are momentarily distracted by the birds in the trees and the sweat gathering around the back creases of your knees. When you look back at Jack, he's still looking at you.

Shit, Jack, you think. *I love you, too.*

In a place far, far away, the volume of "Shit!" looms most loudly.

Not "love" but "Shit."

15

WITH SEPTEMBER COMES the resuming of your regular Tuesday evening hustle, finishing up at work at five of five, so you can walk from your office in midtown to Elaine's office on the Upper West Side. She has been away on vacation, and now you are on your way to tell her about your summer, wondering how you can possibly spill all that it is you have to spill in less than fifty minutes. Your route strings together like a puzzle, turning up Fifth Avenue when you have a walk signal, walking as far and long as you can until you hit Central Park, another stop sign, or an immobilizing cluster of after-work crowds. You could have taken the subway, but walking brings you peace, a breather from another uneventful day in the office, where you can look past carefully planned storefront displays and over the traffic to the between-building slivers of sky. You rationalize it's a necessary corridor, moving from routine work-you mind-set to the internal, questioning-you. Besides, somewhere in the middle of your forty-five-minute stroll, you will take note of panhandlers with open faces and sad stories, petitioners asking you to save the children, a woman laughing on her phone—reinforcing that the nature of it all is simple: Keep moving. You can't be late.

This morning, on the phone with Paula, she asked a very Paula question. Paula has recently returned from her summer in London, and you are happy to have her presence back in the city, even if you have both been too busy to actually get together. This morning, you were going on and on about moving into your new apartment with Jack's help, how you discovered a built-in closet and bookshelf you hadn't even noticed when you went to look at the place. You were telling her about the drive from the Bronx to Brooklyn, how Jack had followed your car, driving the sketchy van with an expired sticker. Filled with relief at having the move half over, you were staring at him in your rearview as you both waited in traffic to get on the Brooklyn-Queens Expressway. It wasn't enough to see each other. You heard your phone buzz and opened it to find a text message from Jack. "You're the best," he wrote. You wrote back, "So are you." The next one was, "I can't wait to hold you." And you went back and forth, grinning at each other, even as the cars inched along, until he finally wrote, "There is something really wrong with us"—with an e-smiley face tacked onto the end, of course. In the middle of telling Paula this, she abruptly said, "Can I ask you something? What makes you feel beautiful?"

The last time Paula interrupted you with a non sequitur was when she called you from London. As one does when one rambles, you'd started talking about whether or not the new HPV vaccine promotes promiscuity in teen girls, its target market. A frequent cause of cervical cancer, HPV is a sexually transmitted disease, which, incidentally, is estimated to affect one in four women. This is a fact you always include when you tell lovers or potential lovers that you, ah, contracted it in your

early twenties (thinking its prevalence will make this information slightly less shameful). Your gynecologist thinks the virus
has been dormant years since, but you and she both agree that
when it comes to sex, better to err on the side of full disclosure.
Paula, instead of commenting, had said, "Um, do you know
anything about getting a Fulbright? I want to go to Turkey next
summer."

Paula's cues are clear, simple. When she cut you off, with
your obsessive details about the move, to ask you about beauty,
you didn't hesitate: "When I feel good inside, I feel beautiful."
Of course you'd said that. It's the easy answer, the logical answer, and what one should say in the posturing of having good
self-esteem. What does that even mean?

Paula is a smart girl. You'd heard her take in a heavy breath
after your answer and go on to explain that she had moments
of feeling not beautiful with Fred, her long-term, long-distance
boyfriend. You'd thought to say something about long-distance
relationships existing sometimes in a high-pressure compart-
ment that doesn't quite gel with the rest of your life. The times
you spend together are limited, colored by the time when one
of you will once again be leaving.

But Paula and Fred have done this for two years already. She
doesn't need you to tell her that the beauty question is probably less about beauty and more about a larger anxiety taking
up residence on this tiny issue. Problems are sometimes just
easier to digest that way, when you start with the random surface stuff.

"He doesn't say it enough," she'd said. "That I'm beautiful."

You, for one, happen to think that Paula is very pretty, with
her fair eyes and rosy skin. You kept this observation to your-

self, knowing that she'd think you're just saying it because you have to. Instead you say, "Hmmmm . . ."

Whether she knows it or not, Paula has given you a home-work assignment. You had spent a greater part of your summer feeling very strong—beautiful, even. Perhaps deceptively so.

Looking back, you've had an ongoing love-hate relationship with the *b*-word, often confusing the issue of looking good to the outside world with feeling solid on the inside. On the one hand, you know that looks don't matter. (And really, does that statement even need further unpacking?) But despite knowing this, you have always placed enormous pressure on yourself to look good—which makes you feel incredibly shallow whenever you stop to think about it. Living in looks-obsessed New York City does not help matters.

When you were in high school, you looked over your jour-nals from when you were a child. On one page, you'd started a "story," a piece of so-called fiction, and the first line was, "It's hard to be beautiful." You were mortified, seriously mortified, when you reread this, imagining your lonely little self sitting up in the tree feeling bad for yourself because you were . . . such a beautiful child? Please.

Like plenty of women you know, you grew up in a house-hold where beauty was prized. Your mother, an attractive woman, was always working to keep it up—with permanents, acrylic nails, fad diets. One fall, she had a very Oprah-like mo-ment before the words "Oprah" and "diet" were synonymous on the pop culture landscape. Family friends were having a barbeque at their house. You were swinging with their dog—whom you'd forced to take a hammock ride with you because he was so damn cuddly—when your mother emerged through the sliding glass doors onto the back patio, wearing skin-tight dark jeans and a T-shirt. "Wow!" others remarked, admiring her recent weight loss. "Look at you!" You'd been with her all along, on the drive there, through the many meals of salad and rice cakes. (Regardless of whether or not she was on a diet, your mother always looked so beautiful to you.) But seeing others see her in her new shape, this was new. She smiled and moved across the wooden patio, owning every inch of her body, as if she had full grasp of every last cell. You watched from your perch on the hammock, transfixed, curious, until the dog started to lick your face excitedly, the shift in his weight tipping the hammock over and dumping you on the hard ground. You spent the rest of the night picking the pine needles out of your wool sweater.

Other times, you heard your mother making comments about spandex-clad women who spend all their time in gyms, perfecting toned upper arms and sweating it out on the Stair-Master. Once she said, "Kind of vain, don't you think?" complete with a click of her tongue. A preteen then, you didn't answer her question—not only because it wasn't really a question, but because you didn't agree with the underlying sentiment, though it seemed like you should.

But all of this is beside the point: Paula wasn't asking about appearance, or looking beautiful *to* others. That's all surface stuff. (How easily derailed you are by what others think!) She was asking the more substantive question: What makes you feel beautiful? And feelings, as you well know, are nothing if not interior.

The real essence of beauty—and, as suddenly as the season has turned, you are once again struggling with this yourself—is strength. What substantiates this? For one, you have not ever once felt beautiful when you were living out an expression of weakness—by either being too concerned with impressions you made on others, or holding on too tightly to the feeling of having been wronged by ex-lovers, family members, or friends. You, a student of philosophy, are bad at recalling names, but you remember one particular theory on aesthetics: that our sense of beauty and being attracted to beautiful things is largely dependent on our own subjectivity, and whether or not these external things—people, buildings, art—resonate with an innate sense of well-being. In other words, if someone calls a room "beautiful," she may as well be saying, "I can see myself here." To extend this to inner beauty, when we feel beautiful, isn't it because we are living up to our full potential, as best as we can define it in that moment? Wouldn't, then, the statement of "I feel beautiful" be the equivalent of "I embrace and approve of myself"? Perhaps it's too pat, but don't forget that sometimes the "pat" answers are the most profound. There are other times in your life when you haven't felt so great about your career or love life or your self (with a lowercase *s*) and you've caught yourself thinking, *At least I'm pretty.* During those low points, your lover's opinion takes on unbearable importance.

This morning, on the phone with Paula, whom you hate to hear upset, you hadn't gone this far in your thinking. Instead, as she told you a story about shopping for cashmere sweaters with Fred, the excursion that had prompted her to ask this question in the first place, you just listened as she vented. (And it is very rare for Paula to vent.) Had there been a mirror present, your option might have been to remark, "Beautiful."

* * *

WHEN YOU ARRIVE at Elaine's, Frank the elevator guy smiles at you and asks in a lilting voice, "How are you? Haven't seen you in sooooo long!"

Frank always makes you a little nervous, ever since he gave you his phone number and asked that you call him if you ever have car trouble again. A nice offer, sure. But you had a sinking feeling that Frank wanted to be more than your mechanic, and so now you keep your answers short and your lips pursed when you ride up to the tenth floor. Going to Elaine's, you always have a lot to think about.

You slip into her office and sit on the chair next to the bookshelf, across from the fresh flowers she has delivered every week.

"Hi! So good to see you," she squeals. For the most part, you like Elaine and her familiar way. She does her best to make you feel welcome and cared for. She looks tanned and rested. From the glow on her face, you suspect she's gotten a lot of fresh air during her time away.

You ask her about her vacation, to be polite, and she tells you it was wonderful, putting great emphasis on the first syllable, so much that you feel like it's for your benefit. That's the trouble with you and therapy—you are too damn analytic for your own good, even if you don't always turn that eye inward.

"Well," she asks, "what's new?"

"Well . . ."

What's really new, technically new, is that you have officially moved into your new place. After the move, Jack and you celebrated; you took him out to dinner and then the two of you fooled around in the sketchy van on an empty side street for an hour—all that was wonderful. The following morning you woke up alone in your unpacked room, looking out to a view of two-family rooftops and one fake owl perched on someone's chimney. Apparently, fake owls are commonly used to deter birds, rodents, squirrels, and rabbits. So far, you've spent a decent amount of time in your new place wondering if the faux-owl actually works. That all counted as "new"—oh, and you had sex with Jack for the first time, which was sooner than you two had planned. You were half joking when you told him that you should wait a year, thinking that the pace of your relationship was already on fast-forward and that delaying sex might force you both to take things slower. But after moving and eating and drinking a bottle of wine, waiting suddenly seemed very stupid. Being with Jack felt better than you could have imagined, the brushing of his skin against yours, the sound of his voice in your ear. *Oh!* You love to hear him happy.

Unfortunately, this is not the place you feel compelled to start when Elaine asks you, "What's new?" No, instead of diving in to where you are, you go back, weaving your way through the end of summer, telling her exactly what happened with Marco and Jack, exactly as you remember it. From beneath the surface of your email details and descriptions of your first date with Jack, you hear a voice saying, "Is this necessary?" You are literal, too married to minutiae, and so the honest answer to "What happened?" will not be summed up in five sentences or five minutes. In fact, you are probably boring her.

"Oh, and so then I called Jack back and said . . ."

"So when I went to Marco's, he was getting out of the shower, and he looked adorable, so it was even harder than I imagined, but at this point, what else was there to do?"

"Then Jack and I took the day off to go to the beach and his parents were really surprised because he's a workaholic and known for hardly ever taking time off, even on the weekends . . ."

By the time forty-five minutes have passed, forget boring Elaine—you have bored yourself. So you veer off in another direction.

"I was telling my parents about him, you know, completely gushing, and my father said that he'd never seen me talk this much about a guy, which is true . . ."

Often, you are silent about love interests, mostly because you feel like if you are going to declare, "I am in love!" that it absolutely, positively has to be right, like there's no room for error in your feelings, this statement will live forevermore carved into the stone of Truth. And if you were wrong, well, then you will feel very stupid. And you hate feeling stupid.

With Jack, you are open, or at least more open. You'd emailed your parents a couple of the pictures that he emailed to you, one in which he's wearing your favorite Jack-expression of incredulousness. You think it's very adorable that he is sitting on a chair with his hands out, jaw open, making a very passionate point—and that when you look in the bottom left-hand corner, you see he's talking to his five-year-old nephew. Over the phone, your mother had said, "Oh, he's handsome. You two have the same smile." Both your parents sounded really happy that you are happy.

Of course, your first thought in telling Elaine this is to say, "See, look, I'm becoming more open because Jack is really special." But you are quick to think about alternative reasons, especially when you see the skepticism wash over her face.

"Maybe"—you clear your throat—"Jack isn't the reason I'm more open, but an indicator of being more open. I have been pretty closed with my parents in the past."

You sit, sigh, hold on to that thought for a moment, when Elaine interrupts to say, "Yes, and for good reason."

Oh, the good reason. You'd rather not talk about it, the childish feelings of hurt or neglect, even though this is the reason, ostensibly, that you are in talk therapy. You are twenty-nine, completely responsible for your own well-being, and going down that old road is scary. Being stuck terrifies you and so with an eye-roll you mean to tell Elaine that the family of origin story is old; its shelf life is over, being a useless tale that really just makes you feel a little sad for everyone. Okay, fine. A lot sad.

Letting Elaine's "good reason" comment hang in the air, you are slightly pissed off. Why did she have to ruin a perfectly good story? You were doing just fine without her all summer, feeling beautiful and free.

No one understands. No one seems to understand how badly you'd like to forget. Your mind skips back to your walk here, the zigzagging across the southern area of the park, the stopping to admire a woman dressed in a long, flowing skirt, the time-check that you did every few minutes because you didn't want to be late. But that was silly, trying to check the time, because you'd already chosen the scenic route. There was no turning back. By the time you passed Columbus Circle, the subway, like other modes of transportation, was no longer an option. You had your legs and your imagination, and that was all you needed to keep moving. You have always been a dancer.

* * *

ON THE TRAIN home that night, you sit next to a girl with dark eyeliner. After thinking about the level of skill it must have taken to apply evenly those thick black lines of kohl, you drift off. If you were feeling a bit more confident, maybe you'd ask her if she had an embarrassing story. But these moments you want to capture, they are the ones that people usually like to forget—and so if you must ask, you also must exude sureness.

Besides, if the defining characteristic of an *Oh, Shit!* moment is wanting the ground to open up and swallow you whole, then why would anyone want to relive it? You are not sure. You have a whole line about some catharsis shit, but really, you don't know. You seem to be waiting to capture a story that will break open the safe, unlock the jewels of embarrassment, and set free the diamond dust of secret-keeping. But, alas, you still haven't found those stories—at least not yet.

16

UNPACKING IS BEST done in one task-driven stretch. But you and your issues with task-driving have become rather apparent lately. (*Oh, Shit!*, anyone?) Boxes are strewn around your room, half opened. Books spill across the floor. You know that unpacking these first would help you feel at home, which is something you desperately need.

The first Saturday in your place, you wake up to Jack lying next to you in his white T-shirt. It's not even nine o'clock and already he's reaching for his BlackBerry. Though you are not fond of this behavior, you don't say anything. Jack has a lot going on. He moved out of his apartment midsummer, although he never really explained why. This would not have seemed strange, only he didn't directly move into another place; instead he's been staying with friends and family. He's made some vague noises about not jumping into a new apartment situation until it's absolutely the right one. For reasons that you cannot pin down, you suspect that Jack had been living with someone and that he moved out because they broke up. Whatever the reasons, with the unsettled living situation and his mounting work, you know that he's in a time of transition, too. *Better to not push him,* you think.

Last night, when you two drove up the FDR to the Cloisters, Jack had sat in the passenger seat, singing a country song in an exaggerated, off-key twang. Shaking his head in time with the music, he slapped the back of his hand against his knee, over and over. Witnessing this new, carefree side of Jack, your chest got a little tight. You thought, *Oh, my God—who is this person in my front seat?*

Once you parked your car and the two of you walked through the gardens, looking out at the Hudson from your high perch, Jack grabbed your hand and your heart forgave the moment of unfamiliarity. He pulled out a box of sparklers and you lit two, watching their yellow light twirl and flutter against a fading sunset. After, you ate dinner at the restaurant near the museum, noshing on scallops and steak on the brick patio strung with Christmas lights. You had two drinks each, and then you drove back to your new room in Brooklyn. You were tipsy enough that you shouldn't have driven. But Jack had had two drinks with his brother before coming to meet up with you, and so he shouldn't have driven, either.

When you parked on a tree-lined street behind your apartment, you leaned over to kiss Jack. Since having sex with him, the physical pull between you has superseded all other connection. Sex has begun to narrate your life. You wait for the moments alone with him. In the car, you were almost there, alone, when your lips touched his. Your kisses turned fast and before you knew it, his hands were on your waist, exploring your bare skin. Before you knew it, you leaned into him and felt the tie on your skirt loosen. You touching Jack, Jack touching you, it's not something you have any sort of restraint with. And so right there, on the street, in your car, you almost had sex.

"Wait, wait, wait," you whispered. "Let's go inside."

"Phew. Yeah, what are you doing to me?"

The street was dark. As you pranced down the street and grabbed Jack's hand, he stopped you on the curb. He pulled you closer and leaned in, so that his eyes were only an inch from yours, and whispered, "You know what? I love you."

Instead of saying that you loved him, too—which you think you do—you balked. You don't know where it came from. Sometimes you do this, pull back when you think the risk of being hurt is great. No, reciprocation wasn't there, but not because you didn't feel it. You were just scared.

"You're telling me this now? The moment after we've almost had sex in the car. How romantic . . ." But your sarcasm does not go over well. Instead, he just looked at you, hurt.

"Let's go home," you finally whispered, taking his hand again.

The rest of the evening had been wonderful. You raced by your four new roommates, still strangers, waving a quick hello as you pulled Jack into your bedroom. In the dark, you'd kicked away some of the books to make a clearing on the floor, turned on some moody, atmospheric music, and asked Jack if he would dance with you. With a gardenia-scented candle flickering in the background, Jack took your body and moved it closer to his. You never got tired of this, the way you felt together.

You remember asking past lovers to dance and you also remember them looking at you like you were crazy, even though you just wanted a little stillness. You recall a magic moment with Ted, in Argentina, where the two of you were staying for a couple of weeks in an apartment just blocks away from the Recoleta Cemetery, where Eva Perón is buried. There, after a large dinner of steak from pampas-fed cattle and copious amounts of Malbec, you asked Ted to dance. He said yes and you will never forget it.

Jack likes the stillness, and so the moment lingered into another and then another, until four hours passed and the two of you had fallen asleep on one another. His skin felt so warm against yours.

As he starts to write an email on his BlackBerry, you think back to the night before. The glow of your slow dance is gone, no longer carving out space on your cluttered floor. Your hours—yes, hours—of lovemaking are, too, gone. You are adjusting to the sun as it blares through your shadeless windows, lighting up a pile of dust in the corner. With a clenched jaw, you scan your wreck of a room, which hadn't bothered you at all the night before. Maybe you should have told Jack you loved him. But you didn't, and so now what? As he buries his head and sighs, he begins talking aloud in response to his emails.

"Oh, my god. They said what?" or "That is completely unacceptable!"

Jack, you are beginning to note, can be a bit of a Cassandra sometimes. He often talks doom and gloom about ghastly situations on the horizon, such as the economic downturn or the growing prominence of *Yersinia pestis*, the bacteria responsible for the bubonic plague. While you are continually impressed by the scope of his knowledge, you can't help but think that he's being slightly alarmist when he tells you, say, that you should ask your father to stock up on Tamiflu, since it's the closest thing to a cure to the avian bird flu that's about to wreak havoc on life as you know it. And seriously, while you're contacting your dad, he's going to start thinking about moving upstate because of the ease with which communicable diseases can be spread on the subway. Jack looks so serious that you have begun to doubt yourself. What's wrong with you, that you're not more concerned? So you emailed your dad and his response was assuring, as it usually is. After pointing out that the media dramatizes the avian bird flu (or some comparable disease) every few years, he adds, "I wouldn't worry about it."

This morning Jack is still shaking his head about the growing incidence of hurricanes.

"This is going to be a serious problem," he says. "Mark my words."

You just listen, feeling inadequate for having nothing to add to this conversation.

Even though you have one hand placed absently on Jack's stomach, your head is turned away from him. You are staring off into space when suddenly he puts down the BlackBerry and says, "I hate to do this, but I should really get going soon. I have a ton of errands to run today." He kisses you on your nose, and you, still naked, reach out for him as he begins to leave your bed.

"Baby?" you say with a yawn. "When are we going to get to spend a whole Saturday together?"

You are thinking: an evening in, making dinner and snuggling on the couch to watch a movie. You will fall asleep in the first twenty minutes, but it's the coziness you crave. Being quiet with one another—it never occurs to you to wonder whether or not it will exist, actually could exist.

"Soon, my dear. All in good time."

When your face goes sour—that was not the answer you wanted to hear—Jack adds, "It'll be so different when I get my own place."

"Yeah, how *is* that apartment search going?"

"Good. I have a couple places I'm going to see today."

"You do? Where?" You are not surprised as much as you are hurt that this is the first you're hearing of his plans.

"West Village."

Now you are sitting upright in bed, your mouth open.

"I'm just going for a quick look. Would be great to find something before I have the surgery." He told you yesterday that the surgery is scheduled for next week.

Your face is still scrunched up. Despite the fact that he told you he loved you last night, something has changed since you started dating. You swear, if you were still with Marco, Jack would *insist* that you go with him this afternoon. But you're not with Marco anymore. And so Jack no longer pursues you with the dogged persistence he once had, no longer responding to any and all emails. The times he can write, however, are still heartfelt and sweet. You need to get a grip. Really.

"Hey, hey," he whispers. "I'll get back here as soon as I can today. We'll see a movie tonight?"

"Okay," you mumble, forcing a smile. "Sounds good to me."

The equation is simple. Jack leaving is bad. Jack coming back is better.

After Jack leaves, you turn on some music and run a damp washcloth over your grimy windowsill. *Ugh.* Your luminous summer—and all its accompanying glory—is definitely over.

AFTER A MINUTE of hearing one of your new roommates shuffle around in the kitchen, you slip out the door, saying, "Good morning," on your way out. Sophie, who lives in the small front bedroom, is hunched over the coffeepot and looks startled, not that you are there, but that you don't stop to say hello. Down the creaky stairs and out the heavy front doors, you realize that you don't have anywhere to go.

You stand on the sidewalk for a minute, realizing that if it's coffee you wanted, your wallet is upstairs. You scan the line of stoops—real stoops!—on your new block. There are potted plants, window boxes with drying flowers, and trash cans— many trash cans. Just then, a man in a gray overcoat too heavy for the weather walks by. He holds his bulldog's leash in one hand and a cigarette in the other.

You pause for a minute. It's not even noon. But the sky is calling and across the street, a wall of trees line the park, your best neighbor yet. The man is scowling, visibly scowling. *Must have had some bad news this morning,* you think.

"Excuse me, sir?" you ask shyly, tentatively. "Can I bum a smoke?"

17

OUTSIDE IS A painting, an Inness painting—gauzy yellow light, barely visible sun peeking through the silhouette of branches— all framed by the worn wooden windowsill, seen through fingerprint-smeared panes. Your eyes are focusing on what's outside, while your brain is steadying on the question to which you have no good answer:

"So, you've looked up the Latin root of 'embarrassment' and all that?"

"Uh . . ."

You are sitting in Dalton's office overlooking Washington Square and peeking out to this snapshot of New York City. The October morning is cold, and you have lied to your boss, telling her that you have a doctor's appointment. In fact, it's not entirely a lie, if you take into consideration that Dalton is a PhD. This is a stretch, yes, but your mind goes to silly, obvious places to save yourself from having to give Dalton a straight answer. Although this is the first time you've seen him since the wine bar, you fall into exactly the same goofball persona in his presence.

To Dalton's straight man, you are a bundle of nervous, chattering energy. You are zany, off-the-wall—perhaps all this craziness is in your head, but you feel it in your most benign gestures, i.e., a perfunctory kiss hello on the cheek or bringing him a coffee and a muffin when, of course, he drinks decaf and is allergic to sugar.

"Pretty day," you murmur from your hard-backed perch of a wooden chair. The air is damp, signaling rain, and really, this is anything but a pretty day. Dalton stops and looks at you, quiet for a moment. His eyes are round, inviting. You don't know why, but you have an affinity for people with big, circular eyes. Maybe it began with your friend's daughter, now three, and the happy blue orbs that dominate her expressions, whether she is pulling the cat's tail or walking around with a pumpkin on her head. Prejudices are so easy to come by.

"The Latin root? Uh, no, I haven't looked that up yet." Then, clearing your throat, you add, "Actually."

"Oh." Dalton looks puzzled.

"Yeah, I'm still collecting—it's been kind of a hectic time, with moving, work . . ."

"Are you still seeing the Czech boxer?"

"Ah, no, actually, no. I'm seeing someone else, um, a literary agent, actually." You fidget on the chair and reach down into your bag, making a show of pulling out your notepad and recorder, as if this extra pause you take to ensure that your tools are in place makes you a more determined person.

"Is that how you met him?"

"No, no." You are flat-out lying to Dalton because you are too ashamed to tell him the truth, *Yes, that's how I met Jack.* You know you've been stupid in leaping into this relationship, crossing professional lines that weren't so firm to begin with. No need to broadcast it to the world. Besides, your worst fear is that Jack only "took you on" not because of your writing, but because your ass is kind of okay-looking.

"But we may work together," you add. *May?* This is either (a) a lie or (b) a premonition. Your menstrual cycle is about to begin and you read somewhere that the days before a woman gets her period are when her intuition is stronger than normal. You have noticed this over the years, a voice getting louder and louder as your belly bloats, sometimes saying things like, "Just admit it! You and Ted are more friends than lovers!" or "Don't you dare try to blame that weight loss on some imaginary celiac disease—you've cut down on wheat because you like being skinnier!" From quiet corners, you are thinking more clearly about Jack and his role in your life, whether you want to or not.

"Well, that's great," Dalton says. "It's going well? You're happy?"

You are not happy, actually. You are not happy at all. Ever since Jack's corrective nasal surgery a few weeks ago, you have not seen him. What was supposed to be a normal procedure took an unexpected turn when he got an infection in his nasal cavity. Even a hefty dose of Cipro didn't seem to help. Convalescing this whole time at his aunt's house in Westchester, Jack has been more or less miserable-sounding. The painkillers have kept him groggy and unable to conduct business as usual. Every day you call and say, "Can I see you?" and he says, "Oh, I would love that!" but then comes up with a reason why it's not a good idea. He's had a persistent fever. She lives too far for you to go to that kind of trouble. You are tired of saying, "Okay, babe, just let me know if there's anything I can do . . ."

You've sent him get-well cards and a DVD of *Rumble in the Jungle,* a documentary that covers the historic boxing match between Muhammad Ali and George Foreman. Though Jack is not exactly a boxing fan, you thought that the film would help keep his mind off his health. You don't understand why he has continued to put off your offers of a visit. Is it because he doesn't want you to meet his aunt or other family members? Or is it because he doesn't really want to see you? In other respects, Jack is acting somewhat normal, calling you affectionate names, writing you heartfelt responses to your emails, telling you he misses you.

Your eyes flicker when you think about telling Dalton that you aren't happy. Your eyes—sometimes blue, sometimes gray, sometimes green—are too large a presence on your face for others not to notice when you're uncomfortable. With someone else, someone you know better, you may have fessed up about your unhappiness, but not to Dalton.

"Uh, yeah, yeah . . ." Your eyes wander around his office, looking at the piles of papers and notebooks and textbooks scattered over his desktop. You can't look over at the bookshelf again. You've only been here five minutes and you've already done that too many times. "I mean, he's cute."

Dalton looks at you with a big-brother concerned face, as if to say, *Oh, no. Is everything all right, young one?*

God, you hate that look.

"Oh, and the other great thing is that he speaks English."

Now Dalton is the one looking around his own office as if for the first time. From his expression, you guess that your answer has sufficiently confused him.

"Yeah, you know, like, Ondra, the boxer, he didn't speak English. Then I dated an Italian, lovely guy—and that was a step up because, while he was not a native English-speaker, his mother is American and so he speaks English very well. And now, with Jack, he . . ." You are realizing that you sound like a fool, a total fool. "Well, I guess I mean to say that it's going well . . . we have marathon conversations, you know . . . he's very bright and it's, uh, great."

Even though it is cold, a layer of sweat has formed on your skin. You feel it right where the capped sleeves to your slate-green angora sweater cut off on your arms—a pool, as it were, welling.

Dalton is too formal to make proper fun of you. You wish this weren't the case. You wish that he would just call a spade a spade and you could both get on with the business of collecting his *Oh, Shit!* story. (After all, your rambling should make him feel more comfortable in sharing his story; sometimes you ramble and reveal with intention, but this is not one of those times.) Instead, you are left with this awkward silence and his returning stare that is too present.

"Um, so anyway, your story? I brought my tape recorder this time . . ."

Dalton leans back into his office chair and your eyes drift outside again. Rain has started to fall, and you can see umbrellas bobbing across the park at varying heights. As you sit with your notebook open and pen poised, you are struck. Melancholy, the feeling you've been shoving under the rug for the last five or so weeks, surfaces. You can't pretend to be anyone other than you, only you have yet to accept this. The absence of mirrors in Dalton's office pleases you.

"Okay," he begins. "So, I was in junior high—seventh grade . . . it's a little fuzzy, and I may have changed the details to make 'the incident' seem more legitimate, so . . ."

This is precisely what you like about Dalton; he has an easy way of admitting that maybe he's not on top of every last detail, but that he'll give you what he has, to the best of his ability. It's refreshing.

When Dalton was in the seventh grade, he went to a public school in Manhattan. The student population was a mix of rich kids and poor kids (your understanding being that Dalton fell somewhere in between). As a self-respecting seventh-grader might, Dalton often cut class, spending hours and hours in front of a stand-up video game in the back of a deli. *Defender* vied for his attention far more successfully than the college-track classes he was supposed to be in, and after a few months of truancy gone unchecked, Dalton was dropped to the . . . other . . . track. In other words, AP chemistry and calculus for geniuses were replaced with sewing and shop.

As Dalton reminisces about those days, his tone is assured. This is a time and era to which he has obviously devoted a lot of reflection. You imagine that even young Dalton would have found some pleasure—obvious or otherwise—in being "different," i.e., a college-track kid spending his days making animal-shaped pillows and overly shellacked wooden signs with his family's names drilled across the front.

One afternoon in sewing class, Dalton was sitting at his desk. He raised his hand and asked if he could go to the bathroom. Well aware of his truancy issues, the teacher said, "No. You have to wait." And so the lesson went on—a pattern was projected onto the chalkboard and the teacher pointed to the different types of stitching that the students would learn in this lesson.

Consumed with the growing stitch in his side, Dalton was not going to learn much. He started to fidget in his seat. This was not good. He raised his hand again. "May I please go to the bathroom?"

"No."

A few more minutes passed. Dalton tried to take his mind off the only thing that he could focus on: *Must. Go. Now.*

When Dalton got up to leave for the bathroom anyway, the teacher yelled, "Where do you think you are going?"

And then right there, in the middle of two rows of desks, Dalton froze. Even though he cut class, he wasn't entirely resistant to authority.

"Uh, uh . . ."

And just as he stopped to think of a good argument—his fellow students staring at him—the good argument appeared, most unfortunately, in the form of a puddle around his feet.

The teacher, a youngish, inexperienced woman, ran to Dalton's side with an apron.

Twelve is the age when hormones burst onto the scene. Pimples appear not daily, but hourly. Everyone spends their days feeling stupid and awkward, making twelve-year-olds a pretty harsh audience.

But as Dalton stood there, his face getting hot with shame, no one said a word. No laughter. No, "Baby!" Not even an, "Ew . . . gross." And it was the quiet that killed Dalton even more than the fact of his peeing on the floor in front of his fellow seventh-graders.

Class dismissed. Someone—likely a janitor—cleaned up Dalton's mess. And, after finally getting a pass to use the bathroom, Dalton learned that his teachers would not allow him to go home and change. He had to spend the rest of the day with an apron wrapped around his wet jeans.

Ever resourceful, Dalton thought about his predicament carefully, deciding to channel all of his embarrassment into a shrewd strategy: he would pull every student aside, one by one, and explain what happened, placing the blame on the teacher. Of course! It was the teacher's fault that Dalton peed on the floor in front of everyone. Dalton was sure that no one would actually make fun of him to his face if they understood. Even though the student population was about eight hundred, Dalton actually thought that he could speak to each and every student.

When Dalton started, the exchanges went something like this:

Dalton: *Man, it was that teacher's fault—that's why I wet my pants in front of everyone.*

Student X Caught in the Embarrassment Cross Fire: Nodding sympathetically. No actual verbal response.

And so it went. For the rest of the day, Dalton tried to get all the students on his side, and although he will never really know what they thought or said behind his back, the responses, muted as they were, remained pretty much the same the whole day.

Embarrassment—derived, you will later learn, from the French word "embarrasser," meaning to block or obstruct, a term first used by Montaigne in 1580—is emotional in nature. You think about Dalton's embarrassing moment, which, like all other cases of the emotion, requires the presence of at least one other person. (For example, if you were alone and judging a quality in your personality as unappealing—such as, say, self-involvement—you would not feel embarrassed. You would feel ashamed. You know, hypothetically speaking.) With regard to Dalton peeing his pants, one doesn't have to dig too deep to see that, hey, losing control in such a socially unacceptable manner is not something to be proud of.

If *Oh, Shit!* moments are universal in the acute feeling of embarrassment—the abashment that rises up, involuntarily, when we've done or revealed something that we hadn't wanted or intended other people to witness—how people deal with that universal feeling is completely subjective. Most people want to run away from their very own embarrassing moment, but not Dalton, who faced his head-on. With this approach, Dalton seems to be saying, "I may not be in control of what happened, but I sure can control the aftermath."

WHEN DALTON IS finished, you turn off the recorder.

"Thank you," you say, while packing up your bag and thinking of a suitable conversational thread that will tie in nicely with your exit. You are a total freak around Dalton, and you know it.

"Oh!" you exclaim, acting as if this just came to you. Really, your "Oh!" is more about having found something to say, as opposed to what you are actually going to say. "What do you want your name to be? Since these are anonymous, I let people choose their own names."

Dalton swats an imaginary fly as he stands up to walk you toward the door, a warm smile on his face.

"No fake name. That's my story and I'm proud of it."

18

Outside Dalton's office, you are standing on the edge of Washington Square Park, bundled and shivering in the rain. You were supposed to visit Jack at his aunt's house, but you need to call him again, because he has turned you away so many times over the last few weeks that you can't imagine this plan actually working out. You are glad for the miserable weather.

"Hi," you start, breathless. When you are breathless with Jack these days, it's because you're scared, nervous, and no longer because you're excited. Coming from the same part of the brain, there is a fine line between nervous and excited, but you have not seen the "excited" plane in several weeks.

"You coming?" is the first thing he says. Now, not quite ecstatic, your breath slows, feels fuller.

"Yeah, yeah."

"Are you sure? I mean, it's so far and I know you don't have much time."

This is true. You are on your way to a wedding in Massachusetts. Jack was supposed to be your date. But he hemmed and hawed, not sure if he should go because of his lingering infection. Finally, two days ago, he told you he wouldn't be able to make it. Your heart sank, of course. You had planned a very romantic weekend, just the two of you. The wedding was on Cape Cod, and you had already spent many an hour thinking about the dune walk you would take him on, the sloping cliffs in Wellfleet that you so desperately needed to show him. And instead of a fun-filled weekend with Jack, you were going to the wedding with . . . your mother. That was nice and all—you knew that she would have a blast—but it wasn't quite the weekend you desired. You have to leave New York on a five o'clock bus bound for Massachusetts. When you counted travel time to and from Jack's aunt's house, this left you with all of an hour and fifteen minutes for an actual visit.

To you, it's worth it.

"Baby, just let me come, okay?"

"Okay, I can't wait to see you." His voice sounds soft.

Yesterday, you'd forwarded him an email from an ex-boyfriend, who had attached a photo of himself shirtless, standing next to a Harley. When you'd forwarded it to Jack, your message was, "How funny is this?!!?!," adding a note that you hoped Jack-your-boyfriend would appreciate this as much as Jack-your-friend might have. Jack assured you that Jack-your-friend and Jack-your-boyfriend are one and the same, but that he wasn't exactly laughing at the moment (although he'd like to someday). Suddenly you felt like an asshole. Here Jack was, with post-op blues, sick with fever, unable to work out, and here you were, showing off photos of your exceedingly buff, forty-year-old ex-boyfriend. Nice. Real nice.

You head up to Grand Central, where you buy an over-priced bouquet of sunflowers. You buy magazines and tea and chocolate ice cream, too. You cannot afford this, but you have no rational control over anything when it comes to Jack. In fact, your spending habits should be the least of your worries. What's the difference of a few dollars?

The difference—after it's all spent and gone—is actually substantial, you calculate as you are sitting on the train, oblivious to the off-hour commuters sitting in your train car, on laptops and cell phones, with newspapers spread across their laps.

You arrive at the train station and pull out Jack's directions. The town is quaint, sleepy, and you wish you had more time to stroll around, maybe sip a cup of tea and read the paper. But you do not have time, and so you hail a cab and can barely punch in Jack's number while you give the driver his address.

"I'll be there soon!" you squeal. The time apart has been too long, putting an abrupt halt to the rocket pace of your relationship. Maybe this slowing-down is good, although neither you nor Jack have addressed it with one another. It just hangs there, like a loose tooth that needs to be extracted.

Five minutes later, as you are pulling a ten-dollar bill out of your wallet to pay the cabdriver, you look down the driveway toward Jack's aunt's house, a large white Victorian with forest green trim. You're supposed to just pay the cabdriver and get out of his car. But when you see Jack waiting outside for you, looking rather adorable in flannel pajama pants and a worn T-shirt, you forget everything else, where you are, what you're doing, who you are.

"Miss?" the driver asks.

"Oh, sorry . . ." You throw him the last of your money and jump out of the cab, balancing your weekend bag, a water-filled vase, and some get-well items for Jack.

Jack must be cold, but his arms are outstretched, and you

cannot stop. You just cannot stop looking at him. All your stupid neuroses are quieted, momentarily, by the look on his face—so appealing—your Jack is so handsome. His nose looks a little swollen, but for the most part it's exactly as you'd remembered it. On the stone walkway, you lean into him, inhaling his skin and falling, practically falling into his arms as if you were the one who was recuperating.

"Whoa! Whoa!" he says. "Hold on, baby. Just hold on."

He takes your heaviest bag and your dress, and then steps back. "It's so good to see you."

You repeat this. He repeats this. You repeat it, again and again. You walk into the house and put all your bags down. The house is dark, save for the glow of a television in a far room. Jack says he's spent too much time there over the last few weeks and what he really wants is to hold you, as far from CNN as you two can get.

You have always been nosy, and in spite of dim lighting and shadows, you look around the living room, scanning the bookshelf, the stacks of books, notebooks, and piles of paper scattered around the perimeter of the room. In front of a large bay window there are many plants—a tall bird-of-paradise, smaller ferns, dramatically arching bromeliads, one lone fuchsia orchid.

"Come here, just come here."

Jack has you by the hand and pulls you onto the couch, where he places one arm around your shoulder, his other hand cupping your chin.

"Are you okay?" you ask. You want to cry. You don't know why. This lonely lighting on a rainy day with this man that you spend more time craving than you do actually enjoying—it's starting to get to you.

"I'm better now . . ."

Of course he would say that.

Since when did you become so cynical? Since when do you question everything, staying remarkably clear of the question that really needs to be asked?

Why are you in this place?

Jack shifts and pulls his BlackBerry out from under a pillow. Why he needs his fucking BlackBerry now, when he hasn't seen you in ages and you've made it all this way in the pouring rain with nothing in your wallet to see him for what will amount to be a little more than an hour—why he needs to see who's emailing him now, at this point, is completely beyond you.

Instead of saying, "Do you have to?" you say nothing. You drop your head because you have not one ounce of dignity left. You have been here less than five minutes and already you feel dropped.

The phone rings.

Jutting his chin out, he says, "I gotta get this. It might be my doctor."

You shift away from him and walk over to the plants, feeling the leaves between your fingers. Normally, you would be taking note of the thickness, the texture, but now your mind is only on your broken heart. When are you going to admit this to yourself?

A minute later, he hangs up the phone. It wasn't the doctor.

"Come back here," he says playfully. "I want to get fresh with you."

Like a zombie—you don't remember ever being this much of a nonthinking person—you walk in a trance back to the couch. You sit and place your head on his shoulder. You don't want it to feel good, to inspire any more confusion than you already know. But it does. His lips lean in to brush your forehead. You once read in one of those women's magazines that when a man kisses your forehead, it means he values your intelligence. It's one of those random factoids that's not really a factoid that bubbles up in conversation or consciousness every so often. Marco kissed you on the forehead all the time, probably because you were significantly shorter than he and so maybe this was the most convenient location, on the forehead. But you do think he valued your intelligence; you took his kisses—whether there or on your cheeks or ready lips—to be affirmative signs.

Looking at Jack looking at his BlackBerry, you think, *This script is in serious need of a rewrite.*

His phone rings again. This time, Jack jerks back away from you to answer it after he looks at the incoming number.

"Hi—how are you?" he asks the anonymous caller on the other line, his voice going into charming mode. Your stomach flip-flops.

God, you need to box again. You have forgotten about your own power.

While Jack makes small talk with a woman—you can hear a faint female voice—his eyes light up. You try not to stare, but you are surprised. His doctor is male. You have a sinking feeling.

As he goes on, chatting about the weather and his busy job, you look up at the Roman numeral clock on the wall. Ticking. Time is ticking, and yet this period of feeling like a total schmuck seemingly has no end.

In a desperate attempt, you scan Jack's face, looking at him more closely than before. What is it about him that has you so crazy? Your first glance of Jack was not so noteworthy. You didn't think he was so attractive at first. Or rather, you didn't notice. And now you look at the little brown mole underneath his eye with awe. But wait. The nose. It used to be fuller around the bridge. Now you are leaning in, and Jack, aware of your keen interest, moves farther away and wipes his free hand over his eyes, covering his nose. In a flash, you remember the afternoon at Blue Ribbon, when you were talking about boxing and the prospect of getting your nose broken in the ring. To ease your mind, Jack had said breezily, "You can get it fixed. I know the best plastic surgeon."

Shit. Was this more than just a "deviated septum"? Isn't that the term celebrities use when they want to cover up the fact that they've had a nose job? The prospect is so weird that you can't even laugh.

By the time he hangs up the phone, you are shaking your head. Maybe the surgery wasn't supposed to be cosmetic. Fine. But where has your Jack gone? Something about him is so different. This disturbs you, more than just a little bit.

A moment later he closes the phone and says, "Sorry, that was Marla Maples."

"Marla Maples?" you say, totally confused now, that the person for whom he put *you* on hold for a good ten minutes, even though your time is so limited—this person is Marla fucking Maples? And please God, he isn't name-dropping here, is he?

"Well, what? Are you working on a book with her?"

"I don't want to talk about work right now."

As you start to say something—you don't know what will come out of your mouth, but you need to say something—he interrupts you. "She is so beautiful. I mean, she is one of the most beautiful women I have ever seen."

Well, good for Marla Maples. Good for Marla fucking *Maples.*

You are the fool who spent your last dime to come out here, sitting on Jack's couch with your wet, rain-soaked hair matted to your face, not only feeling ugly, but utterly rejected as well. Did he just say that to get back at you for emailing the half-naked photo of your ex? You put your hand on your stomach—not only are you queasy, but you're bloated, too. And waiting to burst on your chin is none other than . . . a big fat pimple.

You are so not you. To his comment about beauty, you might have responded with a sharp and admittedly sarcastic, "Great." Instead you are deflated and therefore silent. You have too much wrapped up in Jack—both on the personal front and with your writing—to risk doing or saying something you don't really mean. Isn't this whole fucked-up dance predicated on the desire for permanence, to never ever be left, obviously at any cost? Besides, you have him for less than twenty minutes now—would just enjoying your time even be a possibility?

Jack sees the cloud over your face.

"I'm so glad you came," he says, eyes peering. "I know it's been hard for you . . . but this made my week." When you give him a skeptical look, he adds, "Really, it did. Thank you."

You nod the uncomfortable nod of someone who, after getting herself all worked up, knows it's best to give up the fight. With Jack, with everyone, what will be, will be. Que sera, sera. Your mother loved singing that song.

"I'm glad you feel better," you finally say, after searching for words that won't be lies. Just a few days ago you had been on the subway watching a woman leaning into her boyfriend, envious as they kissed and spoke to one another in half sentences.

When the woman exited the subway, she turned back to her boyfriend and said, "To come . . ." with a big smile. You suspected that she meant the best was "to come," but you don't actually know. You are waiting for what is "to come" with Jack. Hell, you are waiting for what's "to come" in life . . . but no longer with a sense of hope, which was exactly what had drawn you to this woman.

"Come here," Jack says, looking at you with Mr. Seductor eyes, a look you are beginning to question. " I wanna get fresh with you . . ."

Even putting your suspicions and hurt feelings aside, there's something about this situation that doesn't quite "do it" for you: (1) getting "fresh" has a childlike connotation to it—and he's said it twice now; (2) even if she's not home, you are in his aunt's house; (3) despite your presence in his vulnerable state—or maybe because of it?—he has still put you, his lover, below Marla fucking Maples; and (4) he's wearing flannel pajama bottoms that are covered with ducks.

You close your eyes and let him kiss you. You close your eyes and hope that he soon realizes what an ass he's been. He covers the back of your head with his hand, pressing his palm on the crown of your neck. You breathe into him, feeling the tension in your neck release, second by second.

But then you have to go.

"Let me call you a car," Jack says.

"But I—"

"No, no, no. Let me get it—please."

The fare will be at least seventy dollars, and you don't have that kind of cash. It makes you feel uncomfortable, this whole situation, and yet you let him handle it anyway, at the expense of any self-respect you may have left. For the last ten minutes you have together, he tells you over and over how much it means that you made this effort to visit. But when you close your eyes, his voice sounds far away. As you hear him say, "Thank you, thank you for coming," you imagine a sliver cut straight down the front of your chest, tearing at your skin to let his words in, so that they mean more than an echo. Even in this state, your body is somehow telling you exactly what you need. The last time you had a vision like this you'd drunk too much caffeine and saw yourself with a coffee-soaked wooden stake dividing you in half. You make a mental note not to open that Frida Kahlo art book whenever you are having, or think you might have, a hard time.

"You made my week," Jack whispers into your ear. He traces his new nose across your cheek. "Really."

When you smile, he adds, "And don't forget about Vancouver!" He's been telling you for weeks that he wants you to join him on a trip to visit his oldest friends, reminding you that when you go on job interviews you need to tell them that you have a trip planned for the first two weeks of December.

"Okay."

You are so intent on changing this channel that, by the time you are sitting in the back of the cab blowing kisses to Jack, you can only think one thing: all of this—feeling rejected, being rejected—yeah, you're pretty sure it's your own creation.

19

ELAINE'S FACE IS wrinkled in mock horror. It has to be mock. You mean, all Jack did was take a call from Marla Maples. In the two weeks since that visit, you have decided that you were reading too much into things, that you were really the one who was afraid of love, that it was your own fear of abandonment that kept you from living fully in relationships. With Ted, you had told yourself this, too. And it was, in part, true.

"That's . . . that's . . ." You rarely see her hold back. And she is holding back, as opposed to speechless. If you had told your mother the truth about that visit with Jack, her face would be making similar contortions.

"I mean, we've had nice visits since?" Your voice lilts upward at the end.

Well, maybe "nice" isn't the best word choice. For example, the evening you returned to New York from the wedding weekend, you'd gone straight to meet Jack, his sister, and his parents, who were in town for a benefit. The night before, you'd gotten extremely carried away during a raucous sing-along to Mariah Carey's *The Emancipation of Mimi*, which had been blasting from the speakers of Annabelle's new car.

Needless to say, you went to meet Jack's family in a very sorry state, with a bad hangover and nicotine-induced nausea. You even had whiplash from all that dancing. Jesus. Despite feeling physically spent, you'd forced yourself to go. Jack's family is important to him, and you didn't want to let him down by flaking. But gosh, you were terrible company. In addition to being very nervous—how desperately you hoped you wouldn't say the wrong thing—you were very shy and barely touched your salad at dinner. When Jack's father asked you what you wanted to do with your life, you disingenuously tried to paint fund-raising at the nonprofit as your one true calling (even though the whole reason you were there in the first place, with Jack, was because of your writing aspirations). And if all that weren't bad enough, you'd stayed glued to Jack's side the whole time. Clinging. In some parallel universe, you'd like to believe that you and his down-to-earth parents got along just . . . swimmingly. Oh, and in this same alternate universe, it would have been some *other* chick staring into her boyfriend's eyes and giving him heated kisses on the lips. In front of his mother. You would never do *that*.

By brushing this mortifying little experience straight underneath the proverbial rug, you seem to be telling yourself that everything is just ducky. Why you are so determined to live out a version of the relationship that doesn't even seem to be based in reality, you don't know. It can't just be the business of *Oh, Shit!* There has to be something else.

"I can't explain it," Jack had said over the phone one night, talking about how he hasn't felt like himself since the surgery. "I've wanted to talk to you about it . . . but . . . it's kind of awkward."

And you, self-selected embarrassment lady, were hit in your weak spot. Jack admits vulnerability. You sigh into his words and say something syrupy: "Oh, baby, I know. I know."

It's a crock of shit. You don't know, though you have sensed that this has affected his masculinity. Due to the circumstances, you two haven't had sex in weeks now. It wasn't happening in his aunt's house, that's for sure. The weeks just before his surgery, you had noticed sex was ruling your relationship. For example, one afternoon, during your lunch break, you arranged for you and Jack to have a "quickie." You know it wasn't respectful to the friend whose apartment you "borrowed," but these days you are admittedly more intent on pleasing Jack than maintaining your own integrity. The more Jack has drifted from you, the more important your sexual connection has become. Which is why not having sex since his surgery has been such an issue. What other ways do you even have to relate?

Even though he's opened up some, expressing his feelings about the nose thing, Jack is still moving, constantly moving. No matter how hard you try, you just can't catch him. At this point, you are in a perpetual state of breathlessness, turning metaphorical corners and thinking, *Is he here?* only to see the back of his head fading into the midtown lunch crowd, where every man looks the same, even the ones who have recently had their deviated septums corrected. You will never find Jack.

But his apparition is here. He calls you every night. Although you don't see him as much during the week—his work has become busier, he says—you still manage to let him hold your calendar hostage every time Friday night rolls around. His new habit is calling you Friday morning and saying, "What are we doing tonight, baby?" Then he picks you up after work, takes you out to a nice dinner, and after that you see a movie. (Even though he's now started to complain about his lack of adequate money to suit his thread-count-conscious lifestyle, he still won't let you pay. You know that if he were to let you pay, then he would also not be able to insist on restaurants with raw oysters and foie gras on the menu. After all, you've suggested peanut butter sandwiches and shown up with McDonald's.) Then he wakes up Saturday morning, talks about how much he has to do and how he wishes you could spend the day together, but that he'll have to settle for seeing you again that night. Mostly, he never sets a time for his return to your house, but then frequently calls to tell you that he'll be there "soon." When you tell him you hate waiting around, he says, "So do I." It's the kind of statement that you suspect might make you feel castrated, you know, if you were eligible for that sort of thing.

Worse yet, for two weeks, you haven't wanted to eat anything except for the occasional small McDonald's french fry. Since you stopped boxing, all your muscle has disappeared. One of your maternal coworkers has, in fact, this week pulled you into her office to ask if you are eating, because she doesn't want you to "disappear before my eyes." You told Paula this morning over the phone that you feel like "a sheet of paper—ready to blow away in the wind." (Her response was exactly what you were hoping for: she laughed, her voice bubbling up. "A sheet of paper? A sheet of paper? That's crazy. Crazy.") After your appointment with Elaine, you are having dinner with Henry, because you'd recently also told him that you are too depressed to eat. Now, despite sitting in front of your trusted therapist, despite the many, many books about eating disorders on her bookshelf, you do not mention any of this to her.

Elaine is looking at you, as if to say, "Yeah? What's so 'nice' about this relationship?" She doesn't say it, though. Instead, when you comment on her bouquet of irises and lilies, she says a genuine, "Thank you," and goes on about her garden at home for a few minutes. Any other time, this might have bothered you, but this isn't like the time she started rambling about her 9/11 survivors, a group she ran just after the World Trade Center attacks. If you were reading about such a group in *The New York Times*, you may have been gripped, wondered about the strength of that therapist, if the effects of guiding such a group were life-altering. But you are not reading about this group on your leisure time. This is your time, your therapy. Elaine is overly generous with her time and reduced rates. You are pretty sure she's never granted a client the measly fee of $20 per session. In some ways, when you watch her mouth move and head shake fervently, the phrase "You get what you pay for" comes to mind. This is not entirely fair. She's a nice woman, a smart woman, who sometimes talks too much about herself. And you are a wannabe anorexic. Go figure.

LATER, YOU LEAN back in a pedicure chair, a fancy one, complete with massage settings that roll and vibrate all over your back. You sit there, watching a young woman leaning over your feet. The lighting is dim, pinkish, and the running water is the only sound you hear. Your eyes are sad, and you should know better than to stare at someone with sad eyes. She smiles at you periodically, but you don't buy it. You wouldn't want to be that close to anyone else's feet, and especially not your own. You are the fool who left a two-hour gap between therapy and dinner with Henry. Your open time is daunting, empty. You called Dan. No answer. You called Paula. No answer. Just recordings, no real live people to be found.

And so here you are, passing the time in an empty, nondescript nail salon in the middle of nowhere, only you are not in the middle of nowhere. You are a resident of a city with 8.5 million people all around you, fighting for the same resources; and you dare to call this nowhere? But you guess, sighing into the vibrations on your shoulder, ruing the pink walls, sometimes that's just what it feels like.

An hour later, Henry grabs you with a close hug and then teases you about the restaurant name. You'd called it "Larry's," "Eddy's," and "Bobby's"—none of which is its proper name. Henry, with his luminous skin, deep brown eyes, he is so beautiful. You don't see one another very often, but when you do, you always have a momentary flash of: *Wait—now, why did I break up with him?*

"It's 'Frank's'!" Henry says, with a playful jab to your right shoulder, which incidentally does not make you feel like you might topple over—guess you're not just any old flimsy sheet of copy paper. More like manila card stock. " 'Larry's'—who would name their restaurant 'Larry's'?"

"Leave me alone," you say with a light smile. "I'm very fragile, you know."

"Bullshit. You look fine to me."

At the bar, you and Henry take two seats by the corner. You order several small dishes: handmade gnocchi, roasted eggplant, mozzarella di bufala with basil and tomatoes, anchovies in olive oil, grilled calamari salad. The young punk-rock-looking bartender with spiky red hair plunks down a small dish of ol-

ives in front of you as she hums along to Blondie's "Dreaming."
She smiles as she serves you two glasses of red wine.

"So . . . what's going on?" Henry asks.

"Nothing. I'm fine. Just . . . feeling a little crazy, you know?"

"What's happening with the dude?"

"Well, it's . . . okay. Just okay."

Three months ago, you were raving to Henry about Jack.
You were shuffling around the disorganized video store by your
house, on the phone with Henry, when he asked you about Jack.
You caught your own reflection in the front window. Your eyes
were shiny and bright. Your squinting eyes made your crow's-
feet extra visible and you thought with an air of melodrama,
Now, if these are a price I have to pay to live this life, so be it.

A short time later, and now your thoughts about aging go
more along the lines of, *Well, if my boyfriend had corrective
surgery . . .*

"Oh, what's going on? Come on. Tell me," Henry says, resting
a firm hand on your shoulder. Even though you have two older
brothers, Henry is as close as you've ever come to having a protective big brother—while your own brothers are both sensitive, they are not particularly aggressive individuals. When you
showed Dudley, your boxing coach, a family picture, he looked
at your brothers, with their slight frames and gaunt faces, and
said, "Damn, girl. Don't you go knocking those brothers out,
now . . ."

You turn your head to look at Henry, your chin hanging low.
You love that he asks. But, really, can you really tell him? Even
though Henry is a good friend, sometimes a great friend, you
feel guilty telling him how unhappy you are with Jack. You, uh,
haven't even told Jack yet.

"I'm just having a hard time in general, you know? I need a permanent job. I'm stressed. I do like my new place, but . . ."

You take a sip of your cabernet and then another. For someone who barely drank in grad school, you sure do order glass of wine after glass of wine after glass of wine . . .

After a few minutes he says, "You're not that skinny—don't go trying to create some neuroses on me . . ."

Henry has accused you of this before—last month, in fact, when you casually mentioned that you needed Nicorette gum to put a final end to your "occasional" cigarette. "That's nonsense—you barely smoke!" he cried.

Henry is doing well. He has a new job and is recording music. His life, as he paints it, is serene. He's doing a lot of yoga and often spends Saturdays at home composing songs. His world sounds tranquil, complete. You can't help but place it in direct juxtaposition to your own increasingly sad and muted existence. No one has accused you of being too much lately; and conversely, no one's going to tell you that you've become too little, either.

You remember why you called Henry. You have a theory that in the worst of times—hey, wait a second, when did this become the worst of times?—people know what they need, and so the friend they solicit for advice or comfort is a good indicator of direction, even when one feels directionless. You didn't call your friend Amy, because you knew she would have advised dumping Jack immediately. She would have told you, "Yes, you have variables. Yes, you are stressed. But being with some jackass surely isn't going to help matters."

So, instead, you called Henry, someone to put his arm around your shoulder and remind you that you aren't crazy. Well, okay. You are crazy, just not *that* crazy.

An attractive woman whose auburn hair is pulled back into a ponytail sits on the other side of the corner, sipping her wine and obviously listening to your conversation. A smile creeps across her face. You sense nervous, even frenetic energy. Eyeing her, you call out a tipsy, "Heeeey, got any embarrassing stories?"

Perhaps she's just uncomfortable dining alone, but she overlooks your lack of social grace and Muppet-like delivery to respond, "But of course."

The easy answer surprises you.

Henry looks uncomfortable and politely turns to the woman. You put your arm low beneath the countertop and squeeze Henry's side. When he looks at you, you mouth, "Sorry . . ." You are not, though—sorry, that is.

"Well?" you ask, holding a forkful of gnocchi to your mouth. "What is it?"

"Well, it's a great one. But, just out of curiosity, why are you asking?" she asks.

You briefly pull yourself together, trying to change gears and sound official as you describe *Oh, Shit!* When you are finished with your handy elevator speech, she nods her head. "Okay, sure, sure. I got a great one."

The woman is in probably in her late thirties, and though her skin is youthful, there's a fearlessness in her eyes that indicates, perhaps—just perhaps—she's been a few places, seen a few things. She taps her empty wine glass and nods to the bartender to give her a refill.

"Well, a couple years ago, I was single and had developed this little habit of making out with my cabdrivers," she says with a wicked expression, as if she's just waiting for your shock. Or horror.

In fact, your eyes do bug out: "Whoa, whoa, whoa. Nail-biting is a little habit. Singing in the shower is a little ha—"

"Oh, it was no big deal," she says lightly, cutting you off. "In fact, I don't even remember the first time it happened, but once it did, it became a little obsession of mine."

Just as your eyes are narrowing—*does she not know that this was dangerous?*—she adds, "It wasn't here. This is when I lived in Boston . . . So anyway, yeah, I would have these nights out with friends—at clubs, bars, parties. I think in the beginning I just wanted a little excitement, you know? So I started coming on to the cabdrivers who were bringing me home. Once I practically did a cartwheel over the front seat . . ."

Your mouth is agape, and Henry, you can tell from his tight expression, is not really finding this as amusing as you are. Maybe it's a girl thing.

"At least tell me they didn't charge you."

"Girl, you'd better believe it," she says, flashing a grin. "It became this big joke among my friends for a while. Once, when I left a bar early, I was standing in the street with some friends who were going on to another party. One friend tried to hail a cab for me, and I was like, 'Uh, excuse me. I think this is my domain . . .'"

She is enjoying telling this story, you can see from the way she straightens her posture and leans in.

"Yeah, so anyway, one night I am driving home with a new cabbie—very cute—and when we stop in front of my house, I ask him if I can sit in the front seat. So I get out, and sure enough, we start making out and it's all well and good, until I hear the front door of my house slam shut. It's three o'clock in the morning. And I look over to see my landlord, Randi, looking suspiciously into the cab, although she's not wearing her glasses. Randi seeing me making out with some guy would have been embarrassing for more than just the obvious reasons. See, before I'd moved in there, when I first went to look at the place, Randi told me, in so many words, that I needed to be a lesbian to live there. I'd caught on real quick and even said things like, 'Oh, yeah, men suck! I hate men!" Even though I don't. Anyway, I got the place and made sure never to be seen with the opposite sex. This place was amazing—cheap and huge and so well worth the lying. So when I saw Randi, I slid down the front seat and asked the cabbie to pull around the corner. He wasn't too happy when he realized that I was just embarrassed to be seen with him . . ."

"Oh, poor guy," you say, shaking your head at the number of innocent victims caught in the embarrassment cross fire. That's a lot of people out there, unwitting witnesses to moments of lost control and secrets reluctantly revealed. Turning to Henry, you see him shake his head, too. He's been quiet this whole time and so when he speaks up, both you and your new red-headed friend sit at attention.

"Sounds like . . ." he begins slowly, lifting his glass to his lips. "Sounds like you had some fun."

An hour or so later, Henry gets up to go to the bathroom. You have long since stopped chatting with the redhead, and so with this quiet, the mood in the restaurant comes into sharp focus—its soft lighting, the overhanging chalkboard, the garland strung up around the walls. The music is low, and you are sitting in this small pocket of the city, warm and tipsy. Jack, he's never far from your mind. You take out your cell phone, hoping for a phone call or text message from him. But when you see that no one has called, you sit back, shoulders slumped, and sigh loudly.

Things just haven't gotten back on track, yet you two are still talking that ridiculous "together 4-eva" crap. But there's plenty that you are not telling him. You've recently been wondering what really happened with his ex-girlfriend, the one with whom (you think) he had been living when your flirtatious summer began. Through this lens, you recall your early meetings, such as the Fourth of July, when you met at the Peninsula for drinks. Because the roof deck was closed for a private party, you two lingered for hours in the tony lounge, surrounded by bouquets of calla lilies, drinking martinis, and continuing the conversation that seemed to have no end. At the end of the night, you stood on an uncharacteristically quiet Fifty-fifth Street and offered to give Jack a ride home, which he turned down. While this had all seemed very normal at the time— hello, you *had* been drinking!—the thought now crosses your mind that maybe, just maybe he didn't want you to drive him home because "home" then referred to an apartment that he was technically still sharing with his girlfriend. Was he? Technically, it's none of your business. And technically, you two just had some drinks. So what's the big deal? You know, aside from the fact that your insecure heart doesn't really give a shit about technicalities?

From her sideways glance across the bar, you can tell that the make-out lady sees your disappointment, possibly more. Funny, this thing about embarrassing situations. Don't they really point to things that we don't want exposed? If you could take a million steps back, you might be able to see something rather significant in this brief yet revealing eye contact with her.

You asked her for a story. She gave you one and that was nice and all, but by virtue of just sitting near you for an hour, she is already privy to some very personal information about you—namely that your appetite has been wrecked for two weeks over unexpressed heartache, that you are anxiously checking your phone, waiting for a message from someone else to tell you that you are okay. So, comparing your story with hers, whose is of more consequence on the scale of chagrin? All she did was make out with a cabdriver—which, not incidentally, appears to be a point of pride. Of your own situation, you cannot say the same.

Turning your head toward the window, away from her, your thoughts drift to what pleases you. Memories. The exact moment in the Peninsula lounge when, oblivious to the fireworks outside, you'd stared at Jack's handsome face, enthralled, and thought, *This is the man who will never bore me*—the moment just before you settled the bill and then descended that grand staircase in the lobby, the one that—on the way up, at least—had seemed to hold so much beautiful promise.

20

YOU NEED FUN.

You need late-night dancing on tabletops. You need skinny-dipping in the ocean on a rainy day, to return home to warm, thick towels and a pot of homemade chili. You need a motorcycle ride through Tuscan vineyards while holding on to the back of a young, sweet-faced Italian who, before taking you exactly where you wanted to go, had to call his mother and tell her he'd be late for dinner. You need making out with your college boyfriend in the movie theater because even though you find him a little boring, he sure is sexy. You need a night of shrieking laughter, when nothing anyone says is as funny as everything everyone does. You need drinking several bottles of wine with a lavish grilled fish dinner and a high-up vista, overlooking a purplish Lake Manyara—with company so loud and boisterous that an uptight American tourist from Arizona calls the group of you "Aborigines!" You need a night of wild dancing when you pull out moves that you haven't let anyone see since you were in the seventh grade (at least that you remember), and if that means doing the "Roger Rabbit" to the Beastie Boys' "So Whatcha Want," so be it. You need to be dragged to Pasadena, Annabelle picking out your outfit and demanding that you rise to the occasion of a party with her friends, only to find that once you open your eyes and apply a little red lip gloss, everything festive follows suit, most notably a karaoke rendition of "Boogie Oogie Oogie," during which you and your sister disco-dance and sing, holler, and clap—yes, clap—like you did when you were kids, behind closed doors, thinking that no one's watching, only everyone is, at least everyone in the packed Chinese restaurant some random Saturday night in Pasadena. You need a night when you have never, ever lived so loud, that is, until the next night comes along.

In this muted place, you may not recognize your fun-loving self of the summer—fine. But please stop moping about it. You have a job. You have shelter. You are in good health, despite your insistence on smoking cigarettes and overindulging in wine. Your parents gave you everything you ever wanted, including a pricey private college education. So then what is the big goddamn deal? If you're not happy with your job raising funds for charity, just *do* something about it.

Since when did you become so inert, anyway? Since your measure of life and all that shines is still Jack, you cannot believe that you have not been to karaoke once since you started seeing him. This is clearly not Jack's fault—what disturbs you is that you haven't *wanted* to sing karaoke in a few months now. You are *so* karaoke—so all about the release you feel when you dance and sing like a fool. In an early karaoke experience, you and Alana, your college roommate, were at the cozy Japanese restaurant where you got free sake and sushi. (You still haven't figured out why.) One night you both said no to the sake, since you were planning on studying. But it was Friday night, so eventually you caved in and drank the sake. Three hours later, Alana was sitting on some old man's lap, crooning "New York State of Mind" in a deep voice, and you were up next—so caught up in the rhythm of "Little Red Corvette" that you decided to throw the microphone across the room, but not before shouting, "I just wanna dance!" Yes, karaoke. That's your magic.

Dammit, girl! That is exactly what you need, and you need it now.

But even your pep talks, from yourself to yourself, don't really seem to go anywhere. Instead, you are rolling along through your life with less grace than you would bodysurfing waves during a riptide, always thinking that one phone call, one email, one letter, any message from someone other than yourself, thinking that this is what you really, desperately need to fill yourself up. You have an idea, though—*Oh, Shit!* will be your anchor, and you use it as a point of focus.

A friend of a friend forwarded you an email about an all-female entrepreneurial group hosting a cocktail party at some bar in the Meatpacking District. Female entrepreneurs? You are so there. You need a little uplift, and besides, Jack has been nagging you about not having enough *Oh, Shit!* stories from women. (How many more times will you listen to him say, "You need women to read that book. Interview *women*.") So you head out to the party, even though you think that what you really need is not female stories, necessarily, but a stronger direction for the book, more intellectual heft. If that's even a possibility.

WHEN YOU CALL Dan from outside the cocktail party and mention that you're meeting up with Phillip Lopate the following morning to "pick his brain," he repeats, " 'Pick his brain'? Ew. Could you have chosen a worse visual?"

"I don't know, but guess what? I couldn't have chosen a worse setting."

Dan is laughing before you even have the chance to finish telling him that you, with your one-track mind fearing credit card declination, have invited Phillip over to your house for omelets. In fact, you hold the phone away from your ear, and can still hear Dan's guffaws for a good few minutes.

"Omelets? Dan, I don't know what I was thinking!"

"Well, I would have said that asking him to your house was the weirder thing, but hey, maybe that's just me," Dan said.

Dan's new boyfriend is in Denmark for the semester. Although you live on the other coast, you are picking up some of the slack as his stand-in when Dan needs to talk out stresses of school projects or postgraduation plans. Without Jason around, Dan's life revolves around school—stories through which you are living vicariously, remembering how it felt to have ready-made structure and purpose in your life. At twenty-nine, Dan is one of the older people in the undergraduate architecture program. Last night, after a particularly stressful week of midterms, Dan went out with all of his school colleagues to blow off some steam. He is telling you that, um, apparently he went too far, ordering a fourth pitcher—which should explain his headache. As per your daily chats, Dan recounts even the smallest details of his evening, including when he taunted his new friends by saying, "What's the matter? Can't keep up with the old guy?"

As the fall moves along, you feel yourself leaning on him more and more heavily. More often than not, when you pick up the phone to call him these days, it's because you need to vent, about your dissatisfaction at job or your own anxieties around your relationship with Jack. Dan has this way about him of always making you feel comforted and heard, though he doesn't indulge you in long rants. Whether or not he means to, by keeping your bitching short and contained, he sends you a positive message: be mindful of where you put your mental energy.

A young woman walking by in an oversized sweater and jeans is smoking a cigarette while she walks her dog. With Dan on the line, you keep quiet and motion to her, putting your index and middle finger on your lips in a V shape. Barely looking at you, she pulls out a Parliament Light and hands it to you, you nod thank-you, and she walks away. You pull out the matches you've become accustomed to carrying and light your smoke.

After hanging up with Dan, you are standing by the door minding your own business when the bouncer makes a point to open the door to tell you that you are "too pretty" to smoke. You don't know what the hell that means and so you raise your right eyebrow, the action that used to impress Jack, and say nothing.

Inside, you search for women. They are not hard to find; women in suits with smart haircuts are scattered all down the length of the bar. In fact, there are probably only five or six men in the room. You order a $1 apple martini at the bar and start sipping away, holding the oversized glass in front of you like armor. You do like strangers, and you can usually pull your weight in conversation, but this does not mean you feel free and easy about walking into a cocktail party by yourself. You had imagined finding an interesting group of women and sitting down at a table to chat. But by now the tables are emptying, with papers and empty glasses strewn across the tops. There had been an earlier conference part of the day, which you guess, from the tired, glazed-over faces, was attended by 99.9 percent of the women here.

One woman with straight brown hair and freckles spread across the bridge of her nose appears to be in between conversations. You see her scanning the room, and dive in before she has a chance to talk to anyone else.

"Hi, did you attend the conference?" you ask, stepping closer to her, your eyes brighter and wider than normal. You are putting so much effort into being "present" that her answer barely registers. (She's responded in the affirmative and said something about inspiring presentations, blah, blah, blah.)

"So what is your business?" you ask.

"Well, I don't have one, but I just came for the influence."

"Smart," you say.

"You?"

"Oh, me, not exactly. I mean, I'm working on a book, but it's not a business—yet."

She smiles. "Well, good for you. What's your book about?"

"Actually . . ." You launch into the description, and how you are collecting embarrassing stories. As always, you finish with, "Do you have any?"

In the best of all worlds, you finesse the question, give it a more seamless entry into the conversation. But not today. You assure her that you won't use her name.

"Well, okay," she says with a smile. "When I was in the first grade a noodle flew out of my nose in the lunchroom. That was pretty embarrassing."

After nodding for a few minutes, trying to come up with something interesting to say about an errant noodle, you spot an empty stool at the bar.

"Excuse me," you say to the woman. You sit down, removing your jacket. Your new strategy? Let them come to you.

An hour and two drinks later, you realize that this was a really bad strategy. Still on your stool, you are surrounded by men; in fact, you'd wager that the group of men standing in a semicircle around your stool are likely all the men in attendance. This happens to be a pretty night for you, and yes, you happen to be wearing a shoulder-baring dress that both men and women usually take a liking to. But really, couldn't you have done better than this? Even though you started talking to a very nice married lawyer and were actually enjoying your conversation about life choices, family dramas, and the efficacy of wheatgrass shots, you realize that your current perch will make gathering stories from women near-impossible.

Screw it, you think, as you lift your glass to your lips. *I'm tired.*

Just then a man wearing a black T-shirt underneath his black blazer steps aggressively in between you and Walter, the lawyer.

"Hi, hi. I'm Rick. You gotta know me. I swear, you are so beautiful. You gotta know me," the man says in a raspy voice that makes you pause: you should stop even the "occasional" cigarette. His dark hair is slicked back. Looking at his perpetually lifted chin, you think it's safe to say that this man probably doesn't have a self-esteem problem, at least one that he's aware of.

"Thank you, Rick," you say—and this is absolutely sincere— whether you feel great or not-so-great, you have always appreciated someone brave enough to say what he's thinking, even if it comes in the form of aggressive Rick. (One day, when you and Jack first started your regular rendezvous, you had run past a construction site to meet him on time. He asked you how you were and you said, "Not great. I'm so tired I couldn't even smile at those nice construction workers when they whistled.") Rick answers by lifting your hand to his rough lips. *Ew.*

"Uh," you manage, looking over at Walter, who looks uncomfortable for you. "Got any embarrassing stories for me, Rick?"

"Do I ever." Then, giving Walter, easily standing a foot above Rick, a snide sideways look, "Listen, I'll let you finish here with . . . with . . . him, but just know that when you call me, you'll be reaching a real man."

"Um, okay, then, Rick. Nice to meet you," you say as you take his card.

After he leaves, Walter says, "Would you really call that guy for a story?"

"Do you doubt he has some good ones?"

Walter hasn't offered you any embarrassing stories. He's tried, but then keeps shying away. You gather, from the talk about his wife and their separate jogging, eating, and working habits, that he'd rather not be married. But what do you know? You're just a hack with a notebook that has lots and lots of space left in it.

Just then another man taps you on the shoulder. "Excuse me," he says. "I just have to tell you I love that dress."

When Walter smiles, looking down, you say to both of them, "Wow—guess this is my night. I have no idea what I did, but . . ."

All the while, you know exactly what you did: showed up at an all-female cocktail party and managed to attract a group of complimentary men with enterprising interests of their own. *Duh* . . .

This man is far less forward than the last. In fact, you get the impression from the ease in his voice and his relaxed stance that maybe, just maybe, he actually does just—as in only—like your dress.

"I'm Joey," he says.

"Hi, Joey," you say, adding your name and Walter's to the introduction mix. "How's it going?"

"Good, good. Just on my way out, but here's my card. I do a lot of networking, so . . ."

"Cool," you say, admiring his business card. When you flip it over, there is a photograph of Joey on the back.

"Say, Joey, I'm working on a project collecting people's embarrassing stories—fun ones, ones that might not have made you laugh then, but definitely make you—and possibly others—laugh now . . ."

The bartender grabs your empty martini glass and slides it across the bar. Walter motions to you—another? You nod, of course.

"Oh!" Joey smacks his forehead with the palm of his hand. "Yes! Yes! I have the best one, but I'm on my way out . . ."

You hand him your card, too, and ask him to call you, but then add, "Do you have time for a preview? Short version?"

"Oh, okay, this one's great—I was working in an office and—this is in the nineties, when the techno version of "Total Eclipse of the Heart" was huge . . . you know, the one by Nicki French?"

You shift in your seat. This one's going to be good.

And so there's Joey, in his nondescript and slightly depressing office, sitting in an area very removed from the rest of his coworkers. Because he was so far away, he could often play the radio and sing along without worrying about anyone hearing him. On this day in particular, his boss was out, so he was close to certain that no one would be stopping by. He had free rein to belt out radio songs, whether he was in tune or not.

So, he's on speakerphone, dialing a coworker, when he gets his voicemail and leaves a quick, "Your order's in. Call me." Then "Total Eclipse" comes on and Joey, a karaoke fan himself, starts singing, loud and proud.

"I neeeeeeeeed you more tonight / Yeah I neeeeeeeeed you more than eeeev-ah . . ."

Joey sings along for a few more minutes, when he looks down at his phone. Because he was on speakerphone, he had absentmindedly ended his message without actually ending the call, and therefore hadn't ended his message at all.

"Noooooooooooo!" he yelled, racing up to the department of his coworker, to see if he could somehow get the coworker to erase the message before listening to it. Maybe he could catch his breath and calm down enough to say, "Uh, yeah, that's me, but really, I was just telling you the order's in . . ."

Only, once he made it up there five minutes later, he was approaching the door when he heard shrieking laughter.

Oh, shit!

This confirmed his worst fears. Obviously, his warbling had already been played, not just for the intended recipient, but for everyone. When he looked inside the doorway, though, he saw that people were not only laughing. They were falling to the floor on their knees because they were so overcome with amusement—this was when he just turned around and snuck back down to his office.

He made a silent promise to limit contact with that department until the situation blew over. Yes, Joey thought, hanging his head low—now he had a situation.

The next day, Joey was back in his office, this time with the radio turned on low volume. He was sitting there going over a spreadsheet when someone walked by his office door, singing quietly, "And I need you now tonight . . ."

He looked up for a minute, thought, *Huh, that's weird.*

A few minutes later, another coworker walked by, also singing, "I really need you tonight . . ."

And still, weird.

But the third time a coworker walked by singing, "Forever's gonna start toniiiight / Forever's gonna start to . . ." Joey knew that this was no coincidence. You imagine him clearing his throat, acting distracted by his work. Even though his face got hot at the thought of people talking about his message behind his back, Joey still thought, *This will so blow over.*

Around midday, while eating the lunch he brought from home because he was too shy to go down to the company cafeteria, an email popped up in Joey's inbox: "Joey, just thought you should know: so-and-so just forwarded your 'Total Eclipse of the Heart' message to everyone on this floor . . ."

Noooooooooo!

When Joey estimated the number of people on that floor to be between one hundred and one hundred fifty, he shook his head and tried to think fast. How could he get everyone to turn off their phones, in a way to somehow erase his hugely humiliating mistake? Well, the answer to that came easy: he couldn't.

And so Joey needed to live with being the butt of an office joke. He took the next day off to recoup and just avoid the general feeling of horror that crept in when he was at his desk, inevitably his thoughts drifting to, *If only I had hung up that phone call . . . if only . . .*

When Joey walked through the doors of his office the following day, the sun was shining, and he forced himself to say, "Okay, I guess this situation's going to be okay." Soon after, he discovered that some of the employees would begin their week or day by listening to his rendition of the Nicki French cover of Bonnie Tyler's "Total Eclipse of the Heart." His little gaffe turned into a ritual, where after hearing his gravelly-voiced singing, they might sigh relief and say, "Okay, now I can begin my day."

Knowing this made it all the more bearable when the random coworker would stop by his office and say, "Hey Joey, who sings 'Total Eclipse of the Heart'?"

When Joey would respond with an intentionally monotone, "Bonnie Tyler—" he would get cut off by the coworker, who would take great relish in saying, "Good. Keep it that way."

WHEN JOEY IS finished, he says, "Hey, look, I gotta run. But definitely call me if you want more details."

"Yes, and another thing . . ." you can hear your own speech beginning to waver. You shouldn't have said yes to another drink. What is this one—number four by now? Joey and Walter are looking at you expectantly.

Yes?

Your mind has skipped, dipping momentarily into the place where you think of Jack. You told him you'd call him later. He has lots of "client" dinners this week, and part of you thinks that he's avoiding you. You are sure he once told his last girl-friend that you were a client, too. But that part of you needs to be silent. Because, really, you are warm and jolly and have had a nice, innocent enough time tonight and because you finally remember what the "other thing" is.

With Joey and Walter still waiting, you blurt out, "It's okay. It's okay. I love karaoke, too."

With this, you stumble off the stool and weave a creatively drawn curlicue through the crowds to the restroom, leaving Walter and Joey staring at you, confused.

21

THE NEXT MORNING, you wake up in a panic, thinking about Ted. Ted used to make the fluffiest, prettiest omelets. He used herbs, fresh cheese, always taking great pleasure in cooking breakfast for the two of you. He was so good at whipping up entire menus from a seemingly empty refrigerator. You were so good at putting on your coat to go buy the coffee.

Head cloudy, you, in the habit of rising around 4:30 AM to write, have now officially overslept by almost four hours.

You crawl out from under the covers and shake your head. *Why did I have to have that last drink?*

Your breath stinks, your bedroom floor is cluttered with your clothing, some of which you threw in a haphazard pile when you got home last night. Your lacy cream bra is halfway out your bedroom door.

Jesus, you think, removing your undergarment from the hallway, hoping your roommates haven't seen it.

But then your cussing takes a turn for the worse. Not only is your place a mess, you don't have any food in the house and Phillip will be here in less than thirty minutes.

Sophie is in the kitchen making coffee. She says hello and

smiles impishly. She saw the bra. But out of all your new roommates, you are sure she would care the least. You haven't spent
much time with any of them, to say more than hi in the kitchen
and make small talk about their classes and projects and your . . .
well, you really don't have anything to talk about, but you are
good with the weather and the occasional weirdo factoid, like
how the sex of alligators is determined by the temperature at
which the egg is incubated. (Below eighty-six degrees, they will
be female.) But with Sophie, sometimes you talk a little bit longer. You clean the countertops and extend your conversation,
when otherwise you would have rushed off, back to your room,
out the door. She talks about "boys" a lot, even though she has a
long-term boyfriend overseas. Sometimes she says things like,
"Well, I guess I should have waited, but I liked him, so we had
sex . . ." and then throws her arms up in front of her, as if to say:
What's a girl to do?

"Gotta run! Having Phillip over for breakfast this morning
and I . . . have . . . no . . . food!"

You are at the store, looking through the aisles of Potato
Buds and ketchup bottles, when it dawns on you: *Why would
you assume Sophie knows who Phillip is?*

You are back at your apartment, walking through the door,
armed with eggs, fresh fruit, yogurt, and milk for coffee. You
throw your plastic bag of supplies on the countertop and rush
into your room to throw all the clothing clutter elsewhere—
making new heaps in your closet is a fine solution. Phillip
won't see in there. The layout of your place is such that when
he walks up to the kitchen, your bedroom will be in full view.
You can't just ignore it. Lucky for you, the kitchen has a layer
of crumbs by the toaster but is otherwise clean. The living

room, where you will eat, is always clean, because no one ever seems to use it.

You then throw on some clothes and put your dirty hair into a ponytail, stopping to wipe the eye makeup still smudged under your eyes. You look like shit.

Well . . . not what I would have planned, but whatever . . . I'm the one who got drunk last night.

You pull one of your little pink pills from the plastic prescription bottle. You do what you always do: shove it in your mouth before you have a glass of water handy so that the chalky pill begins to disintegrate in your mouth, tasting awfully bitter. After filling a glass of water in the kitchen, you swallow, washing the unpleasantness away. You begin prepping, cracking eggs in an aluminum bowl, your head drifting into fogginess. You need coffee, you think, only this will amplify the fogginess. Soon you will be wired and saying things that you shouldn't say. You know the story a little too well.

This can't go wrong. Not again.

Your mind skips over your imaginary "culinary" file, only there is no omelet card. No omelet card. No omelet card. No omelet card.

Shit!

So not only do you need better, more restful sleep, but you also need to figure out how to make the dish you've promised your guest. You've never actually made an omelet before, only watched Ted.

Rrrrrrring!

It's the doorbell. Looking down at your aluminum bowl with three lonely unbeaten eggs, you are demoralized. Phillip is here and you've done zero prep work.

"Hi!"

Phillip is standing in an overcoat on your front steps. You think back to the first essay you read in his *Against Joie de Vivre*, and, remembering how in awe you were of his excavating via words, you feel sick. The brain that concocted that essay is standing on your front steps and you don't even know how to make an omelet.

"Come on up," you say, motioning toward the stairs. "You find the place okay?"

"Yes, it was quick. How nice that you are so close to the park!"

"Yeah, yeah, it's great," you say. And it would be if you actually used it.

As you lead Phillip through the second floor, you see Serdar peek out from his office. The look on his face is very: *What is going on?*

Once upstairs, you show Phillip around the top floor—the living room with its expansive bay windows, the dining room with its delicate stained-glass panels, your room with barely anything on the floor, save a bottle of sea-green Happy Penis Lotion. Oh, the misguided efforts to let Jack know that he's on your mind.

"Uh, uh . . ." You are hoping that he does not look down. "So that's that—want to join me in the kitchen?"

Phillip takes a look outside, to the fake owl on your neighbors' roof. When he's done with the pause, saying, "Sure, that sounds fine," you are ready to once again breathe.

"So tell me about the film festival. Anything good?"

Phillip is on the New York Film Festival Committee, and you remember that he usually has good film recommendations.

"Did you see *The Squid and the Whale* yet?"

Thankfully, you have. You loved it, in fact, for its brand of distinct humor, making the audience laugh while adequately revealing the darker situations that almost necessitate comic relief. So you move on autopilot and try your best to nod and listen, when in fact you're very nervous about the status of your meal. You've already added several eggs to the bowl. (It doesn't need to be mentioned that you, clearly, are not thinking.) You are in your tiny kitchen, with Phillip standing awkwardly at the far end of the counter by the coffee machine and the sink. His hand is pressed against the countertop, and you really, really wish that your kitchen were big enough to include a place for guests to sit.

Phillip is going on about the film's director and you are having a mild panic attack. An interested smile is plastered all over your face, belying your hunched-over, tense body. You don't remember how many eggs you added, but as you stir the egg mixture around your skillet you think it looks like too many.

Oh, crap—here we go again . . .

As he speaks, you nod. "Mmm-hmmm. Oh. Interesting."

But facts are facts and your omelet looks like hell. You think back to all Ted's rules for making the perfect omelet. Often he recited them, proudly. You were usually sitting at a nearby stool, too wrapped up in Ted's rapture to actually file those rules away in a safe space. You are pretty sure that rule number one is to have an appropriately sized pan. In these terms, your pan is unwieldy and not hearty enough to produce something you are going to be proud of. In the presence of a white-haired man old enough to be your father, you say an internal, *Fudge!* You give up on rules number two through five. You are officially, hopelessly screwed.

"Yes, so you knew, uh, I mean, *know* the director's father? . . ." you say, trying to pretend that you aren't nervous—trying so hard, in fact, that you barely notice the acrid whiff of burning eggs and the smoke rising from the pan.

Phillip, even though he's still answering your question, looks somewhat concerned and points to the stove: "Um, should you—"

Just then the buzzing, beeping smoke detector sounds off. It's a new smoke detector, the kind that comes with the harsh and grating *ehhhh-ehhhh-ehhhh* sound. Whatever happened to the good ol' beeps? Before moving to New York, you were working in an upscale pizza restaurant, waiting tables. You hated closing. One night, after twelve, you were moving the empty garbage cans to their spot by the back door. Your eyes were heavy and you carelessly tossed one of the plastic bins across the wall. It banged into the fire alarm, setting off the worst buzzing noise you'd ever heard, replete with flashing lights. Your manager just shook his head as you ran around the restaurant, dropping checks for all the customers, all of whom were covering their ears and none of whom wanted to stick around to wait for the fire department to debilitate the alarm.

Remembering the glare of the alarm, like a strobe light, you think, *So this isn't that bad.*

"Shit!" you yell, junking your cool and calm attitude. This—your rattled reaction—is so unlike you. Before the pizza place, you used to waitress in a place where you were constantly putting out fires, including the time your boss threw a patron's dinner into a Styrofoam container, called her a "bourgeois motherfucker," and then "suggested" she never return. At the time, you'd nodded to her slyly, and when your drunk and probably high boss was out of view, you apologized over and over, told her that you understood if she never wanted to come back, but really you would comp her meal, treat her like gold, and make sure that the boss wasn't in. Besides, even if he was, he wouldn't remember being so rude to her. You've been in far more stressful situations where you stay calm and don't panic. But here, with Phillip, you are panicking, and evidently so.

You rush past him to fling yourself across the sink, unsuccessfully reaching for the window's bottom lip.

How . . . on earth . . . did I burn the omelet? How?

Years ago, for one of your dating anniversaries, you'd cooked tuna steaks for Ted in his perfect cast-iron omelet skillet. By the time you sat down to eat them, you realized that they were cooked almost the entire way through. You'd muttered over and over, "But, baby, it was sushi-grade tuna." (Ted joked that phrase was going on your gravestone when you died.) Life moves on, but some things don't change. You don't know Phillip well enough to say, "How the fuck did I burn the omelet?" but you wish you could.

As you struggle with the window, Phillip runs into the hallway and pulls out a broom from beside your washing machine. Taking the broom by the bottom of its handle, he starts swatting at the smoke detector, so that the grating *rrrrrr-rrrrrrrrr* will cease. Even though the sounds are urgent and the scent is bad, you have to stop and feel very, very regretful that no one seems to have removed the dust bunnies from the bottom of the broom, and then even more regretful that they are falling in fast, determined tufts all over your guest's face. He's been here less than twenty minutes.

At the sight of Phillip Lopate, again in a tweed jacket—maybe even the same one that you dropped marinara sauce all over—jumping up and down in your hallway trying to help you recover from your disaster, you shake your head and think, *Dear God, this isn't happening.*

But it is. And really, you should say something. So you lie. "Phillip, I—I swear this never happens."

Just then, Serdar, faithfully on cue, rushes over to the landing. (Presumably, the smoke detector has taken a wrecking ball to his concentration as he grades midterms.) He raises his voice. "Hey, you have to turn on the fan above the oven—just like when you did this yesterday, remember?"

By now the smoke traces a path toward the open kitchen window. Even with the stressful *buzz-buzz-buzz*, your neck starts to loosen and you take the broom from Phillip's hands, calling faintly in response to Serdar's question, "Right. It's all coming back to me."

MIRACULOUSLY, PHILLIP ROLLS with it, even suggesting, after you've given the omelet another try, that you send the more burnt one down to Sophie. You take the least brown one and cut it in half, slap each half of your sad-looking creation on two plates. *Oh, fuck it,* you think, holding the plates tight as you move toward the living room. When you place them carefully on the coffee table, the only thought on your mind is how ashamed—how very ashamed—you should be.

AFTER PHILLIP LEAVES, you think back over your conversation, sitting in the rickety rocking chair, facing outward toward the green of the park you have yet to enter, and filling your notebook with thoughts and impressions that popped up over the morning. You are forcing yourself to write only about thoughts and impressions that relate to *Oh, Shit!*, initially thinking that this will include all of your conversation with Phillip, his recommendations on what to read, his thoughts on what approach might best suit your writing style, based on what he's seen. Your intention has been to exclude the burnt-food panic-mode situation. Only, as you think more and write more, it becomes very clear that there is nothing else from this morning that is more *Oh, Shit!*—related.

You are not sure why you're not more chagrined. Is it because you play the role of the klutz well? A former restaurant coworker, Joe McGuirk (one of those people who, for inexplicable reasons, always goes by his full name), once responded to one of your "Whoops!" slips on the floor (hands full of plates, of course) in his Boston, rough-cut accent, "I love how you are both klutzy and a graceful dancer. It's wicked sexy." Funny, though, you don't feel sexy when you're burning things and running late and trying to grip the railing so that when you fall, it's not all the way down. Then again, you don't necessarily feel bad in the oh-this-really-changes-how-I-think-of-myself-in-the-world kind of way. You make time for a lot of ridiculous things, but feeling bad about minor foibles like this is not one of them.

Maybe it's because these things—having plans go awry—are not really, truly "embarrassing," in the sense of having exposed something about yourself that you don't want Phillip to see. Dumping marinara sauce on his clean coat was probably your most panicked moment of the three, only because you were trying to make a good first impression. Once that failed, the subsequent gaffes were in line with something you'd been putting into careful place ever since, whether or not you meant to.

With Phillip, you have had no time to think, only time to act. As you write it all out, you realize that in each and every one of your so-called embarrassing moments with Phillip, you have never actually felt bad. You tell jokes. You roll your eyes, in a grand gesture of "Oops." You talk about it—the burning, the spilling, the lack of funds in your bank account—as if none of it were any big deal. You do know in the end none of it is, in fact, any big deal.

But then you think of Phillip and how you greatly admire his work. You can't waste an iota of time worrying about what you've just done. (And my God, sometimes you've stopped to think just that, *What have I done?*) No, you cannot, because you hold him in too high esteem, paradoxical as it may sound. Nor can you give up the fight. And so rather than turning to Phillip (or anyone, for that matter) in one of these moments and saying, *I'm mortified*, you have figured out an alternative response to your very own *Oh, Shit!* moments, something as simple as:

Let me entertain you.

22

UGH. ANOTHER BRIGHT and sunny day.

That sucks.

You roll over in bed. Jack lies beside you, his stomach rising and falling. You are annoyed that after all of this you still find his closed eyes, his fair skin, his slack cheeks so . . . adorable.

Last night was a disaster. You were tired of his last-minute Friday morning phone calls of, "What are we doing tonight?" Only, you were completely incapable of resisting. That conversation went something like this:

Jack: What are we doing tonight?

You: Uh . . . Jen is having a birthday party at Pescatore . . . but I'm tired. Feeling (barely audible) *like I need to be alone.*

Jack: Oh, well, I have to go see a friend's baby on the Upper West Side. I'd bring you, but I don't think they want too many people there, since he's a newborn.

You: Uh-huh.

Jack: So, let me call you later and we'll figure something out.

* * *

You didn't stop shaking your head for a good five minutes after putting the phone back on the base. When Jack called back later, you were resolute: "I need to be alone tonight."

"Okay. But I have my sister's car tonight. Why don't you at least let me give you a ride home?"

You'd agreed, halfheartedly. With every step down the hallway, you were aware of how much energy you didn't have. Sometimes you are almost thankful for the dulling effect of fluorescent lights.

In the car, going south on the FDR, you finally admitted to Jack, "I have this persistent feeling of heartbreak."

The moon was low and the night darkened early. Daylight savings just passed. Around you, cars were zooming by. Jack seemed to be slowing down, looking at you while he drove. His sister's car smelled new—bland, beige, and new, only it wasn't.

"Why?" he asked, suddenly looking over at you, while still trying to keep his eyes on the road.

After running down your list of excuses—mostly that your job is unsettled and so is your writing—you shrugged and said what was really on your mind. "I don't feel as close to you anymore, either. I don't know what happened."

You were thinking about the then—the walks through Bryant Park, the late afternoon coffees, the trips to the beach, all of those goddamn emails, blurting every last thought you had, feeling blessed and full because there was someone on the other end, someone who cared enough to blurt back.

"Well, I mean, we couldn't sustain that—how could we sustain that and function in our lives?"

You were quiet for a moment. Jack had a good point.

"Why haven't we talked about it until now, Jack? It's been like this for almost two months . . ."

There is no resolution. Just sad, heavy agreement. By the time Jack pulled up in front of your apartment, the air between you felt lighter, less charged. Your relationship was not on the mend, exactly, but at least you were finally talking.

"Hey, do you want to go get dinner?" he asked. "You have to eat. How about Blue Ribbon?"

With one hand on the car door and your body angling to get out, you thought of how he always paid for dinners, pricey ones. "Why don't you let me cook for you, Jack?"

"Wouldn't you rather have oysters? You love that mignonette."

At Blue Ribbon, you'd sat at the bar, what had once felt like "your" bar, and ordered two glasses of Sancerre. After some small talk, Jack sat back in his chair, and, with his hands clasped on his lap, he said, "So I booked my flight to Vancouver."

He was smiling, looking at you closely for reaction. Vancouver? Wasn't that the trip he'd invited you on? The trip he'd been nagging you to tell potential employers about so that no one was surprised when you were gone the first two weeks of December?

"That's nice, Jack," you'd said, lifting your glass to your lips. All of your inaction—everything you didn't do or hadn't said to Jack—was starting to amount to something, and it wasn't anything of which you were proud. Quite the opposite. "Do you remember inviting me?"

"Yes." Jack's response was firm, looking you in the eyes. Instead of finding his gaze heartfelt, you had one of those unfiltered, involuntary, judgmental moments: *Could he be any more disingenuous here?*

"And so you really think that telling me like this is okay?"

This was the pitiful end of the line. Your bags were packed. You could already hear the freaking Gloria Gaynor record playing—until Jack started crying.

"I'd hate to lose you," he sniffled.

With this line, you took a good deep look—into your wine glass. You drank until it was empty, in hopes that if you became tipsy, it might make his words seem more sincere. But even with your head abuzz, they didn't. His eyes were red and watery, and you thought rather coldly that you could now file this experience away, under the heading of "Crocodile Tears."

But Jack promised to do better next time. In the car, you looked out the window at a "Flats Fixed" place on Fourth Avenue and said with the heaviest heart, "If we break up, it is going to be a long time before I can date again."

Jack snorted. "Ha! Doubt that!" This didn't make things between you two feel any less tenuous.

Nevertheless, he'd taken you home and pulled you close in your bedroom and even told you he loved you, for only the second time.

"I know you don't know it now," he'd said in the flickering candlelight of your room, a moody, yearning song playing in the background. "But you did at one point. I know you did."

You let him hold you for this one time, this last time, and you hoped that everything would be as easy as waking up in a new life, one where your new linen sheets were neatly folded in the closet, waiting for you and him to stretch them out over your mattress, making the seemingly impossible fit work. And if not linen sheets, then baseball, poker, anything, as long as it's something light, something that doesn't make you think about all the wrong moves you have been making.

Jack didn't know it, but when he told you he loved you, you cried into his shoulder. You were not crying because he was an asshole. You were crying because nothing in the world—short of actually feeling it in that moment—could make you tell Jack you loved him back.

AND SO HERE you are, with a bright, sunny morning, the man you've been pining after in your bed, and you lean across him to play a CD. Your chest pressed over Jack's, he opens his eyes, lids slow to rise.

"Hey," he says, leaning up to bite your nose. "Whatcha doin'?"

Fuck his playfulness. Fuck the sun and blue sky. Heavy winds and dark clouds and terminal rain and sleet are pouring down all over what had been your faulty idea of clinging to a near-dead relationship. Last night, after Jack told you he loved you and you said nothing, you'd had sex; while it was nice—always bearing the semblance of depth, Jack's eyes never veering from yours—you couldn't quite get over the queasy feeling when you remembered Jack's delivery of the disinvitation.

I booked my flight to Vancouver.

"Playing a song. Sophie gave me a new CD."

It was not a new CD, though, not entirely. You had owned this Me'Shell Ndegéocello CD before, only you lost it. And now the resurfacing of *Bitter* could not be more timely.

Jack smacks his mouth together, squinting his eyes and waking up.

You press play. "This is a great song."

When "No One Is Faithful" starts to play, you say, "Okay, so . . . listen to the words."

You are naked in bed and naked in life, although the latter state is not entirely apparent to you now.

"*No one is faithful . . .*" you sing, lying back on the pillow. "*I am weak. You'll go astray . . .*"

After a few quiet and bizarre minutes, Jack running his fingers mindlessly against your shoulder, he turns to you and says, "Okay, so I need to go home and pack up some stuff for my move tomorrow. What time are we going to see Rebecca's show?"

Your childhood friend Rebecca is acting in a play upstate, and Jack has said that he wants to go see it with you, to "support her," which you find somewhat odd, since he's only met her once, and that was in passing, after another play. Sometimes, when Jack makes comments like these that don't exactly resonate with your reality, sadness wells.

"Um, the play starts at seven." You are leaning toward him, too, with your head propped up on your elbow.

"Maybe I can pack up some boxes and then we can head up in the early afternoon, do a little shopping and have dinner?"

Tomorrow Jack is moving into a brand-new one-bedroom apartment in the West Village—finally. Although it's not exactly close to your apartment, this situation promises to be better than Jack staying at his aunt's place in Westchester. You two keep looking to this event—his moving—as the imaginary line; after it's crossed, everything will be better.

"Sure," you say.

The moment Jack steps out your front door, you close it behind you and sigh. Nothing feels right anymore.

You need to call him back—immediately, to tell him that you need to go alone. You need to go alone. You need to go alone. Why are these words so hard for you to say?

Instead, you decide to suck it up. You can hold your breath for just another minute, right?

On the way to Rebecca's play, you stop at an outlet shopping mall, off the highway, somewhere in New York State. Devoting a block of time to going shopping is low on the list of things you like to do, period—never mind with your boyfriend. You'd rather watch a movie (especially at home!) or take an aimless joy ride through the countryside. Hell, you'd rather clean your gutters than spend a few hours bargain hunting. So, when are you going to tell Jack? This is so not you, and therefore when Jack parks the car and offers you a hit from his small glass bowl, you say, "Uh, sure," even though you hate pot, too.

Pot is a bad idea, you soon discover. Once you get out of the car and stand woozy in this blank parking lot that inspires nothing short of depressive feelings, you and Jack split up immediately. He says, "While I would love to shop with you, I think in the interest of time we should separate."

Jack says this phrase far, far too often: "While I would love to . . ." and you know, by now that it's a crock of shit, and instead of calling him on it or finding your own way to the play or just plain admitting to yourself that this is the end of the line, you move in another direction, floating through poorly lit retail stores, rifling through racks of clothing—silk dresses, wool coats, mesh undershirts, none of which you can afford, so why are you in this place, pretending that you can?

Your mind is racing. You call Paula. No answer. You leave a message on her machine, while meandering down the paved path of generic-looking storefronts. God, shopping sucks in general, but especially shopping like this. "Hey, girl, in shopping hell, or, um, just hell. My main objective of the day is not to break up with Jack. Call me."

Breaking up with him would seem . . . *wrong.* You are in his car, hostage to his whims, and if you were to dump him, wouldn't the ride home be terribly awkward? Besides, you need to do this when you are in the right state of mind. Sure, you haven't been there in a while, but there is a part of you that, even in the face of your hurt, has lapses of fairness. Besides, now you are high. Paranoid and high. Jack isn't the bad guy here, or even *a* bad guy. You are the one who has become quite skilled at breaking your own heart.

You sit down on a bench and watch people moving in a steady stream, from store to store, clutching shopping bags, eyes focused and determined on finding the next big deal. You close your eyes and wait for this to go away, the dizzy head, the racing mind, the shortness of breath. None of it belongs to you anyway.

Later, at dinner, you are looking down at the tablecloth when Jack lifts his glass of wine to make a toast. "To our first shopping trip."

Yeah, and our last.

The marijuana-heightened anxiety is still with you, and, in fact, worse. Your head is whirring, moving in a million directions, and you think that you are capable of doing and saying very inappropriate things, like eating off your neighbor's plate because you are too hungry to wait for your sushi, or asking the neighbor what to do when you think that you're falling out of love with the man sitting across from you, this stranger who has yet to introduce you to his friends, likes to shop, and seems to be completely out of tune with your anxieties about the relationship. Lucky for Jack, you do not lose it in this way.

Instead, you keep your snarky little comments to yourself. Jack has mentioned that his ex loved to shop and now you are piecing things together.

Oh.

Is it that he misses her, so much that he will smother you with these semblances of togetherness and familiarity, casting this idea over your relationship, even though it's not a fit, not at all?

Jack is going on about something, and you have completely, thoroughly checked out. Maybe it's the pot, but suddenly you are fifteen years old, that girl slipping easily underneath your skin. In this memory, you are standing in your parents' bathroom, applying mascara in the mirror. A hot curling iron is set on top of the molding around the porcelain counter and one of the medicine cabinet doors is half open, revealing all of your mother's makeup. You have permission to use it, but only for tonight. It's not often that you get a night out with your dad, just the two of you. The occasion is the annual Father-Daughter Dance, and your dad is a great dancer. He will outshine you on the dance floor. You love this night. But you hear your mother's voice downstairs. It's not the same enthusiastic, generous tone that she had with you just moments ago, when she'd put everything out on the counter and said, "Help yourself, honey." From the edginess in her voice, you can see her, sitting with her head in her hands at the kitchen table. This image is heavy on your heart, and it does not matter that you haven't actually seen it . . . this time. Your parents are having another fight, this time about why your father walked in the door looking happy. Why doesn't your father buy her flowers or get excited when he takes her out on dates? Her voice is sharp, can-opener sharp, and you feel it cutting through your skin.

Jack interrupts your memory, leaning forward to ask, "Everything all right?"

You are startled back to the present moment, absently picking up a water glass to remind you where you are, in this crowed room. As you nod unconvincingly to Jack, your mind trails back to the worst part of this memory: hearing their fighting in the background, you had allowed yourself just one moment of private frustration. Before leaving the bathroom, you looked deep into your own eyes in the mirror, like only a child might. A small, plastic smile washed over your face. You've done pretty well on the outside.

THE NEXT DAY—surprise, surprise—is busy for Jack, but not for you. He's moving into his new neighborhood, and he's going to a movie premiere with his friends. Not surprisingly, you aren't invited. You will probably spend the majority of your afternoon staring at a blank computer screen, sipping too many cups of coffee, and eavesdropping at the dog park, listening to the dog owners gossip about the recent fling between Fido's mom and Sunshine's dad.

You are sitting in your bedroom, full of tears. Jack dropped you off last night and when his car sped away, without waiting to see if you got in, even though it was after midnight, you called out to the empty, cold street, "Fuuuuuck you, buddy." That small bit of self-amusement was the highlight of your evening.

"Hi," you say when Jack answers the phone. You should think of something smooth to say. Instead you blurt, "I can't do this anymore . . ."

"Uh . . ." Jack draws out the sound, buying time for a response. "Okay. Let me get this last round of boxes together and I'll be there soon. I still have my sister's car."

You know that for him "soon" could mean two or three or four hours, but for the first time, you don't care. You step outside, looking at the trees in the park, and think, *It's a nice day . . . for a cigarette.*

You walk toward the corner store. A young man works there in the mornings. He smokes Parliaments, and you know this because he always gives you one when you ask; the two of you end up puffing away by the piles of shiny apples and luscious oranges. Today you will buy your own pack.

You stand there, lighting the cigarette outside the store, looking up at the top of the building across the street. A man walks by with a Labrador and you blow your smoke in the other direction, smiling at him with your arms folded tight against your body. It's cold out. Damn cold.

Later, you are fiddling around with papers in your room, things that need to be straightened out. You have lived here for two months and have yet to change your address on several bills. No time like the present.

Jack enters your room. You hadn't heard the doorbell ring and so you look up, confused.

"Sophie let me in."

"Oh."

"So . . ." His hands settle in the back pocket of his jeans and he is looking at you, seeming genuinely concerned.

Surprised he even came at all, you think angrily.

"Look, I just . . . I can't do this anymore. It's like we have this relationship in name only and . . . it's really hurting me. I mean, the other night, telling me you bought your ticket to go to Vancouver instead of acknowledging that you'd invited me but needed to go on your own—what's that all about?"

Jack moves across your bedroom and it makes you so sad, really, to remember all the good that was supposed to come from being in one another's lives. You'd promised one another! Jack takes a seat on the bed next to you and sighs, putting his hands over his eyes.

"I . . . I don't know. I really don't. I . . . I just don't know how it's even gotten to this place."

You are facing each other and he is running a hand through his hair, shaking his head at the same time. You are wrapped in a memory of being delighted and close on an empty beach.

"I told you," he said. "I get involved in my work . . ."

In this moment, you are numb. You see the memories like quick snapshots, sliding through your mind, but they are no longer attached to the acute feeling of loss that has been slowly creeping up on you for the past month. Or two.

He looks at you and his eyes start to water, only you don't question his sadness like you did the other night.

"I mean, I really worry that I'm not going to be able to have a traditional life . . ." His eyes drift across the room and up to the ceiling. He is not crying for you, and you are strangely grateful—touched, even. *At least it's honest . . .*

"Work isn't your problem," you say with succinct know-it-all-ness.

Jack shakes his head. *You are wrong,* he seems to be saying. Moments of stillness are punctuated by nothing, nothing at all. You probably are wrong. At this point, does it even matter? Early afternoon light spills across the floor, coloring everything. This suddenly feels so permanent: an ending. You are quiet—not because you don't have anything to say, but because you don't have anything to say that wouldn't just be filler. After your months of obsessive email exchanges and marathon phone conversations, this is what the reality has become: silence.

"I really think the surgery affected me, and . . . and it caused me to take you for granted. I don't want to do that anymore."

The words sit there. Jack is just about as straight with you as he's ever been: he's been taking you for granted, something you know, but it stings deeper than you could have imagined to hear it from his own mouth.

You put your head down, remembering this exact same sentiment—"once one partner takes the other for granted, it's all downhill from there"—Jack had actually spouted off. He said it himself.

You are tracing a line along the plum-colored branch pattern on your silky duvet cover when Jack lifts your chin up with his hand. "Hey, I mean it. I really don't want to lose you. Can we try, here?"

You are utterly hopeless. Your rational mind flies out the window when his hands are on top of yours, when your lips brush his, even when your shoulders meet side by side.

Inside, you are screaming to yourself, *No! You are not well. Leave, leave, and quickly.*

But when he takes your hand and kisses you, you turn soft, passive, filled with indecision. "Okay," you finally whisper.

After you and Jack move toward the edge of the bed to lie down, he looks at his watch. You've been in repose for all of three minutes.

"I would love to stay here," he says, " but I have to finish packing before I get ready for tonight. I also need to pick up a box of books that I left at my cousin's house."

"Who's going to the premiere?" you ask, sitting up and brushing out the comforter around your thighs. It's something to say. You expect Jack to say it'll be just Jack and a friend, maybe one or two other people.

"Oh, so-and-so and her boyfriend, so-and-so and his wife . . ."

His friends have all invited their significant others, and he has, most conspicuously, not invited you.

"Oh."

Realizing what you've realized, Jack says, "Yeah, ah, I really, really wanted to get you a ticket, but there weren't any extras . . ."

"So I'm going to write this afternoon," you say, changing the subject for him, even as your head drifts to why he didn't invite you. Somewhere in the last two months, Jack has gone from adoring everything about you to picking apart your wardrobe and noticing when you're wearing too much makeup. Maybe he didn't invite you because he's been mentioning your need for new shoes, a new bag, that ratty wallet. Maybe, but then again, maybe not. You have a feeling you will never really know.

JACK AGREES TO drop you off at the café. When you are driving, you ask if you can go with him to see his new place.

"Oh, I would love to show you my place, but I can't. I need to pick up those books first."

"Oh," you say, looking out the windows to the piles of rust-colored leaves on the sidewalk, in front of houses that you imagine are all lit up from the inside.

After Jack drops you off, you are not sure why you agreed to stay with him. There was only one other time in your life when you knew down to every cellular inch that the man was wrong for you and yet, every time you saw him, you had the hardest time saying no. When you were with him, a cloud would settle in, surrounding all exchanges and interactions. It stifled you, mesmerized you. That lasted for three weeks, and you had never felt more ill in your life, moving like a yo-yo between the extremes of knowing you had to leave him and confusing your bodily connection with love. At the time you finally left, you'd been full of regrets, sure that that waffling hadn't served any purpose but to make you more upset, more likely to spend an afternoon crying in your bedroom instead of out there enjoying the world. But now, when you watch Jack pull away from the café and you think about it, you know that this past heartache is something from which you can draw upon now. You know this feeling. It's not good.

You feel frozen in time and space, and wish someone would stick you with a pin, right in your belly button or the middle of your forehead, and break through the frost crystallizing over your skin.

The brownstones outside with their stately, constant presence make you think of history, and all that has gone before you and your trivial neurotic concerns about falling in and out of love. A few days ago, you lugged home two bags of apples and dropped one on the corner, where two older men, one with lesions on his cheek, stopped to help you pick them up. When they insisted on helping you carry your load, you learned about how much times had changed on this street. They told you of muggings and how even the police were scared. They told you how lucky you are, a young woman like yourself, and you had believed them.

From the café window, you see families gathering outside on stoops, saying goodbye or hello to houseguests. Mothers roll their babies in strollers down the tree-lined street, nodding to passersby. Your environment is beautiful, but you can't shake the feeling that it is not a part of your world, that it is some flat, lifeless movie set that's not really there for the taking, at least your taking. The only thing in relief is you, your body, your worrying mind.

After getting a cup of coffee, taking a seat on a sofa, and watching your neighbor blow her nose, you open your computer and write the words, "I will break up with Jack—for sure—the next time I see him. No exceptions."

For the next forty-five minutes, you let your head move through various thoughts and feelings, giving yourself free rein, i.e., *why doesn't that lady go to the bathroom if she's going to blow that forcefully? Why didn't Jack invite me to the premiere? Coffee is always better with cigarettes. Make this go away.*

Your phone rings, and you see Jack's number.

"Hi, there," you say tentatively, sighing loud enough for him to hear, in spite of yourself.

"Hey, looks like there's enough time to stop by my new place—do you want to come see it? My cousin and I are

in the car and I can pick you up in three minutes. I can drop
you both back in Brooklyn after, too, if that makes a difference."

Could you really drop everything to go to his new place?
The West Village, his new neighborhood, seems so far. Besides,
you just promised yourself that you would wrangle free the
next time you saw him and you aren't about to do this in front
of one of his family members.

"Actually, it's not a good time. The writing is really coming,"
which is a total lie. You only wrote that one junior high sentence about breaking up with Jack when you see him next. "But
thanks anyway."

When you hang up the phone, you add, *Jerk.*

Two hours later, you leave the café, your bag slung heavy
over your shoulder. In total, you wrote five sentences. *Oh, well.
There's always tomorrow.*

It's a beautiful fall Sunday, and you remember the time when
the leaves were a freshly turned green on the trees, how the sky
had looked different then.

When you feel your phone buzzing in your pocket, you almost don't even look. If this is Jack, who cares? You need to
acquaint yourself with the idea of not caring when it comes to
him. But it's not Jack. It's Dan, and so you answer.

"Hello, my dear," you say dejectedly. Wise words from Dan
could really come in handy here. Or even a joke. Hell, you'd
settle for hearing Dan say, in an exaggerated Boston accent,
"Park the Car in Harvard Yard," ten times. Anything you say to
lighten the mood.

"Hey, I have a favor to ask," he says. "I'm writing a piece
for my elective, and I'm basing the character on you. I want to

explore this theme of endings or departures. Do you have any relevant stories?"

Wow. Dan really is your best friend.

"Do I ever . . ."

So you launch into the story of your weekend, running your mind over every last sorry detail. You are not even halfway up the block when you see Jack, driving by you in his car, presumably coming back from dropping his cousin off.

"Oh, shit, Dan. Can I call you back? I promised myself the next time I saw Jack I'd break up with him, and, ah, he's right here."

Dan starts laughing, "Oh-boise . . ."

You fold your phone shut and walk over to Jack's passenger side, where he has rolled down the window. He has a big stupid smile on his face.

"Who's that?" he asks.

Leaning in, thinking about what you're going to say, you respond carelessly, "Dan. Guess what? He asked me for a story about departures and endings for his class, and, ah, I told him I have one."

Did that really just come out of your mouth? Did you really, really just say that as if it had no intended import? If so, you are lying, lying, lying.

Jack's eyes are all glazed over. He doesn't respond in a way that indicates he's even heard what you said.

"Oh, cool. Well, the apartment's great. I have to run, just came back to drop my cousin off. Have to get my tux ready."

And before you can even say, "C-ya!" he's speeding down the quiet side street on his way to a movie premiere to which you are not invited.

When you call Dan back, the first thing he says is, "Well, did you do it?"

You are completely deflated. Now you will have to wait another night, another day of thinking about how he's taken you for granted already, how you are a mere broken-off piece of the person you were trying to be this past summer.

"No. He's on his way to a movie premiere."

"Do you think he's been thinking this carefully about your feelings all this time?"

"Yeah, well . . ."

"And I mean, you've given him every clue that things aren't going well. Frankly, it's his own fault for not dumping you first."

"Yeah. Okay." You sigh, deeper than before. "Can I call you right back? I need to at least get him before he's in the theater, okay?"

You are full of vibrations, ringing unhappy sounds. Ringing, ringing, ringing anxiety, and there is nothing, it seems, that will make it go away. Your heart has never felt so heavy, not that you can recall, anyway. Breaking up with Ted was a long process, one that you're still processing. Oh, God. Has this whole path been a diversion? An inevitably messy road taken because you've been still reeling from the loss of Teddy? Sometimes, even now, you wake up in the middle of the night and expect the bedroom door to open and see Ted's silhouette. All you have now is Jack's shadow, imagined and blinding. When will you learn to be your own first love?

You dial Jack's number. You are walking along and your stomach is getting increasingly tight. You have backed yourself into a corner. There is no way you can stay with him now and feel good about it. You had hoped that this might be an option. But now you are here, looking at the bus pulling away from the stop, and you are crying out, "Wait, wait for me!" even though you don't really want to go on that tour.

"Hey," you say, your head spinning.

"Hey, there. What's up?" Why does Jack still sound so familiar and easy with you? Does he not get it at all?

You lean one arm on a parking meter, bending forward, as if you have a stomachache.

"Look, I just can't do this. Every inch of me is saying, 'Don't do it.' "

"What? But—but—why?"

"Gut instinct," you say.

You throw your hands up in the air, aware that you are standing in front of a hospital, where several medical professionals are taking smoke breaks from rounds or whatever the hell they do to make the world a better place. "Jack, we both know where this is headed . . ."

"I . . . I don't know why you think that." This is the first time that you have seen Jack at a loss for words. A feeling of sickness swirls through your chest, rising in your throat as he continues: "It, it doesn't have to be—"

"But you said it yourself! This summer, when I was telling you about my friend whose boyfriend took her for granted. You said that it was always over after one partner starts taking the other for granted."

"I did? Well . . . well, I was wrong."

His answer is perfect. But too late.

"Jack, I'm sorry. I just can't do this."

"Whatever," he says. "I have to go." Click.

"Whatever," Jack said. "Whatever" is the Berlin Wall of communication stoppers and you—guilty of some communication-stopping verbiage yourself—have just heard it, from your now-former lover's mouth for what you hope will be the last time. You ended it abruptly because your heart couldn't handle another second. You'd rather scratch your own skin raw than put up with one more moment of living under this unbearable weight of your fantasy falling short of reality. You waited so long to tell him how you really felt and so now, in theory, you should feel relief, but no. The pressure is still there, heavy, throbbing, even.

The path home is bleak. You are bleak, walking by the restaurant where you and Jack used to eat. Your world lens has a sad, gray filter. You walk by the movie theater, the fire hydrant he'd declared with much zest that you should be able to park in front of. You and Jack spent far too long looking at a fire hydrant on the corner of the street. You were so enamored then.

With a sigh you realize, lighting up your cigarette, *It's all over . . . it's finally all over.* You think of all the times that you should have felt good, but didn't. This is right up there with your college graduation, your mother waving the program wildly as you walked by, you gripping your stomach and hoping you could at least wait until after Madeleine Albright's speech to vomit.

When you get home, Sophie and her brother are in the kitchen cooking. You smell the whole fish roasting in the oven. Rosemary fills the air, and you assume this to mean there are potatoes in the pan, too.

Your hand heavy and gripping the wooden railing, you stop.

If you fell back, even a millimeter, you would go tumbling right down those stairs. You are tempted.

Even when they are not associated with the situation at hand, scents are reminders. Your nose opens, pulling you back to places that were marked, punctuated, heightened—just because you decided to start paying attention. You go to the places of remembering, feeling, filling up. You are not only here, with these scents. You are everywhere at once, and nothing could disturb your numbness more.

"Hello?" Sophie calls out when she hears you at the top of the stairs. Here is this other person that you have to talk to, to pretend that you are fine when in reality all that you can think about is what a colossal wrong turn you have made by dating Jack, being indiscriminate in drinking in his praise and adoration, until you got used to it, needed it, thought that your life as you knew it would be over if he were to turn his attention elsewhere. However did your life get so small?

You could cry. You should cry.

Sophie comes out to the hallway to see if you are really there, or were the creaky floorboards just ghosts? She finds you, still teetering at the top of the steps. You are a puddle.

"Oh!" she says. "Come here."

You drift into her hug and put your head on her shoulder. She is shorter than you, much shorter, and so not only does this look awkward, it feels awkward, your head crunched at an impossible angle. You can already feel the pain in your neck; the sharp physical discomfort relieves you from the nausea.

"Is it Jack?" Sophie asks, a question that you cannot even bear to answer, especially not now that she is holding you so close, rubbing your back. The tears begin and flow, and they don't stop when you want them to. They keep pushing out of your eyes, pushing, pushing, pushing. They are here, these tears, and they feel like they might be sticking around for a little while. You need a good cry—or fifty.

You can't answer Sophie's question. You make no sense to the outside world, but you stop, sit still for a second, and think: *IS it Jack?*

You don't even know anymore.

PART III

There is as much difference between
us and ourselves as there is between us
and others.

—MONTAIGNE

23

You have decided. You have decided. You have decided to become a different person. This is America—land of easy transformations. You want to be someone else? Read a self-help book. Quit smoking. Watch *The Secret.* Think positive. Take up a new hobby. Or, hell, don't even bother doing any of that—just say you are someone else, and thus it will be true. This is the age of Oprah, and you can do anything you damn well please.

The memory of your failure with Jack feels like, well, a big embarrassing failure, and so you decide simply to change the channel. You moped for all of eighteen hours before deciding that being a sad lonely-heart is not for you. After shooting off a "Don't call me!" email to Jack (written in more gentle terms, of course), you invited friends over and cooked an apricot- and apple-stuffed pork loin. And even though you called it your "Celebrate Heartbreak" party, you were actually a bad host, forgetting to cry or even mention the name of that guy you'd just as soon forget. You did lots of things that week: went out for oysters, danced all night at a club. You were going to be, as Paula reminded you over drinks one night, "Absolutely fine. Just fine."

So for now, first things first. You have a book to write! In lieu of cardiovascular activity, you have taken to walking the streets of Manhattan every night after work. Every night, you step out onto Lexington Avenue and meander downtown, peering inside the wrought-iron gates of Gramercy Park, crossing Third Avenue, sniffing various candle scents at the home goods store on Second Avenue, and, of course, stopping to ask anyone and everyone you can, "Hey, got an embarrassing story for me?" Sometimes it's more like, "Excuse me? Can I have a cigarette—and an embarrassing story?" It's an imprecise science, which works perfectly for imperfect you.

Night after night, you collect *Oh, Shit!* moments from unsuspecting New Yorkers. Night after night, you hear horror stories. Good lord, humans are nothing if not survivors. For example, one guy thought it was bad enough that he had anal warts. But once he was at the hospital, facedown on an examination table, the lights went up, the curtain opened, and there stood an entire med school class, ready to learn about how to treat anal warts—*his* anal warts. Standing next to maroon marble columns, outside a building just blocks from your office, another smoker told you about his days as a model. His agency held a workshop on how to walk the runway. Ninety-nine percent of the attendants were female, and this guy was doing his best to impress. Most of his work was found as a hand model and at the end of the workshop, when the head agent asked if there were any questions, he blurted out, "How much for that hand job?" before realizing just how wrong that sounded. In a seedy bar on Second Avenue, a young woman, visiting from Michigan, told you how she'd worked at a sex shop and how horrified she had been when her mother's best friend walked in one day, arms full of toys. Her mother's best friend dropped everything and ran when she saw her best friend's young daughter.

The moments of strangers are blending into one after another after another. Life before New York City, with its diurnal rhythms and enveloping architecture, is beginning to feel like a dream, an imagined time and space that never could have really worked out for you anyway. In light of this, the collection of other people's stories gains new importance.

As part of your determination to move on, you have banished all downer thoughts, and if you must mention the heartbreak, you cover it with performance, your shield of choice. For example, on one of your nightly walks after work, you bumped into Robert, a boisterous Englishman you'd met months ago when you were with Marco. That night, you weren't surprised that Robert took a liking to you and your sheer leopard-print camisole with red lacy trim. Marco liked people just as much as you, and so he listened to Robert's stories about his dying mother as you leaned back into Marco's shoulder. In between painting scenes of his mother taking care of her nine children, Robert would pause to say, "Look at you two, so in love!" So here you were—broken up with Marco for Jack, broken up with Jack for life, and what did you have to say for yourself when you saw Robert having a pint at the Telephone Bar on Second Avenue and he asked you what, exactly, you mean by "heartbroken"?

"Well, Robert"—you cleared your throat for dramatic pause, then sipped your beer, batting your eyelashes—"let's just say . . . I was tied to the railroad tracks and I still didn't see the train coming."

In glibness, certainty becomes you, and you are in no position to turn it away.

With a wicked grin, Robert responded, "I'm sure I can help you with those ropes."

When you patted his shoulder while turning your head to watch the after-work crowd hurrying to their respective Friday night destinations, Robert added, "Now, tell me that you're not going to keep on working with this guy."

"We'll see," you said nonchalantly. "Anybody up for buffalo wings?"

"That's a terrible idea," he said with a fair amount of paternal concern. "Just terrible."

"Quesadillas, then?"

TONIGHT IS SATURDAY, and you are sitting with Henry and Cash, a friend of Henry's, in a dark, crowded bar, huddled in a cozy half-moon-shaped booth with a fiery-colored glass orb hanging overhead. Background music is inching up the volume knob, and you find yourselves shouting as anonymous bodies periodically bump the table. The crowd is a mix of hipsters and straighter-looking folk. With your plain jeans and T-shirt, you count yourself in the latter group.

Despite barely knowing him, you like this Cash character. Not only does he have hands down the sexiest voice you've ever heard, but he also has heart. In the span of the one hour you've spent with him so far, you've seen him bust out "Use Me" at the karaoke place across the street, to wild success. Strangers asked for an encore, something that is never heard of in the karaoke trenches; you've seen him step to and manage a self-described Bob Fosse jazz move swinging his foot on the floor in a semicircle and moving his hips accordingly. ("Bob Fosse?" you'd repeated over and over. "Excuse me, did you really just say 'Bob Fosse'?") You've seen stageworthy performances of simple stories from his everyday life, with firm attention on you and Henry, taking steps in closer with his eyes, always looking to engage his "audience."

You assume Cash to have the good-natured, does-not-take-oneself-too-seriously gene. As you settle into the round booth between Henry and Cash, you clutch your beer and turn abruptly toward Cash.

"So, do you have any embarrassing stories, Cash?"

Much to your surprise, his face turns a deep red. He looks down, averring that he, indeed, has some embarrassing stories for you.

"No pressure," you say, explaining the book that you've come to explain one thousand one times. "No pressure at all."

"Maybe later," he says with a wink.

"Well, whatever it is," you say, laying your hand on his, "I assure you that it won't shock me. It can't."

After six months of collecting stories, nothing surprises you anymore. You almost wonder if embarrassment, so haphazardly covered by you with the thoroughness of a term paper written entirely from random Post-it notes and ideas sketched out on the back of envelopes stained with coffee remnants, even exists at all. Or is it just in your/his/her/my head?

"So, how is the book coming, anyway?" asks Cash. "Where are you with it?"

"Oh, it's coming," you mumble. You don't want to explain your botched agent situation—again. Technically, you still have an agent. His name is Jack, and the main problem is that, despite your best intentions, you can't dial his number or send him an email without thinking longingly about his sparkling eyes. (Big problem.) Therefore, when he tells you he'll call you right back and then waits a day or two, you take it very, very personally. Yeah, it's not really going so well.

"Yep, coming along," you repeat.

"That doesn't sound good," he says, leaning forward to look you in the eye. You cast your eyes downward and you start twirling the base of your glass on the shredded cocktail napkin. After a minute of silence, you look up.

"Well, the writing is happening. It's just not going so well with the agent," you say loudly. You have turned your own volume up, so that Cash can hear you and so that you can make the point that you're not really open to talking about this.

"Why?" Cash asks. "What happened?"

"Well, we, um, had started dating," you mumble, much too low for the music.

Cash shakes his head, tapping his earlobe with an index finger. "What?"

At this moment, the DJ lifts the needle off the record, only you don't notice the song coming to an abrupt end.

Your voice full-throttle, you shout, "I slept with him!"

Silence. Dead silence.

Several people turn to look at you. Cash, oblivious to the staring, is frozen, his mouth wide open. You can see from his pained expression that he is about to, or trying to, say, "You *what?*" as in, "Didn't you know better?"

The truth is that, at almost thirty, you certainly did know better. But you'd done it anyway. (Often you think, *If only I'd taken Davida's don't-shit-where-you-eat warnings more seriously.*) When you feel Henry laughing beside you, you elbow him. Before Cash can say anything, you smile within inches of a wink and shrug your shoulders. Who are you, anyway? You lift your hands, palms outward, and exclaim with exaggeration, "Oops!"

Sleeping with Jack was, indeed, a big "oops," one that clearly fits within the theme of *Oh, Shit!* It's an easy enough piece of information to turn into both shtick and strategy—*shtick* because the admission is cast through a ditzy-yet-cavalier affect, and strategy because you are hoping that, by sharing something about yourself, you will get Cash to talk. You are in a bar, for god's sakes. You're not about to tell Cash or anyone else that the situation with Jack is, in fact, eating you up.

A few weeks after the romantic breakup, you met with Jack at the café outside your office, to discuss the professional relationship. For whatever reason, he had wanted to keep working with you, and despite your reluctance and despite the advice of your parents and friends, you agreed. In that first meeting, he'd looked at you with those expressive eyes, as if he were asking you to believe, and said, "I have strong feelings for you that aren't going anywhere . . ." This one little sentence had sent you into a tizzy. This one little sentence gave rise to an inordinate amount of false hope—and bullishness. Despite all your posturing to the contrary, you'd never really given up the idea, however buried it might now be, that you and Jack could go back to the summer, to those months of foolish bliss, to the time before you even kissed. And so after this ostensible work meeting, you plowed forward with subsequent emails asking him to meet with you to discuss the personal relationship. But he kept putting you off. First he could. Then he couldn't. You sensed that your forcefulness made him nervous. Humiliated by the realization that he was never going to act on those so-called "strong feelings," your attitude fast became, "Well, then, put up or shut up, buddy!" When you two finally did meet to tie up the loose ends of your personal relationship (at Blue Ribbon, of course), you asked him never to say those words again. Sitting at the bar, his hands clasped tightly in his lap, Jack signaled his agreement with a closemouthed smile and a faint nod. He looked down, like he wanted to say something. Only he didn't. So you picked up your glass of champagne and tried not to choke on your own toast. "To the fun we *had*."

MOMENTS LATER, CASH pulls you outside, ostensibly to smoke cigarettes. (Henry has not had enough drinks yet to partake in the tobacco.) You saunter across the concrete patio. Yes, saunter. You have nothing to lose anymore. You cannot touch this thing called embarrassment. Despite a new focus on gathering and recording stories, your neediness with Jack is still cause for shame, something you'd rather not dwell on. You cannot penetrate that which you don't really understand.

Screw it. Gimme a cigarette. Or twenty.

Cash reaches to pull two stools together, side by side. The stools are awfully close, even for you, a normally close-talking woman. Alas, you do what you must, and brace yourself, hoping that if Cash needs to obliterate the American concept of personal space, then maybe, please, hopefully, his breath won't smell bad.

"Okay," he whispers, planting his ass on the stool, while his hands are ready for the catch: A football? A baby? Something. His head is hunched forward, giving him the air of a turtle. The upright, strident, and expressionistic Cash has been replaced by a somewhat timid, perhaps chagrined, and definitely muted one.

Smoke billows around you. It is now late enough in the evening that the whole crowd generally seems drunk, all together inebriated. You are not quite there, but you like it, this sense of oneness. You meditate on the conversations all around you, managing not to focus in on the play-by-play ("So then I told him that I am really, like, really over it!") and instead hearing the voices in chorus, a sound of togetherness. Humanistic failure is all around you. And more important, so are support systems. Your eyes drift off, past the railing, past the sidewalk and the clusters of friends all out for a good night and a good time. You are out for a good time, too. Isn't that what this is all about?

"This story is pretty bad," Cash says, still quiet. He hands you a cigarette distractedly. You see his eyes looking past you and he waves. When you turn, you see two women, both pretty, with defined dark eye makeup.

"Hi, Cash!" they say in unison.

"Hi, hi," he says, and turns back to you. They obviously want to talk to him and he obviously wants to get this story off his chest.

Years ago, he was visiting his friend in Barcelona. It was summer. They spent their days going to the beach and their nights eating big meals and frequenting clubs. One day there was a big party planned on the beach—and everyone was supposed to wear white. Cash found some white linen pants and a particularly tight T-shirt, one that undoubtedly showcased his biceps. Picture it: DJs, drinking, dancing, lots of beautiful Spanish women with whom Cash could mingle. But Cash noticed one woman in particular. She had long brown hair and big eyes. The night wore on. They danced together, got closer. So close that when someone bumped her from behind, she went flying forward and spilled her full glass of red wine all over Cash's white outfit—the largest quantity of Rioja landing around the zipper of his white pants.

Flash back to earlier in the day: Cash and his friend were heading to the beach when Cash realized that he had left his bathing suit at another friend's apartment. The friend he was with offered to let Cash borrow his extra suit, which happened to be a hot-pink Speedo emblazoned with white stars. Since he was in Europe, Cash thought, *Oh, what the hell?* When in Rome . . .

Or Barcelona.

The trouble was, Cash hadn't changed after the beach, so when his date spilled her wine, making his pants see-through, his girlie Speedo became visible to all partygoers. Having imbibed enough, Cash didn't really care as he looked down at his stain. In fact, he decided to take the pants off and throw them to the side, continuing to dance barefoot in his body-skimming T-shirt and very teeny-tiny swim trunks. Which were pink. And this was not even close to being the embarrassing part.

As the party wound down, Cash and the girl stumbled across the sand, making it to a taxi and going back to her apartment. In his drunken stupor, he'd left the pants behind, which was too bad because in the back pocket was his wallet. But this was the last thing that Cash had on his mind as he escorted her home.

They stayed up for most of the night, having what he says was really "hot sex." (Of course, if it were just so-so, then it wouldn't necessarily add to the story, would it?) Finally, they fell asleep, peaceful in each other's arms. Or, they passed out cold from drinking too much. You decide.

Cash awoke a few hours later to the girl shouting at him, "I have an appointment. I forgot! You have to get out of here—now." His head foggy, he began to get up, thinking that this was all a bad dream. But she kept shouting, "Now! I mean it."

Slightly put off that the girl wasn't nearly as friendly the morning after as she had been after some drinks, Cash felt around at the bottom of the bed, looking for his clothing. His clothing, however, consisted of only the Speedo and the T-shirt. Before he could even ask her if she had some pants or shorts or something, she was clapping her hands, universal for, "Get a move on, buddy."

When he had the shirt and Speedo on—and no shoes, which had been left at the beach as well—Cash was struck by the distinct sensation of humiliation, because she was kicking him to the curb in this outfit; the girl didn't really care. He waved goodbye and snuck his hand into her change jar, realizing that, with no wallet, he'd need money to take the subway home. He'd rather steal from her than beg on the street.

Ah, the subway. It was a weekday rush hour, to be exact. Big burly Cash hopped on the crowded train, forced to hold on to an overhead bar with one hand, covering the Speedo area with the other. Some commuters laughed, others just stared. But they all inched as far away from him as humanly possible. (You can imagine a young woman snickering over in the corner, maybe looking at her best friend: "Ewwwww!") Barefoot, half-naked Cash stood there, exposed with a silly grin on his face. He was so preoccupied with his lack of clothing that he didn't realize that he'd missed his stop.

ON THE SMOKY patio, Cash leans toward you and adds, "By the time I got back to my friend's place, it had taken me two hours." His eyes widen as he purses his lips.

Now working on your second cigarette of the story, you inhale, raising your eyebrows, and so Cash repeats it for you: "Two hours."

A tall woman with a wicked smile walks up behind Cash and rubs his shoulders. "Hey, baby . . ."

"Hi." Cash barely turns around. His story has put him in a state of please-don't-touch-me."

You shake your head a few times. You don't laugh. This is not a laugh-out-loud story. It is an "Oh, honey . . ." story. Sometimes, in the retelling of these stories, you can almost see the ghosts lifting, people moving in and out of old stories and places that they've kept hidden for too long—creating not mere cobwebs, but actual ghosts.

You and Cash sit to honor the story for a moment. Music blares from the inside and people are in high social mode, squealing and talking all around you. Neither of you says anything. You let the smoke flow and remember where you are. Cash's not in Barcelona anymore, and neither are you.

"Okay, Cash, so what would you like your fake name to be? I gather you'd like this one to be anonymous?"

"Cosmo," he says without pause. In his deep, radio announcer voice, again: "Call me Cosmo."

Cash is wise to go with the fake name. You know you. You don't keep quiet, and so his story will be pouring out of your mouth, at least a few times, before even writing it down. And you are not one of those fools who think that New York is a big city. It's not. In the interest of protecting "Cash" and all his future dates, you are happy to keep his name a secret.

You are beginning to wonder: How honest can we really be with ourselves? You mean, Cash was traumatized by the memory of this story, clearly. But is there more to the story? You can only guess.

Take Jack. On the surface, yes, embarrassment exists in the blurred lines between your professional and personal lives. Oops. A big oops. You can make silly jokes and shrug your shoulders and perform, perform, perform in the presence of others like Cash and Henry. You can send emails to acquaintances in the industry, explain your situation of working with someone you've been shamefully obsessed with, and write, *So, do you have any sage words for me? Besides 'Don't sleep with your agent'?* You can try to be funny all you want. You can throw your hands up in exasperation, wink, and smile, because you know you can be charming if need be. But what you really need is to get real. And putting on a show isn't your ticket to reality, no matter how entertaining you think it might be. How can you expect to know what's beneath Cash's story if you have no idea what's beneath your own? Can you peel the layers back? Or would that be too much?

24

YOU'VE SPENT THE New Year's days of your young life in a variety
of settings: on an herb farm in central Massachusetts, strolling
the snow-covered grounds and inhaling the chilly New England
air; exceedingly hung-over at Doyle's Pub, eating eggs Benedict
and drinking Diet Coke as your mind went fuzzy over the details
of the night before; mildly hung-over at Ted's apartment, cooking hoppin' John and curling up with him on the couch.

Today is a new New Year's Day. As it approached, you viewed
it as an opportunity to let go, really let go. In a new effort to
rid your body of all toxins, you decided to eat nothing but veg-
gies and rice for two weeks. The drive to cleanse your system
is strong, and so you kick all habits of alcohol, sugar, and complex carbohydrates with relative ease. But one stinking habit remains: the cigarettes. You don't plan on giving them up anytime
soon—nor do you plan on feeling bad about it. Besides, more
than tobacco, the biggest toxin you need to rid yourself of is Jack.
Although you are through talking about Jack to your friends and
family, you are not over him in your head—or heart. And now,
two months after the breakup, you really think you ought to be.
Talking about it would mean failure. You failed to get rid of him,

even though he is not a part of your physical life, except for some brief book-related emails here and there.

Contact between you and Jack is limited to talk of *Oh, Shit!*—and always uncomfortable. Every time you ask about feedback or how the other reads are coming (at his agency), you feel as if you are bothering him. Beyond knowing whether or not this is all in your head, you do know one thing: it's not pleasant.

As you see it, the main trouble with this professional relationship is that you are thinking less of the book and its development and more of how annoyed you get when Jack doesn't respond immediately to your emails. You know it's irrational. But that doesn't stop you from being annoyed. When you'd sent him the first draft of your proposal, he intimated that he would give you written feedback, but later said that perhaps you two should just have a phone conversation about the feedback. When you tried to schedule something via phone, he said that his week was packed. He had started signing his emails with the line, "Talk soonest!"—which, of course, you found irritating. (What the fuck does that even mean anyway?) But soon enough, he did make time for you, only it was when he was in the airport, waiting to go to Vancouver—the trip you were supposed to have gone on together. In addition to needling you, these circumstances did not aid your Sisyphean efforts to keep the personal and professional relationships separate. Paying more attention to the background gate announcements than Jack's actual "feedback," you sat more or less mute, completely deflated.

AND NOW HERE you are on New Year's Day, with a different ex-boyfriend in your bed. You'd met Henry at a party the night before, danced a little, and then brought him to your house, which wasn't exactly your plan, but when all the other party-goers started moseying home, inviting Henry to your house seemed like a good enough idea. You made two cups of Bed-time tea, which you sipped in your dark bedroom as you forced him to listen to Shakira on your computer. He sat on the floor and you sat on the bed, which changed when he asked sweetly, "May I kiss you?"

Now Henry is lying next to you, naked, with his hand brush-ing hair away from your forehead. You are overwhelmed by the memories of someone else. You can't even bear to say his name, you are so ashamed that you are not over it. What is your problem?

"Just let it out. It's good to cry," Henry whispers.

You do. The sobs are real, not stifled. Somewhere between the increasing volume of your cries and the comforting prox-imity of Henry in your bed, you begin to calm down. This sense of shame—of not being where you think you should be, on so many levels—starts to fade.

"You wanna talk about it?" he asks. But you, in your own bed with a friend who is more a friend than a lover, could not possibly tell Henry that you are crushed beneath the weight of being with him and not feeling even a smidgen of the deeper connection you had with Jack.

When you open your eyes, you crawl over Henry's torso to get closer to the window. The sky unbearably gray, the weather is a bad omen. The rooftops on your block are empty, the only semblance of life being that fake plastic owl. When you see birds and squirrels running amok on that particular roof, you think, *It's not working.*

*   *   *

LATER, YOU ARE settling into a comfortable armchair at Starbucks. You have been collecting and writing up *Oh, Shit!* stories
now for months, but still you are struggling with the concept.
In an effort to improve your proposal, you settle in with some
green tea and write snappy sentences such as the following:

The beauty of embarrassing moments is that everyone has
them. Of course, some are greater than others. For example,
trying to pass off some unexpected snot on your lip as tree sap
when you're about to have your first kiss is decidedly not the
same as having your former intern's Gap dress DNA-tested
and entered as official evidence into a judicial proceeding to
prove that you, indeed, fooled around with her (ahem, Mr.
President). But no matter how grand the scandal, after the
memory fades, the universality of the mortifying moment
remains.

Your book is becoming the best excuse in the world to avoid
your problems. A free hour stretched out before you? Work
on *Oh, Shit!* Struck by loneliness on a Friday night after work?
Make it your job to collect stories of other people's embarrassment, roaming the streets, bumming cigarettes, and asking other people to fess up. This way of gathering stories has
worked pretty well, at least as far as it's kept you occupied.

You don't even want to imagine the trouble that would start
brewing if you weren't occupied.

The cursor on your Word document blinks. What if you
classified the embarrassments? This might make it at least
more palatable for you when filing stories. Classification never

hurt anyone, right? In your attempt to understand your place in life, the mere act of creating a structure, even if it's only for the book, is incredibly pleasing. In keeping with the "snappy" theme, you come up with subheadings for *Oh, Shit!*

1. Oh, Shit: Bodily Function Mishaps
2. No You Di'n't: Being Embarrassed for Others
3. Get Me Out of Here: Social Humiliation
4. Who, Me?: Past-Self Mortification
5. Professional Roadkill: Workplace Chagrin
6. Here We Go Again: Dating Mishaps
7. Ouch: Personal Grooming Gone Awry
8. Sometimes Hot, Sometimes Not: Sexual Gaffes
9. C'mon, I Know You'll Like Me: Efforts to Impress That Took a Wrong Turn

When you pause, trying hard to think of more categories, you go blank. Is nine enough? Will it be funny? Are your titles too dumb? Clever and quick has never really been your thing. When you scan back down this list, you realize that you have a personal story for every single heading.

Oh, brother, you sigh. *Does everything I do have to have some sort of personal resonance?*

You don't ask this question aloud. For one, you are in public. For two, you already know the answer.

25

ALTHOUGH THE NIGHT is chilly, you are standing in front of the mirror in your fishnet stockings, pulling black velvet pants over your legs. Except for the fact that you have a date with William, the guy you met at the Starbucks in SoHo a couple weeks ago, this night is an ordinary Friday. You are enjoying yourself, inhaling the gardenia-scented candle and humming to a new CD. Last week you wore this same outfit to visit Ted at his school's Open Studios program in Chelsea. You hadn't seen him or his artwork in almost one and a half years. When you arrived and found him in a very lived-in space, with empty beer bottles and scattered palettes around the perimeter of the room, you jumped beside him, tugging on his sleeve, a surge of excitement coming over you. In this way, he will always be your baby. *My baby!* This visit, it was hard to comprehend that six months earlier he had called you one hot July afternoon and said, "Hi, look, I wish I were calling under better circumstances, but my mother just told me you cheated on me with some Czech guy. Is that true?" You could only say, "Uh, yeah," wondering how his mother knew. But Boston is a small town, and you'd figured a mutual friend had learned about Ondra through gossip, and that this news eventually got back to Ted's sister, who must have told his mother, who obviously told Ted. You don't ask. What's the point? After your confirmation, he'd cracked, "Great. All I can picture is you with some really buff Viggo Mortensen–looking guy." *Shit,* you thought, sighing audibly into the phone. You had hoped that Ted would never know. With this phone call, you had to face the fact that maybe you and Ted would never be friends after all. But there you were, just a short time later, invited to his studio to see his new art and celebrate his near-completion of graduate school.

When he turned and saw you, he said in a monotone, "Oh, hi . . ." about which you teased him later—"What's up with the flat, 'Oh, hi'?"—to which he responded that you (implication being: "you, the cheater") should really cut him some slack. He had a point there. You and he had sat on folding chairs after all of his other visitors had left, one by one, leaving you two alone. You thought it was because he was introducing you as his "ex-fiancée" but Ted explained that he just wanted people to know that you held an important place in his life—an explanation that put a quick halt to your ribbing. Whatever the reason, there you were, sitting across from one another, wondering in your own ways how the last year and a half could have created so much space between the two of you. Ted was everything to you. You focused on the superficial aspects, the coat he wore with a burned-through cigarette hole on the sleeve (obviously on purpose, mostly because he doesn't smoke and there was a red paint circle around it for emphasis) and his tossed-around haircut, juxtaposed with your three-inch velvet heels, cashmere turtleneck, and ironed-flat shiny hair. But you know, knew, it is often easier to focus on the tangibles as opposed to the unnamed.

William is picking you up in ten minutes. You have exactly enough time to finish blow-drying your hair and apply the finishing touches of your makeup. You don't know much about him, other than that he likes Sudoku, works as an assistant district attorney, and had seamlessly weaved in an invitation to play Ping-Pong with him, somewhere between asking you if he could borrow your pen and commenting on Dick Clark's valiant post-stroke appearance on New Year's Eve. "Ping-Pong?" you'd said, stalling for time while you decided whether or not you could stomach going on an actual date. It's only been a couple months since breaking up with Jack, but deep down, in emotional time, it feels more like only a millisecond away. Dr. Nick, your first therapist, had once commented on how people devote a minimum of twelve years to their intellectual development, but are often less patient in thinking about their emotional development. When you had first heard this, the civil rights movement sprang to mind; in those terms, the movement basically happened yesterday. But now, when you think of the emotional-time argument, you are only thinking of Jack and your impatient efforts to rid yourself of any and all feelings.

Thinking that a little distraction never hurt anyone, you'd said to William, "Uh, sure. I could play Ping-Pong."

When the doorbell rings, you skip by your roommates, all of whom are gathered in the living room, drinking beers and eating take-out Indian food. You wave goodbye, like you always do. With your erratic schedule and lithe frame—getting more and more slim the more you've settled into actually being a smoker and replacing your usual midday snacks with nicotine—you have assumed the role of "ghost" in your own home.

William stands on your front stoop by the doorbell with his hands clasped low behind him. He is tall, with a shaved head, one he probably sports due to early male pattern baldness. In Starbucks, after having known him for all of ten seconds, you imagined him to have almost always a bemused look on his face, as if borrowing a pen from you could potentially be the funniest thing that ever happened to him. On your doorstep, you can see that he holds his head slightly down, with his warm brown eyes looking up. He is already smiling.

"Hi," he says, leaning in to kiss you on the cheek. "You look great."

"Thanks—where to?"

"I'm in your neighborhood—you tell me. Just nowhere with a menu that's heavy on the spice or garlic, because I'm going to want to"—at this point you think, *Huh, that is some assuredness*—"kiss you later."

Everything about William screams "guy's guy." Not only does he probably like football, but he definitely played it—at least in high school. He is not your usual type, but all that means is that you don't normally date the "guy's guy." You shiver in the cold and he puts two hands on your shoulders, the pressure feeling light, comforting. A reminder: you are not in your head anymore—until you drift out to watching your shadows on the street, angling his with yours, toward the park. You are not sure that you will be kissing him, but you suggest a cozy place not too far from your house. The last time you were there, you had an incredible burger with french fries—sans garlic and spice.

Aside from traveling to Brooklyn for your first date, William has already done three impressive things by the time you are seated at the restaurant: (1) he opened the door for you; (2) he helped you take your coat off and hung it on the rack; and (3) he pulled out the table, making it easier for you to slide into the booth. You don't even hate to say it: these gestures, they matter to you. If you ever find yourself with the urge to tell the man you are dating that it would be polite if he opened your car door for you, you have already gone too far in the wrong direction. Now if only you had these markers for all of your decisions involving relationships and the sometimes lengthy process it has taken you to realize that you don't know someone.

You are still on your detox (now extended by a week or so) and so you don't order the hamburger. Instead, you have salmon with greens and vegetables, plus water. When William orders a Diet Coke, you wonder, *Recovering alcoholic?* but don't ask. Something like that is none of your business, especially not on the first date.

After a few minutes of talking, you are reminded of your first impression of William: he is easy—everything about William is easy. Conversation flows at a relaxed pace. Within thirty minutes, you start talking about an article in *The New York Times* called "The Odds of That," suggesting a renaming of what is commonly called "coincidence" to "probability" and how when such instances of probability occur—such as, say, having the same birthday as a classmate or coworker—the tendency is to assign a higher meaning, when in reality it's just sheer probability. After all, there are only so many days in the year, right?

But as you are talking about this article, William, whose body leans toward yours as his elbows are propped up on the white tablecloth, interrupts.

"I love that article! I reference it all the time. In fact, I have a shoebox I keep under my bed, marked with a 'C' for 'Critical,' and that article is in my shoebox."

"No way!" you exclaim, pounding your right palm flat on the tablecloth. "I reference this article all the time and no one ever knows it!"

There is no pause for irony. Or, there is a pause, even amid the bustle of the dining room, plates floating by you on the arms of servers, the laughter of other diners, the imagined hectic kitchen behind those swinging doors. But the pause goes unnoticed, by you, at least. You are too busy chiding yourself for having been so judgmental about the fact that maybe William's guy's-guy-ness would somehow make him less of a contender.

Other similarities between William and yourself include: (1) faith (you're both lukewarm about Unitarianism because you both like to "have a little God in your religion"); (2) volunteerism (you both have wanted to join the Big Brothers/Big Sisters program for, like, ever); and (3) sports (you both love to sweat and have run marathons). In your mind, you take these semblances of common ground and render them *Important.* You, a sweet young thing from Massachusetts, you like a little *Importance,* and so, in turn, you feel somewhat giddy.

My, my, how things change.

Just a few weeks ago, you woke up on a Friday morning with a hangover. You were going to call in sick to work, until you remembered that you didn't need to: you'd already taken the day off for back-to-back shrink appointments, one with Elaine and one with the psychiatrist who was supposed to monitor how you are doing with your antidepressants. Thursday night, you'd brought Paula a six-pack to send her off to see Fred in London. You were upset and didn't tell her that your period was late and nestled in the bottom of your bag was a very inexpensive home pregnancy test, wrapped in a plastic bag. Of course, at the time, you had been broken up with Jack for a little more than one month; the likelihood of actual conception would have been a horribly, horribly bad stroke of luck. You are just completely mad. You didn't tell Paula all about your shaking hands and fluttering thoughts—she was busy tidying up the apartment—so instead you proceeded to drink five of the six beers. By the time you were escorting Paula down to the front door, you couldn't walk straight.

The following morning your headache said, *Please detox. Please.* (Which was, incidentally, what made you go off the booze and sugar for a while—though, admittedly, the sugar seems the smaller of the issues.) The phone rang; it was your mother who, months too late, was suddenly dying to tell you something about your love life: "Look, I was just thinking and you know, I just need to tell you: never ever date someone who has divorced so young . . . when someone tells you . . ."

It took you a minute to figure out that she meant Jack, who wasn't actually so young when he divorced, and besides that, your mother never even met Jack! You were looking in the mirror and cradling the phone against your shoulder, rubbing your old eye makeup further into your skin. You looked like shit. You sighed heavily into the receiver.

"Mom, that's good advice . . . for you. But *I* don't happen to be so judgmental!"

After judging your mother's judgment, you made an excuse to get off the phone so that you could, now somewhat sober, take a pregnancy test. But you were not pregnant (yay!) and so you ran out the door to bum a cigarette before your appointments. You saw a bulky-looking guy in a green sweater smoking outside the townie bar at the end of your street and asked him for a cigarette, to which you'd gotten a somewhat rote response: "For you? Anything." And you smoked it with him and asked for an embarrassing story as he interrupted you to say that he was writing a book of his own called *Places I Shat Myself.* And you actually thought for a moment, *Shit! No, oh, shit!* Competition is not good. But you didn't dwell on it because his friend chimed in to tell you about getting wasted on his honeymoon ten years earlier and going with his new wife back to their beachfront room to do it (which they did). None of this would have been all that noteworthy if it weren't for the next morning, when he woke up in a fog and meandered to their beachfront balcony, and as his wife started to stir, he pulled the curtain back and she started to yell, "No, Jimmy! No!" because, as it turned out, in opening the curtain, he was unveiling his buck-naked self to the crowd of beachgoers, most of whom had a full view of his erect penis. This image had caused in you an internal, *Eeeeeeewwwwwww.* But, per your usual professional face, you laughed it off and excused yourself, turning down their offers for a noontime beer as you stamped out the cigarette with your boots.

"Actually, I am going to see not just one shrink, but two," you said with a laugh. "A beer might not be the best thing."

Jimmy slapped you on the back. "Yeah, or it would be the best thing ever."

You scurried off to the subway and sat next to a young white woman with blond dreadlocks. You don't remember now why you'd started speaking to her—maybe it was the book she was reading—but soon enough you were asking her for an embarrassing story and you were hearing about the time at a party she'd told a woman that she looked just like Anthony Kiedis from the Red Hot Chili Peppers and how this woman had taken it as an insult, when really your new subway friend had meant it as a compliment because not only did she have a thing for Anthony Kiedis, she also had a thing for his female look-alike. You don't remember what else was said, really. You are sure that you didn't mention your two back-to-back shrink appointments or the fact that you were still completely and utterly heartbroken over a man with whom you were still purporting to have a professional relationship.

Yeah, you are sure you didn't mention this to the woman with the dreads and strong jawline. Yet, for some reason, she told you, a stranger, that there was a book you really needed to read, called *Facing Love Addiction*. Although you weren't paying too much attention, you did scrawl down the title and file it away under "Stuff I Will Probably Never Even Think of Again." With this—a story and a suggestion—you moved along your merry way, first meeting the new shrink—a nice, if nondescript, brown-haired young man with a decent sense of humor—and not arguing when he suggested increasing your dosage of the antidepressant, even though you knew exactly what you needed, which was to start working out again. You returned home that night, tired from all your activity and yet still failing to get to the bottom of things. You picked up the empty, half-torn box for the pregnancy test and stopped to listen to the swoosh noise it made as it fell into your nearly empty garbage can.

* * *

WITH WILLIAM NOW, at dinner, that day is a blur, seemingly having happened so long ago, so far away. Yes, you are tending toward melodrama these days.

William is looking at you, asking questions and challenging your answers. ("What do you mean, that you 'want to write'? Write what?") You like him, and are struck by how down-to-earth he seems, especially in comparison—you should not do this!—to what's-his-name. You feel your chest rising, then falling, and think quietly, *Why do I make everything ten times more complicated than it needs to be?*

Ever since you started this detox, you swear that you are even more sensitive to other people's "vibrations" than normal. As William talks to you about his sister and her family, you are suddenly feeling a sadness, a stillness that you would swear belongs to your date, not exactly an easy (or smart) thing to mention before the main course even arrives. For a fleeting second, William's heaviness feels so familiar it could be your own. This, a sense of melancholy, is not troublesome, though—quite the opposite, actually. The subtle mood drapes over you like a blanket, on your shoulders, exactly where you need a little comfort.

"What about your family?" William asks.

Uh, my family . . . my family . . .

You are not a big fan of talking about those people who gave you life, at least with strangers. Besides, one effect of the antidepressants has been a certain detachment from the past. Aside from random memories—clinging tightly to your grandmother's shoulders as she swam in the ocean; posing for an Easter Sunday photograph with your siblings—do you even remember your childhood? A few years back, when you lived with Annabelle, she had a *Greatest Hits of the Seventies* CD, which included songs like "Dust in the Wind" and "The Long and Winding Road." Your knee-jerk reaction to the album had seemed a little out of left field. ("Jim Croce makes me want to slit my wrists—would you mind not playing that when I'm around?") But on further reflection, you'd supposed that you equated the seventies with your earliest years. You're not sure if it was the decade or your own experiences, but God, could there have been a more depressing time? Anyway, no use dwelling on dark feelings. But because they exist, you don't ever, ever feel genuine saying, "My childhood was great!" Which is exactly what you think you're supposed to say.

You resent the grid of "good" and "bad," the preoccupation you and everyone else seem to have with "doing the right thing" (an inevitable offshoot of polarized thinking). Isn't this the fate of perpetual immaturity? Here we are, a young nation, breeding breeders but forgetting about the space in which to take the time to figure out who the hell we are. If that question were answered, in society as well as in your own heart, then maybe the lid on those early memories wouldn't be so tightly sealed. You'd be free to tell those stories about your mother, the ones in which she is less than perfect. Why do we make anyone, especially mothers, bear the burden of perfection? Not everything is the mother's fault. You hate that you can barely have an honest reaction to your own feelings about your childhood in your own head, never mind in a conversation with some stranger. But if you start talking about the time that, say, when you were eleven, your mother returned from the vet one day with news that she put the family cat to sleep because she had "leukemia," even though there had never been a diagnosis and even though the cat had never exhibited signs of the fatal illness and even though you never got to kiss little Jenny goodbye—if you start trying to talk about what that day was like, some asshole's going to say that you had a crazy (implication being "bad") mother or that you're some whiny, spoiled, glass-is-half-empty kid, while all you're really trying to express is this: as someone who grew up witnessing a good deal of detachment, even the smallest shred of connection you've been able to build—with family, friends, and, yes, even with strangers—has been hard-won. That's all.

Um, yeah, William doesn't need to know all this—at least not if you want him to stick around.

"I love my family."

He nods, throws a piece of calamari into his mouth, and says, "That's good."

William is so rough around the edges.

After more silence, you trail off on how the lack of open discussion around David's developmental disability affected you, as his younger sibling. You never talk about this. Why tonight?

William asks, "What kind of disability?"

Usually, when you don't know how to say it plain, you tell stories. You weave narratives so that you can *demonstrate* all the things that you can't bring yourself to define. Silence with strangers can be unbearable, but this one seems okay. You wait a few minutes—only it doesn't feel like waiting. Candles flicker on every table in the restaurant. Besides the waitstaff, you and William are the youngest in the room.

"Well, there is this one memory . . ." You are seventeen, with long curly hair and an excited grin on your face, as you jump into the driver's seat of your mother's car. You just got your license and your parents are letting you take the car out for the first time. Moments earlier, your mother had said, "Have fun!" as she looked up from reading her book on the sofa. Your father walked down the stairs from where he was looking at photographs, to hold on to the railing and say, "Be safe." David had stood at the top of the other set of stairs, just by the kitchen, and said, "Have a wicked fun time." Always, you felt uncomfortable with witnesses to these moments, even if they were wishing you well. (Or maybe that should read *especially* . . .) And still you bolstered your spirits, looking up toward the star-filled sky before you put the key in the ignition, ready to pull out of this oppressive fog you'd been living under—your mother's moods, your father's quiet frustration—on your way to f-r-e-e-d-o-m, fastening your seat belt and feeling your stomach jump with excitement. You were going to pick up your best girlfriends, and then you looked into the front door to the house, the house you'd wanted to be out of for, like, ever. You saw David standing there in the doorway, behind the screen. The outside light was not on and you remember his silhouette, with one arm raised, set just before the dimmed, yellowish hues of the interior. Despite having received his license a couple years earlier, David was not allowed to take the car out, but you, after holding the damn thing for less than three hours, you were. This was one of those times when the ghosts of past loss would creep into your family's present-day life. Your father had lost his younger sister more than twenty years earlier when she died in a car accident; you assumed that, in not letting him take the car, your parents were protecting your brother. Seeing David in the doorway now was worse than the moment he watched as you left for your first prom. That night, posing for pictures on the front lawn, standing next to your date, you'd smiled your same smile, while inside you were fracturing into smaller and smaller pieces. Were you the only one who noticed David felt left out? He went to special schools, with classes of ten and twelve, where there weren't any proms, at least in the traditional sense, with the big-deal chicken cordon bleu plates or DJs who played an inordinate number of slow songs. And yes, pulling out of the driveway was worse than this. You waved back to David, and paused for a second or two before putting the car into reverse. But they were long seconds, ones that wouldn't go away, no matter how loud you turned up the car radio or how fast you took the curves.

With William, you begin to cry. Okay, maybe the emotion is coming out more like mist than rivers, but even this small amount surprises you. This is a buried memory; usually, when you flip past moments like this, you sniff the mood—somber, depressed—and shake it off faster than you can say, "Ice queen!"

"Sorry," you mumble halfheartedly as you take a sip of your water. But you are not sorry, not really.

"Do you ever write about this?" William's doing that thing again, craning his head forward, with his chin down and eyes that are looking straight in your direction. His eyes are deep brown, and very warm. Your grandmother always bought molasses cookies when you were a child, you are just now remembering. They were too sweet for you, but you ate them anyway. Lots of them.

"Can't. He's my brother."

Somewhere inside a voice rises up: *Yeah, but it's also a piece of my life.*

William is shaking his head now, too, putting down his fork for emphasis. "No, you gotta write about the stuff that actually matters."

Tired, you sit back against your chair. First dates are supposed to be full of pleasantries, polite nodding, the withholding of one's real story to insert one's best portrait of the one she wants to be. They are not supposed to involve tears. Well, not "normal" first dates anyway.

While it's true that you are so not normal, you are beginning to suspect, with the smallest amount of cautious glee, that perhaps William, with his quirky perception and plain and probing questions, isn't exactly normal either.

Before his calamari appetizer is even gone, William raises an index finger and announces, "You know what we're going to have? Chocolate cake."

Chocolate is not part of your detox diet.

"Oh, I—"

"What?" he interrupts, again leaning forward, like he might try to kiss you right then and there. Your chest tightens, even as you feel yourself starting to smile. "You think one bite is going to kill you?"

26

Advice. You are not one for giving advice. Of course, if a friend is in need, you will do your best, but really, deep down, you are not assured that you know anything. And this is not just your philosophy degree talking. This is you on the precipice of thirty, with your fleeting boy crushes and adolescent hopes of a prince's rescue. Are you ever going to understand what it is that your own life is all about, without the prince?

This week, Sarah, your friend, turns twenty-five and is having a party, the theme of which is "Getting Prettier and Smarter with Age." You had scoffed at that claim, calling her to say, "Sarah, we may get prettier—sure. But we do not get smarter. Or at least I haven't." She laughed, in an oh-that's-just-you-being-you kind of way. When you show up at her party early— held at one of those nondescript, dimly lit bars on the Lower East Side—you flirt with the young bartender until the rest of the gang shows up, which makes you say, *All right, I'll take prettier with age . . . fine.* Two hours later, after much revelry, to include binge drinking (yep, the detox is over) and loud laughter, Sarah's roommate approaches you and says, "Hey, I really like that guy over there, and we actually went out last week, but now we're avoiding each other because I never called him back. What would you do?"

"Um, sweetie, I slept with the agent with whom I was supposed to be working, remember? You don't want my advice."

But when you try to go back to drinking your champagne and mindlessly moving your head to the music, she presses you, "Come on . . ."

"Okay, fine, if you need more proof, let's see, I said 'All right' to a marriage proposal that I knew—hell, everybody knew—was a bad idea. Then I cheated on said fiancé with a man who didn't speak English, and for a time thought that I was going to make that one last. Oh! And I once dated a recent widower who turned out to be a heroin addict."

Before you can stop and say, "Yikes!" Sarah's roommate actually puts her hand on your shoulder. "Yes, I know all of that stuff—well, um, actually, not the widower/heroin addict part . . . geez . . . but anyway, the point is, I still want to know what you think. So?"

After a few minutes of looking around the crowded bar at the smaller circles of friends laughing, talking, dancing, you have one thought.

"Well, it could be as simple a question as, 'What would be the best move for your personal growth?' Approaching him . . . or not?"

You leave the party before she approaches him but after she makes the decision to do so. You don't get to see how it goes, but this whole giving-advice thing . . . it does make you think. So often, we walk around giving people the advice that we ourselves need to hear, even in those best-case scenarios where the advice does actually apply to the other person's situation.

Always, we are always our own best teacher. You need to pay more attention, in the right way. You know, one that is fruitful.

This week, you are walking around thinking of advice.

When you see a man on the corner of Fifth Avenue and Forty-first, walking outside in twenty-degree weather with wet hair, presumably coming from his gym on a lunch break, you think:

Didn't your mother ever tell you not to go outside with wet hair?

When you overhear two coworkers gossiping rather loudly about so-and-so's "poor" performance at some meeting, you think:

Didn't your mother ever tell you to mind your own business?

When Jack tells you over the phone that you will have a contract by your thirtieth birthday because *Oh, Shit!* is such a "great" project, yet you haven't found any of his feedback to be of substance, you think:

Didn't your mother ever tell you that actions speak louder than words?

Your mother, in fact, did tell you all of these things. (In fact, "Actions speak louder than words" was a favorite of hers, along with "Water seeks its own level.") But instead of applying this guidance to your own life, you have become *pret-ty* good at applying it to other people's situations, so sure in your knowledge of what other people should and shouldn't be doing.

Sitting in your cubicle one afternoon, you think of going home and making a list of all the things that your mother told you. Maybe that would help right about now. But you get sidetracked when you suddenly have a memory of her from a few years back. David had just had open-heart surgery to correct an arrhythmia. In his hospital room, your mother, Ted, and you were standing in a circle around David's bed, when your father walked in with a cannoli, a single birthday candle planted in the center. It was your mother's birthday and before anyone had the chance to start singing the birthday song, she started jumping up and down, exclaiming with exaggerated, gesticulating hands, "Oh my GOD! Cannoli! MMMMMMMM. I just LOVE French pastry!"

Then, amid everyone cracking up, you remember David's face as he sat back in the hospital bed, vulnerable with an incision down the middle of his chest, one you imagined more readily because of the paper-thin johnny he was wearing. Ever since you can remember, David's laugh makes you laugh, more than anyone else. You crack up when he repeats lines from *Anchorman*, especially in the affected, deep voice of Will Ferrell's Ron Burgundy: "We've been going to this same party for twelve years and in no way is that depressing." When you were kids, you slept in the same room sometimes, as a special treat, and the only two things you recall were your covered-feet pajamas and how David's giggle had you giggling all night long, well past bedtime. But in the hospital room, where he was recovering from an invasive surgery, David covered his mouth with his hand and laughed so hard at the cannoli comment that you started to worry that his stitches might burst.

As you think about this memory and the unruly way in which it has surfaced, despite your adamant efforts to think about advice, you can practically hear the collective laughter— David's, your mother's, your father's, Ted's, your own. The memory of this sound surprises you, but not because you had forgotten it. Turning off your computer, you realize you haven't forgotten. Not at all. You zip up your bag and begin to make your way home.

YOU DREAM OF a little boy. You are walking together through an urban neighborhood with mostly drab, concrete three- and four-story buildings, but the blue sky above is all you want to see, all that you do see. Tall stalks of grass are pushing up through the cracks in the sidewalk and you dance through the litter. Your legs are the means to twirl, twirl, twirl. The little boy carries a backpack and is going somewhere. You arrive at a hotel, an airy space with ceiling fans and bamboo furniture. Plants move gently back and forth, with the rhythm of the whirring fans. You step up to the bar and order a cappuccino. You hear the bartender talk about selling the boy to "kind parents," although the bartender will profit, somehow, from this transaction. Wait, this bartender—you know him. He is Johnny C., with whom you worked at the music club years ago. Despite how different the two of you looked—you were gypsy girl to his trailer-man chic—you two were simpatico behind the bar, until that one night everyone on staff, except for you, decided to partake in cocaine in the downstairs office and the next morning you heard the story of Johnny C. (otherwise known in his inner circle as "Booby") flipping out and leaving his wife of three months to run off with their change jar down the street, in the middle of the night, to meet up with his secret seventeen-year-old Brazilian lover whom he met at the pizza shop next door to the club. They hopped a Greyhound to Alabama, and that was definitely the end of some era. Yeah, that news kinda freaked you out. So, in your dream, it is Johnny C. who will be selling off your new friend, the little boy. Weird. When you see the little boy next, you lean down and whisper that the bartender doesn't really care about him. "Run away," you tell the little boy. "I know you need parents, but you'll be better off finding them yourself . . . I promise you." You have never seemed more certain of anything in your life. "Please leave, kid—just leave." When he runs, you are relieved.

WHEN YOU RELAY this dream to Elaine one wintry afternoon, you finish by saying, "Yeah, and my dreams are usually pretty literal, but this one . . . I just can't imagine what this would be about."

Elaine gives you one of those looks, peering at you through her glasses and wrinkling up her face in disbelief, as if to say, "Um, you're full of shit."

"What?" you say to Elaine, looking at her in that "Who, moi?" kind of way. You. Surely she does not require that you implicate yourself here, in the therapist's office. Your tone is part Valley Girl, part defiant teenager.

You sit there raising both eyebrows and you try very hard to resist the urge to look at your well-shaped fingernails. Often Elaine jumps in with her own words of advice or anecdotes clearly designed to direct you, but this time she meets your defensive gaze and raises you one.

"What do you think?" she asks.

Of course, the main thing on your mind as of late is *Oh, Shit!*—big surprise—and how not only does it not seem to be developing into anything you're actually interested in, but being "involved" with Jack, even at this half-ass level, well, that doesn't seem to be working out for you, either. After New Year's, you called him and announced that you were resolved to making the professional relationship work. When his response was, of course, warm and polite, you just felt stupid. But since then, Jack isn't making much of an effort and you are back to your old habit of taking it personally and cussing him out, at least in your head. If you could get there—to writing about something that actually matters to you instead of holding on to this pipe dream that you are banking will wrest you free from your current monotonous, full-time employment—you are pretty sure that you wouldn't want to work with Jack anyway. So what on earth are you doing?

At the end of your session, you pick up your things and wave a halfhearted goodbye to Elaine; she nods at you with her trademark mix of sympathy and tough love.

"You can do it," you hear her say as you trail out through the beige waiting room, with its pictures of seashells and sand and stacks of *New Yorkers.*

Before you make it to the ground floor, even with Frank's incessant chatting, you remember the line from Mary Oliver's poem that you love, and once sent to your family. The words float through your head, as you and your bags spill out onto the Upper West Side tree-lined street. The temperature is cold, but you find your imagination leaping, as if to a space beyond this city, beyond this year you've come to characterize as "shitty."

One day you knew what you had to do and so you began . . .

THERE IS NO more waiting.

This will be easy, you think. *Jack obviously wants out of this just as much as I do.*

It is the day after your appointment with Elaine, and you are at work, assured. You sit in front of the same old monitor where all the trouble—and magic—had begun.

Banking on the fact that Jack will get back to you sooner if he knows he'll soon be free of you, you send a short email, explaining that you think it would be better for you to work with someone else. Promptly, Jack replies that he will call you in an hour.

"Hey," he says, sounding as upbeat as ever. "How are you?"

"Good," you say, curt. "So, you got my email . . ."

You don't want to say any more than you have already said. You have been thickheaded in this relationship—professional and otherwise—imagining that if you clarify your thoughts and feelings more, you can make him love you again. None of this is even about the book, probably never was. Oh, well. You gave it a respectable amount of time, yet nothing has changed. You worry that this will be difficult, but Jack's response confirms what you hadn't wanted to believe in the first place: that he is relieved to be rid of you, too.

"Of course, I understand. Listen, I would be glad to help you find other agents."

Despite your resolve to maintain a cool distance throughout this conversation, you are, for a brief moment, touched. He doesn't have to help you find someone else. You both know this. Maybe he feels guilty. Or maybe he really is just being nice.

"Have you started looking?" he asks, his voice raising a hair.

"Uh, yeah, actually. I have a couple names—one at this bigger agency . . ."

"Well, you need to be careful," he says, immediately going into that big brother mode that drove you nuts. "You don't want to end up with some total nightmare."

What do you think this relationship has been? Jesus, Jack.

You are looking down at the exact same computer screen that you had once checked obsessively for his moment-to-moment emails.

In the interest of making a clean break, you keep your mouth shut, listening to him prattle on, saying lots of nice things you know he doesn't have to say. Unfortunately, even if he did mean them, his words have lost all meaning to you now. Ever since the romantic breakup, all your walls are up, which sometimes makes you, uh, difficult.

"This is a really great project . . ." Jack says.

You start to cry, softly, so that he doesn't hear. *If this is such a great project,* you think, *then why did you give it zero attention?* But it's not just this so-called "encouragement" and its failure to add sincerity to this final conversation. It's you that's making you cry—the hours of frustration that you have wasted over this man, wanting to believe his slick promises and flowery words, even though his actions told you differently—every single time. *How stupid am I?* You feel like you just ran a marathon but through some cruel chemical mix-up don't have even the slightest bit of a runner's high. You have blisters and cramps and breathlessness. You have the desire to close your eyes and go to sleep until you wake up in a less messy life. There was a time you would have imagined Jack as he spoke to you, his eyes you once found so intoxicating. But now you don't care where he is. You do, however, know exactly where you are: hunched over your desk in this god-awful light, holding your entire midsection tight, in a feeble effort to keep it together.

After a few minutes of listening to him suggest some "back-and-forth," where you will presumably send him a list of agents and then he will . . . (well, you are not exactly sure what he will do with this information) you know you have to get the hell off the phone.

"Sure, fine, that's nice of you," you say. But since your dynamic has continued to be you moving toward him, him moving away, the thought of more "back-and-forth" sounds just plain grim. You resist all urges—and boy, are they strong—to say, "Back-and-forth? Oh, because that's worked so well for me so far?" You are in a very hateful place, you realize, as you hang up the phone.

In a flash, you want to just let yourself go, scream at the top of your lungs, rip the phone out of the wall, throw your computer out the window, watch as it falls to pieces, landing eighteen stories below in a scattered, delicate mess of permanently broken hardware that would look something like art if it weren't so utterly destroyed.

Alas, you are at work, young one. Having a breakdown is a no-no in the office. You have never been adept at seamless social grace, but still, you know that having a psycho temper tantrum isn't really an option.

But crying's okay. You rush toward the bathroom, inhaling the moments you spend holding back your tears, gasping almost, with the paradoxical hope that if you take in enough restraint at this moment, you will never again repress yourself.

That night, you go home and celebrate—uh, "fake it till you make it," anyone?—with a lavender-scented bubble bath, richly fragrant candles, and a fluffy beauty magazine that tells you about the perils of too much soy and which kind of bronzer will look most natural on fair skin.

Yep, that's exactly the kind of stuff you need to be thinking about. After your bath, you lie down in the room that Jack helped move you into, and after all this, finally, finally you breathe in relief.

Your good ol' gardenia candle flickers on your nightstand, and you leave your moody music conspicuously turned off. There is silence in your room, and darkness. For the first time in months, you would not call the mood "dark," though. You would say "still."

Thank God he's out of my life. You think this over and over, looking out into the night, tonight barely seeing the silhouette of the fake owl. *Thank God, thank God, thank God.*

27

PLUCK—SUCH A STRANGE concept. "Pluck," as in sassy, witty, never staying for too long in a pause, but always knowing that one needs to stay for at least long "enough." Bite, perfect timing, sense of rhythm, mood, and impeccable footwork. Self-assurance, perceived self-assurance, playfulness in a world where "pretend" does not exist. Pluck, as in lean down and yank that earthy flower from its homey stalk, because that is exactly what you want. Hold the blossom—is nothing more beautiful than this?—hold it close, still, until you are dizzy with the senses and realize, have to realize, that neither you nor anyone else really, truly owns anything.

Whew. You love Saturdays, especially Saturdays like this. You are free! The winter air softens, and you have more than one moment of imagining that your spring might begin as soon as tomorrow. Later, you will have a fourth date with William, whom you are really beginning to like, much to your surprise.

Last week, you went to see him on a Saturday afternoon. The plan was to have lunch, but he needed to drop off his laundry first. As tall William carried an overflowing bag of dirty clothes, he started to complain that, no matter how hard he tried, he couldn't seem to make friends with the lady who worked the counter at the Laundromat. As someone who can and does talk to everyone—waitresses, the guy begging for change outside the deli, the cashier at the grocery store—William just wouldn't accept that he couldn't break this lady's hard shell: "I mean, she acts like she's doing me the biggest favor."

"Are your clothes clean?" you asked, skipping to keep up with his stride.

"Yeah, they're great. The best in my neighborhood."

"So . . . maybe she is doing you a favor."

Inside, there was a man, short and slightly overweight, already at the counter. Shuffling from the counter to the scale, he mumbled unintelligibly. Standing beside you at the door, William gave you a look. The woman behind the counter, who was Korean and presumably in her fifties, said nothing. Her eyes simply moved back and forth, back and forth, following the man as he continued to pace.

When the man stopped at the counter, William looked over the shoulder of the man to see the name on his laundry slip. After the man finally left, William walked up to the counter, put down his bag of laundry, gestured toward the door, and said in a knowing voice, "Ahhhhh, Mis-ter B."

The woman's head snapped to attention. Looking William directly in the eye, she said nothing for a moment. Then a smile crept across her face. Drawing her breath in, she said, a new lilt in her voice, "You know Mr. B.?"

With this, William claimed victory. In the days following, you were getting used to him interrupting silence with what he considered to be the détente of all détentes: "You know Mr. B.?"

In addition to this new relationship, you are still writing *Oh, Shit!* but are free from the strangulation effect you felt "working" with Jack. Instead of reflecting on why you'd even been trying to write from that meek little place, you force yourself to think, *Jack who?*

Last night, Paula made a root vegetable stew with homemade corn bread. "Is this okay?" she asked timidly, using her long, skinny arms to wield a huge, piping-hot pan of stew, placing it on the table. As you ate at her small dining room table for three, you emphatically agreed that it was more than okay in your request for seconds. Your life, it seems, is turning around.

Before diving into your morning writing, you walk down to the coffee shop at the end of the street. Along the way, you pull out one of your own cigarettes, from a pack you actually bought. This week, you lost the battle. If you don't buy them, you aren't really a smoker. This sort of faulty logic can bite you in the ass both ways. You sit outside of the coffee shop when you notice a cluster of cyclists sitting inside. This is not unusual for a Saturday at your regular coffee shop—athletes enjoying a post-workout bran muffin. They are slim, all of them.

After stamping out your unhealthy morning cigarette (as opposed to that über-healthy afternoon cigarette you enjoy), you order a coffee and turn to watch the group. Men, skinny men, with pointy features. Your flash assessment says, *Nah, I'm not going to get anything out of these guys. But then again, what the hell?*

You are feeling just cowboy enough to mosey on over to their table and ask that question you just can't help but ask. You, in your sweatpants with an eau de nicotine emanating from your breath, you stop in front of the guy with his legs out-stretched, and you raise one hand. "Excuse me, I'm wondering if you all have any embarrassing stories to share?"

The three men look at you, each from behind the cover of their loud visors.

One man, with a veiny neck and pointy nose, says, "Excuse me?"

You quickly explain the project, as you have so many times before. After another pause, one of the men looks up and asks, "What are you going to give me? Do we get paid for this?"

Considering your rent, slow recovery from being booted from the shelter of kindly graduate school loans, and a pricey facialist that you have just moved into the "necessary expenditure" column of your budget, you answer, "Sorry—I can't pay anyone at this point. There's no deal, but I can offer you one of my stories . . ."

He waves that off and says, "Oh, I'm a photographer and people are always asking me if they're going to get paid if I take a picture of them. It's just fun to be on the other side."

But you don't buy that, not for one second. "Well, in addition to being able to tell you one of my own—'cause I have a lot—I can also bet that whatever story you tell me, I'll have a similar one."

The cyclists spend a few minutes looking back and forth at one another, and only occasionally in your direction. After a few minutes of further cajoling, the long-nosed man speaks up. "I have one . . . but it didn't happen to me."

His story—or the story of his "friend"—involves picking up a pretty girl at a bar one night, which would have been a completely normal scenario had this "friend" not had a girlfriend.

But the city's a big place, he reasoned. Plus, the regular girl-friend rarely went out on Friday nights and he had no worries about getting caught. He and the pretty girl were chatting each other up at the bar, presumably just letting enough minutes and beers pile up before one made the want-to-go-back-to-my-place? move. She was the one to extend the invitation and within moments the two were walking arm in arm out of the bar, beginning the trek back to her place, where he would most certainly get "lucky." As they inched closer to her place, he realized that this was the very neighborhood in which his girl-friend resided.

Huh, he thought, *what are the odds that they would live in the same neighborhood?* But the more she kissed his neck as they walked, the less he cared about whether or not this one-night stand lived in the same locale as his regular girlfriend.

Moments later, his rational thinking clouded by the promise of imminent sex, he looked up to see that they were, in fact, standing outside of his girlfriend's apartment building. And the one-night stand was reaching for her keys. She lived there, too.

In a moment of paralysis, he thought, *What do I do?* But not wanting to screw up the screw, he said nothing and silently prayed for a quick trip to her bedroom, where they could close the door, turn the lock, and get it on as planned. As they climbed the staircase in the four-story building, they were approaching his girlfriend's apartment, which was on the second floor. For a minute he thought if he held his breath and tiptoed, everything would be okay. Just as he tip-toed past, the door opened: his girlfriend's roommate was going out.

"Hey!" she said to both the other girl and the—what do we call him here?—oh, the louse. "You're here to see Becky, right?"

Before he knew what was happening, he was standing in the living room of his girlfriend, who was wearing wrinkled flannel pajamas, right next to the girl with whom he was attempting to cheat with. He should have just run, he thought as he cursed himself and his molasseslike instincts. As Becky looked at him, incredulous, the pretty-girl-from-the-bar-turned-girlfriend's-neighbor said, "Okay, well, we should be going—you ready?" turning to look in his direction.

What could he do? He waved goodbye to his girlfriend—for the moment, as well as forever—and moved toward his girlfriend's neighbor's apartment. Adding to fortune's cruelty, his girlfriend's bedroom was directly below the neighbor's bedroom. Although he did enjoy himself that night, he tried his best to tone down his usual enthusiastic sounds, nobly attempting to downplay any obvious indicators of sexual gratification. There was such a thing as being a gentleman, after all. He wanted to leave his girlfriend with room to delude herself: maybe they were just knitting partners after all.

When the cyclist finishes this story, you stand there with the group—all of you shaking your heads, as sunlight screams through the window. There is a moment, a collective moment, when everyone pauses. What to think? Pity for the poor guy who couldn't think quicker on his feet? Or empathic horror for the girlfriend? Once it is clarified that the girlfriend broke up with him—you mean, right?—there is silence. You are relieved for her, sorry for him.

The cyclist with the pointy nose looks in your direction. Grinning, he asks, "Well, do you have an embarrassing story like that?"

"Absolutely not." You are still shaking your head. "And I thought I had the topic covered!"

The photographer winks at you.

"Thank you"—trying to find a graceful exit after his messy story, you place one foot toward the door and put on your best I'll-be-going-now voice—"for giving me a good, solid objective this week—maybe I, too, will be unlucky enough to be embarrassed by way of proximity in dating."

They laugh and you think that you are such a geek . . . "embarrassment by way of proximity in dating"? That phrasing is embarrassing all by its lonesome.

You walk back toward your brownstone, lighting up another cigarette for good measure as you sip your coffee. When you think of the cyclist's friend and his very, very bad luck, you shake your head. *Glad that wasn't* me.

But girl, you were born on Friday the thirteenth. Your superstitious self forgets to knock on wood, throw a pinch of salt over your shoulder, and say "Rabbit" a zillion times when you pass the cemetery. (Like all those dead people care . . .) Instead, you work your way home, because it's Saturday and that's just what you do.

AFTER WRITING FOR a few hours and then walking through the park, you go home to get ready before meeting William at his apartment, which is in Manhattan. Every time you see him, you are more surprised by how much you enjoy his company, how you feel so at ease, how you love to hear him laugh his free-wheelin' laugh.

Tonight, rain settles into the neighborhood. When William comes to meet you at the door, he waves a half-silly, excited hello through the door. Once, you'd run into him on the street near where he works. Before he knew you were there, you watched his face, brightening as his gaze skipped over storefronts, babies in strollers, people walking their dogs. He had a wide-eyed way of walking through the world, one that you very much admire. You have not sensed much pretense with this man, and you, one who has never been very good at just dipping her toes in the water, you feel your own face lighting up in a very similar way.

"Hi, sweetie!" he yells through the glass. "I just have to put on my shoes. You want to come in?"

You walk into his apartment, which is located in a regal brownstone. It is a large studio, with a small kitchen off to the side of the main room and a back deck. The ceilings are high, the walls nearly empty.

"Now, should we bring one umbrella or two?"

As you start to answer, "One!" he cuts you off.

"I know, I was thinking that, too. More romantic, right?"

And so you two are walking arm in arm through the rain under one umbrella, as William describes his latest court case. Apparently, a known neighborhood criminal claimed that due process was violated when two police officers demanded to search his bag. Despite the fact that they did find a weapon—a machete, no less—William is explaining to you why the police were in the wrong.

You nuzzle into his side. You like his large frame and especially how your head fits perfectly into the space below his shoulder—an area less gracefully termed "armpit." You jump over corner puddles, but always end up curling back into his side. Eventually, you arrive at a gourmet pizza restaurant. A small current of unease sets in once you are inside the West Village eatery. Jack lives somewhere in this vicinity, but you do not know exactly where, because you broke up just before he moved in. Vaguely, you recall him telling you he was not too far from the Spotted Pig on Greenwich—now, was it Greenwich Avenue or Greenwich Street? You hope, with every inch of your flip-flopping stomach, that you don't run into him, not now, not ever.

You and William share a corner space at the bar and order thin-crust pizza with a side of fried meatballs. He orders a glass of red wine and you order a cranberry with soda. When you tease him, he shoves you playfully, only his 184 pounds have a dramatic effect on your smaller frame and you almost fall off the barstool. Inexplicably, this becomes your favorite moment of the night. Yes, *Teen Beat* you is still keeping score.

On the way home, you stop at the corner deli and pick up some microwave popcorn, plus other sundries. You stand in his kitchen, aware of these different lives you sometimes step into. You like to cite choice, but after your year, if you know anything, it is that you are in control of nothing, absolutely nothing. As William unpacks the groceries, you look out the glass kitchen door. Across the way, you see an apartment building with several of the rear units lit up. That's one thing you love about New York, peering into small glimpses of the ways that other people live. You notice plants, who's watching what on TV, and even giggle when you spy some good impromptu dancing. Life is beautiful—all of it, the ups, the downs, all these lives being lived simultaneously, each with our own set of dramas and ordinariness. You can feel the fog is lifting, and it is not because William is in your life. It is because you made a choice, a small, stupidly long-overdue choice to dump Jack as your "agent." It's your first step toward embracing what is really in front of you and you are sitting there, taking in this view. You would almost say that you are happy, if that word didn't scare the shit out of you.

The apartment building directly behind William's is a black-on-black-looking canvas with rectangular windows lit up in erratic patterns—one on the top floor, diagonally connected to another on the second floor. You used to look into other people's windows like these and imagine what was inside: plants that have been tended to for years, worn bookshelves, the scent of garlic breezing through the apartment. You used to think that this kind of stability was going to be perpetually out of your reach. You will not, cannot claim that you will ever feel truly grounded again, but in this quiet moment, scanning these other apartments all by your lonesome, you are inspired to breathe deep.

But then something catches your eye. Across the way, in the apartment directly across from William's, you see that the lights are on. You see a young man with longish brown hair sitting at his computer—wearing that unmistakable worn blue T-shirt. And a nose that . . . that . . . probably used to be much larger. When your eyes fix closer on his face, you feel yourself inhale sharply.

Jack?

Jack!

Jack.

As you squint closer, wanting to make sure whether or not it is indeed your ex-boyfriend, ex-everything sitting there across the way—hadn't you just declared, with your volume on high, that he was out of your life forever, like, last week?—you feel a little dizzy. Faintly, you hear William's voice in the background, as he tells you about how much he loves this neighborhood. But you are glued to this particular set of lit-up windows. Slowly, you notice Jack's head starting to turn in your direction, as if he senses someone staring at him through his kitchen window.

Oh, my God! If he saw me, how much of a stalker would I feel like?

As his head turns toward William's window, you do the only thing that seems to make any sense: you hit the deck.

"Uh, what are you doing?" William asks, when he sees you suddenly crouching down by his back door.

"Nothing, nothing," you say. "Just keeping you company."

Meanwhile, you are crawling on the floor to the living room, where you yank the blinds down immediately. You are not about to tell William, not in this moment when your heart is beating so fast. You could throw up.

What are the odds? In a city of 8.5 million people—what are the freaking odds? Your mind reels further as you remember what William and you had done on the couch before going out, right in front of his living room windows, windows that you now know look directly into Jack's apartment.

Oh, lord.

As you crawl on your hands and knees into the living room, where you yank the blinds shut with one fierce pull, your mind skips through, over, beyond thoughts that are fast, fleeting:

Maybe it's not him.

Am I losing my mind?

What on earth is this universe trying to tell me?

"Honey," William calls from the kitchen, "what are you doing?"

ONE WEEK LATER, you will tell William over Mexican, between chips dipped in salsa and guacamole. You won't mention the cyclist and his dating-plus-proximity-equals-embarrassment story. When your mouth isn't full, you will give William the bare facts about you and Jack: worked together, dated, broke up love-wise, broke up work-wise, and the truth that none of this has been very easy for you.

"No way!" William will say, incredulous, throwing his head back in laughter while you sit there feeling like a schmuck. You don't find the situation funny. Not like William does.

"Yes . . . way."

"Who broke up with who?"

"Uh . . . hard to say."

"Well, I mean, in a court of law, who would have been responsible?"

Rolling your eyes, you will dip another chip and say, "You are such a lawyer, you know that, William?"

BUT NOW, IN your initial shock, you sit there, alone with the knowledge of this very bizarre, unbelievable coincidence. But wait, is this a mere coincidence, or is there something to be learned?

Well, of course there is. You are too impatient, though, to wait for this lesson to come to you, quiet and still, months down the road when you are in some cool grocery store examining organic eggplants in the produce aisle. Impatient, you stretch one guess over everything, for the sake of convenience and rationalization:

This must just be a reminder.

If there is a part of you that still pines for Jack—and you know that there is—this must just be a very literal reminder: how you feel here, with William, your joy in the mundane, is at least an improvement over how you felt with Jack, all caught up in the mire of fantasy, inhaling the smoke and smiling way too long into the mirrors that you'd really, really hoped would be real. But just weren't.

That's really what this "coincidence" is about, you tell yourself, one too many times for it to be actually true.

28

YOU HAVE NEVER been one to believe that "all good things come to an end." However, it is irrefutable that certain periods come to a close. Hey, just look at your karaoke life, for example. When you started out, you sang Donna Summers's "On the Radio" every chance you got. At a rehearsal dinner for your friend's wedding, you'd taken the mike and awkwardly belted out your favorite music from childhood. And, well, really, it was still your favorite music then. You hadn't had as many beers as you normally would have before karaoke and so all you had was your desire to sing butting heads with your fear of being seen—each influence holding equal power. You wanted to close your eyes, but didn't, because you were afraid that someone might think you were taking yourself too seriously. You wanted to laugh because you found this whole scenario— you, as microphone hog—very amusing. But you didn't laugh, either, not really. Instead, you watched as Ted stood there, closest to the stage, whispering loudly, "Dance, dance!" And you'd been a little distracted by this, first thinking, *He just wants me to dance because he thinks I can't sing.* But then, when you saw the energy in his body, reaching out for you, you realized,

He's here. Teddy's right here. Just one year after that wedding, though, Teddy was no longer there. You broke up and were all alone (as in, single) at karaoke bars, belting out angry Pat Benatar. Who cares if that microphone happened to slip out of your hands when you were twirling the cord around in a circle and simultaneously whipping your head back and forth? Oh, the karaoke list goes on. Just like you don't need to sing Donna Summer every time you set foot in a karaoke bar, you no longer need the story of how you got from where you were to where you are. Right?

Well, not exactly, sister. Whether you "need" it or not, you still cling. You eke out comfort in William's world—and have done so for several weeks now—until one day he just stops calling you.

The timing is strange. You and he had a wonderful Friday night date, during which he prepared you a hearty eggplant parmesan meal for your thirtieth birthday, and even presented you with the red velvet cake that you had requested. He sent you birthday wishes, kissed you, held you, and when you started to think, *Maybe this is actually going somewhere . . .* he gave you a book, with an inscription: "Happy Birthday, Sweets—it's been fun so far . . ."

"So far!" you squealed. "Is there something you need to tell me?" You were laughing, teasing, smiling, when you noticed his normally placid expression take pause. His cheeks went flat.

William has such honest eyes. When their gaze dropped, you wanted to take your comment back. You were just trying to be funny. He teases you all the time.

"Baby?" you said timidly.

By the time William lifted his head, his expression was neutral.

"It's, uh, one of my favorite books."

LATER, WHEN YOU were lying in bed with him, something unsettled you. You just couldn't articulate the uneasiness, more than something's not right. You felt yourself leaning into his body, the way you were leaning into his life.

Why do you think you need a man? You mean, on paper you would never admit to this, but facts are facts. You've essentially jumped from one man to the next to the next. You're not as independent as you keep claiming you are. Wouldn't it just be smarter to stay single, like you keep saying you will, until you figure a few things out?

The next morning, you crawled out of bed and kissed him goodbye.

"Thanks for staying over, baby," he said, still sleepy.

"Call you from the road, William."

You were driving up to Boston to celebrate your birthday with your family when you realized that you'd left your phone at home. You couldn't call him.

By the time you returned back to New York, you had things you wanted to say to William. You wanted to tell him about how you'd brought a carrot cake into the dining room at your grandmother's retirement home, knowing that her very recent bypass would have left her without means for getting you a cake. (Even though she's eighty-eight, she's still on top of these details and was embarrassed when she had to hand you a blank card with a pretty watercolor on the front, chagrined that it wasn't a legitimate birthday card. On the envelope, she'd written, "Please excuse card!") "Here, I thought we'd celebrate my birthday with this," you said as you placed the cake on the center of the table, winking at your grandmother.

When you got home, you found a text message from him on your cell: "Miss you so much, baby."

You noticed that the time on the text message was 4:38 on Sunday morning.

That's odd, you thought. You remembered William saying that he had some friends coming into town on Saturday night, but that he was probably going to stay home because these friends could be "trouble." You assumed that this meant they were party people, probably of the extreme variety. For William, whom you'd never seen have more than two drinks in one night, staying out that late seemed kind of suspect. Then again, you didn't know anything more than this message that he missed you, which made your heart skip— because you missed him, too. So you called him. No answer, no return call.

LATER THAT NIGHT, Serdar approached you as you were making a cup of tea in the kitchen.

"Hey, I need to talk to you about something," he said. The space of the kitchen is so confined that conversations seem more intimate, more grave. Even when Sophie told you about her recipe for roasted eggplant, it felt extra special, in this cozy little corner of your apartment.

"Yeah, what's up?" You were stirring lemon and honey into your mug of ginger tea. This is so comfortable, this place. Even

though you have maintained a certain distance from the roommates, you find it to be perfect.

"We are moving."

You looked at him, confused. What did you miss? Serdar
holds the lease here, a lease he has until the end of May, which
is three months away. When you'd moved in, you were aware
of this, but the way Serdar had presented the situation led you
to believe that they would renew the lease and that you could
stay there.

"Me and Nisa," he added. "It's really bad with the other two.
I am very sorry to tell you this."

He looked so concerned, sitting there with one palm flat-
tened on the countertop.

"What? What do you mean, 'bad'?"

"Oh, I thought you knew. I don't want to go into details, but
it's getting nasty."

Had your four roommates been fighting this whole time,
right under your nose? All this time, you were so happy that you
didn't understand Turkish—when they spoke to one another, it
sounded like white noise to you, which was, you thought, perfect. You could write for hours without ever being distracted by
their conversations. Come to think of it, though, the language
did strike you at times as sounding a little harsher than you'd
remembered from your travels.

With Serdar standing before you, looking truly regretful,
you realized that your reliance on ignorance had seriously
backfired.

"So . . ."

"So I am interviewing people to take over our room and the
office. That way your rent won't go up."

Two new roommates didn't sound promising.

"All right, I'm sorry you've had such a hard time . . ."

"Yes, and also, it seems like now they are moving too."

"What?"

"Yes, we got this place on the Upper East Side, signed the lease, and so we have to go, and now they decide to go, too. I am so sorry. We didn't know they planned on leaving and now we have this other lease . . ."

"You mean to tell me that I am getting four new roommates?"

"Yes, I am so sorry. I feel very badly for you."

"And when will all this take place?" you asked, knowing that the end of the month was in five days.

"Well, soon, I think. They leave tomorrow and we leave in a few days, too."

"Okay."

"Are you okay?" he asked, looking worried, his gaze trying to meet yours, even though you were by now looking out toward the window. You didn't answer him—the truth being both obvious and irrelevant.

Walking back to your room, you thought, *Maybe it's time for me to move on.* But you didn't even know how you would begin.

THIS IS WHERE you are now, only your articulation of beginning again is muddled, probably by all that cigarette smoke you've been inhaling. You are a true smoker now, and it makes you feel kind of good, taking these moments for you in the midst of all this bleeding urban sprawl. But "good" is a relative term.

Sometimes you have a distinct sense that you are ever so slowly wading through the midst of a crime. Its location? Your life.

That night, just as you are settling into sleep, exhausted from a long day at work, your phone rings. It's Annabelle.

"Hi," you say.

"Hi," she says back. "How are you?"

"Exhausted. I just got in. I need to go to bed. I just found out that my roommates are moving in, like, five days and so there will be a whole new crew in here, and now I really, really want to wake up at four tomorrow to write because that's at least something that will make me feel better. What's up?"

"Well," she says, sighing. "I need to talk to you. There's something wrong."

"Okay," you say, sighing yourself. You and Annabelle are in a phase of disconnection and you don't really feel like making time for a "talk" with her right now. It's not your priority.

"Look, something's not right between us."

You agree with her. Annabelle had visited you last month, and things were strained, to say the least. You were on the detox and attributed a lot of the awkwardness to that, because one of your favorite pastimes as sisters was opening a bottle of red wine and talking until the cows came home, or whatever that saying is. You made plans to visit with two of her friends, but after both visits you could tell she was disappointed, like she'd had a hard time connecting with them. You'd thought that this was what the tension was about, but when Annabelle left abruptly the next morning, you called her a few times to see if she was okay. She hadn't seemed to be. But finally, when she did call you back, that was when she told you that something was wrong but that she didn't want to talk about it, not yet. From her voice, from the heaviness, you heard her blaming you. It wasn't a matter of "something's not right, so let's talk about it." It was "something's not right and I'm mad at you for it." When you were at her friend Kay's house, Kay had said to you, "Well, look at your cute little ass." And Annabelle had said, with more than a hint of hostility, "What ass? There's nothing there." Of course, you didn't say a word and instead listened with hearty resentment as she went on to talk about a research study that found a correlation between cigarette smoking and grief. Were you supposed to then chime in and say, "Funny you should mention it—I'm overcome with grief these days," and then start talking about . . . about . . . Oh, right. There is the problem. Annabelle or no Annabelle, can you even face the source of your grief?

Annabelle says, "You are really different."

Uh . . .

"You're abrasive and, I don't know, maybe it's because you live in New York now?"

You bite your lip hard.

You are sometimes abrasive, yes, but hardly ever with Annabelle. In fact, if anything, you think you are too polite with her. Well, except for that time recently, when you told her about Jack and William's shared backyard and you were contemplating whether or not you were going to call Jack, to make an impossibly weird situation less so—or would it be more so? Ugh. It just sucked. You were still trying to figure things out when Annabelle said, "Why do you feel like you have to take care of his feelings?"

Your chest had welled with frustration. You resented being spoken to like one of her social work clients, and so you abruptly barked, "That's not what I'm saying!"

Now you bring that time up. Is that what she means by "abrasive"? The frustration is welling inside you again. You are not the little sister anymore, not in the way that you need her to tell you what to do or how to manage your reactions to situations. Just because you got upset doesn't mean that you don't love her. *She knows that, right?* you wonder.

But before you can go further into this topic of your sisterly dynamic, she continues, "And"—deep breath here—"I think you have an eating disorder."

"What?" She's not the first person to comment on your weight in recent weeks. In fact, lots of people have been making more mild statements. For example, when you called Paula one recent night, on the way home from Blue Ribbon after pigging out on ribs and fried chicken, she said, "Well, I think it's good that you ate so much." When you were a little confused by her comment, she'd clarified, "You just look . . . well, you're looking like you need to eat more these days."

Even though Annabelle knows that you heard her just fine, she elaborates, "You are so thin. You get smaller every time I see you. And you're smoking so much. You haven't smoked this much since you broke up with René. Something's wrong."

Why is she bringing that guy up? That was, like, years ago.

Annabelle starts to cry on the other end of the line.

"I'm just so worried. You're shrinking, and if anything were to ever happen to you . . ."

You could cry, if you didn't suddenly feel like you had to take care of her feelings. Why can't she just talk to you like a normal human being? Why is it, in this conversation in which she is so allegedly concerned about you, do you feel like you're not even a part of the equation? You are pissed. She can't do this. *We haven't had a day-to-day relationship lately, and if we did, this conversation would look different.* Somehow, you can't help but feel like she's blaming your weight on all of the other issues between you.

There is a part of you that likes having lost all this weight. Save for those two weeks when you were still with Jack, you've been eating, just not as much as normal. But your baseline for normal seems to have shifted a long time ago. Yes, it's somewhat less than it used to be, but that's in part because you used to overeat. Long gone are the days of you and Ted settling into his bed for your nightly ritual of devouring a pint of Ben & Jerry's while watching late-night dating shows on Fox. You are different, and so is your body. You see the reasons you lost weight as: (a) you lost your boxing muscle; (b) you take a higher dosage of antidepressants and this particular one makes you lose weight; (c) you moved from the Bronx, where you drove everywhere, to Brooklyn, where you walk everywhere, including for as much as an hour after work every night; and . . . the most shameful reason ever . . . (d) you smoke like a chimney.

THE LIST IS valid, but there is another piece of the puzzle, one that you don't exactly have control over. Something inside is literally eating you up—the stress that has become your powerful second skin—only you are not in a place where you can even begin to guess what that is.

"I have to go, Annabelle."

You hear her sigh, heavily. She is reaching out, and flailing. Finally, she says, "All right . . . I—just know that I am here for you. Please."

You barely hear her as you click the phone shut. The truth is you don't want her to be there for you. You were struggling before, but now, with all this concern that feels more like blame, you just feel lonely, isolated. Sometimes you wish that you and Annabelle—or you and anyone—could have loud, expressed conflict. Instead, you are always so reserved, so careful not to say the wrong thing. Wouldn't want anyone to think you're not nice. And nice people don't say, "Leave me the fuck alone!"

So you dial Dan. As the phone rings, you turn on your bedroom light and put on your socks and sneakers, cradling the phone to your chin.

"Hey, how's my girlfriend doing?" he says.

"Not great. You have a sec?"

"What's up?"

"Annabelle just called me to say, 'Something's not right between us. You're abrasive and I think you have an eating disorder.' "

You are walking down the stairs, buttoning your winter coat and listening to Dan as he says, "What? You're kidding me."

You chose Dan because you believe he is one of the only people who understands you. Annabelle's right. You have become way too fucking skinny. But even though you know this, you don't seem to be able to let yourself see it as a real issue. So you pull out your pack of cigarettes.

"Jesus Christ, Dan," you say, now sitting out on your front stoop, watching the perimeter of the park, where the moon hangs low over the trees. You need to vent, to go over every little detail, every little injustice you have logged into that all-remembering brain of yours. The problem isn't you. It's your sister.

A cigarette in your mouth, you light it, inhale, and still manage to say, "Oh, and I'm getting four new roommates in five days. William's MIA. What on earth is going on? . . . I'm sorry—you're busy. I just . . ."

Dan has a project due for school tomorrow. He's in his studio, and you know it'll be a late night for him, too. But he puts his work down, goes out on the balcony overlooking the Berkeley Hills, where the sky is still light after sunset. Although he will listen to you and actively try to help you get to the bottom of the issue, although he will tell you over and over, "You're fine. Please don't start thinking of yourself as some damaged human being. Everyone has rough times. Let's just take this step by step," Dan will also make you laugh. You rely on him for this. Which is why your breathing gets easier when he says, "No problem. I can take a break for you . . . Karen."

"Karen?" you say, puffing away, as your next-door neighbor lets his dog in.

"Yeah, Karen . . . Carpenter."

29

THE HIGHWAY STRETCHES out before you. To your right is an Eiffel Tower replica, all lit up in glowing white Christmas lights. In your head, you scoff, *Fuck you,* to no one in particular. And yes, you are driving alone. Miles ahead, you see the Manhattan skyline, its jagged geometrical shapes luminous against a pink-filled sky. Oh, this is a view that normally gives you pleasure, much pleasure—at sunset, no less! You think of dreams, hopes, wishes. This is no different today, although you do not believe that hopes and dreams and wishes are actually on your landscape of possibilities. Your life is not rosy, not today.

Today, you stood there, at your work luncheon where people wore silk and cashmere and flawless leather pumps. *Adorned.* You watched as they swirled around you, with their red dresses and smiling faces. You've been hoping and hoping and wondering if today would be the day William would call, to tell you where he's been. You maintained composure and geniality and wellness on the outside, saying all the polite things you have to at a work function: *Oh, isn't this weather just awful? Yes, you're right—she is fabulous. Yes, it's wonderful work we are doing here.* You read rather limply from your own script, until there was nothing left for you to say, except silently to William, *Are you all right?*

And now you are driving, and although your eyes should be fixed on the road, present in this one moment that is only yours for a time, you cannot concentrate on driving. You see yourself folded in half, and this thought—it makes you sad.

Yesterday, when you told Elaine about Annabelle's comments, she first scrunched up her nose and said, "Huh . . . because I see you every week and I haven't noticed anything drastic . . ."

You shrugged your shoulders and pointed at her glass vase of peonies, true pink peonies. "I love those. They are my mother's favorite."

Once, you surprised your mother with a bouquet of peonies in December. She was so excited you couldn't help but laugh as she said, "Are those for me? I LOVE YOU!"

"But," Elaine continued, moving her hands wildly in circles—it's not good, going to this place where you're observing your therapist as opposed to interacting with her—"maybe we should figure out—you know, have a conversation between 'you' and 'you' to make sure that everything's okay."

A conversation between me and me? You didn't even know what that meant.

"So, William . . ." you sighed to Elaine. "I've called him a few times and even sent a text that said, 'I'll take a smoke signal—just want to make sure that you're okay'—and nothing back. I asked for a fucking smoke signal . . ."

"What's the traction here?" Elaine asked.

"What do you mean?"

You are stalling, girl. *Come on!* You know exactly what she means. Elaine used this term—and it's a good one—to question you when you wouldn't let go of Jack, just after the romantic breakup. You hadn't believed in his feelings for you—only the drop-dead certainty of being let down. So you called to tell him so. And when he was busy, you'd written him an email, and when he said he couldn't meet you, you questioned why. This dogged persistence (also known as blatantly ignoring obvious cues that he didn't want to see you) is what Elaine meant by "traction."

"Okay, so the traction is that I'm worried about William."

You were worried, very much so. You had only dated him for a little more than a month, but in this time you have gotten to know him fairly well—and you would have never, ever pegged him as the type to do a disappearing act. After your third date, he'd had some issues with his ex-girlfriend that needed to be sorted out, and he even called you to say that he was otherwise occupied but that he didn't want you to think that he had disappeared. And now he has.

The feeling moves through the middle of your chest, splitting open your heart, running down the back of your spine, growing like vines around your legs—it's all-consuming. You are with coworkers, smiling and looking like everything's fine on the outside. But on the inside, you can feel yourself curling inward, down. You are inside of yourself, kneeling, so desperate that you can't even cry.

"I'm having trouble sleeping," you'd told Elaine.

"This sounds like that 'inconsolable' feeling you'd had when you broke up with Jack."

You don't remember using that word, and probably, frankly, the chances are good you didn't. But all that's kind of irrelevant because Elaine's word, the word, maybe even your word—inconsolable—there's something about it that just . . . fits.

As you sat there thinking about it, Elaine interrupted, "And also, going back in my notes here, it looks like that same session we'd talked about the time your mother left."

You bristled at this mention. Of course—you could have written this script. Present-day issues plus a traditional Western model of therapy equals topical childhood trauma. Having talked about this one event most of your adult and even part of your adolescent life, you weren't really keen on going there again, so you nodded and pretended to think it out, before changing the subject.

BUT HERE YOU are, driving down the highway, still not knowing where William is. Your mind runs through one scenario after another: maybe he's sick. Maybe he's in the hospital. You chide yourself for going this alarmist route. He's obviously just lost interest in you. Face it. But deep down, you know that something is wrong—maybe not with him, but definitely with you.

YOU DON'T REMEMBER when she disappeared, whether the leaves were turning or the front yard crocuses were in new bloom. You don't remember your exact age, although you could figure it out if it were even remotely relevant to anything. (You think you were ten years old.) There was your father's worried face, as he silently contemplated raising his four children alone, after his wife had rushed out the front door screaming, a slightly chewy Sunday pot roast left to chill on the dining room table. *How could she do this to him?* you wondered.

During the week that followed, clues about where your mother was came from indirect sources. You'd eavesdrop as Annabelle, a teenager, called hospitals, police stations, and morgues. Your father stood by the curly phone cord, his worn, wrinkled hand almost always covering his agape mouth. You saw how hard this was for him, and it broke your little heart in two.

Days passed and your absent mother stayed a secret from teachers and friends. One morning, nearly a week after she had gone, she called to say that she'd just needed some space, her midlife, menopausal distress led her to a priory in Newport and she'd had a lovely week. She was to come home that night.

You waited. Your father gained some of the color back in his cheeks as he watched television with you and David. Any minute. But as hour after hour passed, he started to look troubled again. When the clock turned eleven, he reluctantly shut off the TV.

"Time for bed," he said glumly. As he shuttled you off to bed, you felt his pain more than your own. The thought of what happened after death—was it a world filled only with a dark sky, speckled with endless twinkling stars?—was too terrifying, and so you prayed to God, to everyone in your family who died, even the people you didn't know—your father's sister, your mother's father who died three weeks before her wedding. This night, you even contemplated praying to your mother, remembering her pretty blue eyes, this sadness of hers that no one could seem to fix, not even you.

The next afternoon, you sat in the school cafeteria, sipping chocolate milk and eating burnt pizza, when a teacher approached to say that your father was there to pick you up. You remember pushing the carton of milk aside and leaving your friends. You walked to the principal's office, down the dark corridor, past grainy construction paper pictures, and tried not to cry. It was one of the first conclusions that you ever remember coming to: she was dead and your father was coming to deliver the news. This is the only piece of your memory where you are actually feeling for yourself, and so it gets relived in quiet, unacknowledged ways through other places and times in your life.

Your father stood in the front foyer of the building with David, his hands on David's faded red ski jacket. "Ready, Sue?" he said, looking lighter. "Your mother called and she wants us to come pick her up." For some reason, Annabelle got to stay in school, and your oldest brother was already away at college.

You said nothing the whole ride down. It was a blue-sky day, but even the view of the calming ocean brought misery—another reminder of peace that didn't belong to you.

When you arrived on the lush grounds, your mother ran out from one of the Italianate brick buildings and hugged you one by one. There was no apology, no explanation, just an oddly buoyant attitude that neither your father nor David nor you shared.

She nuzzled in close to your cheek, made loud kissing noises, and said, "I love you."

Your body stiffened, jaw locked because you were no longer a believer.

The three of you lumbered after your mother as she took you on a tour of the chapel and nun's quarters, stopping along the way to introduce you to older, white-haired women with names like Betty and Edith.

"This is my family!" she gushed to everyone who crossed your path. "Aren't they beautiful?"

You distinctly remember standing there next to David, feeling foolish and angry. Did no one see what a farce all of this was? The word "bitch" was not in your vocabulary, but if it were, you would have used it, at least in your head. Oh, and that was of course the really hard part. That you kept everything inside. David and you stood shoulder to shoulder when he sneezed, loud. With all those nuns present, he got his fair share of God bless you's. Which led to the best part, the part that somehow made everything okay, that here was this woman pretending like nothing had happened, gushing about her "beautiful" children. Following David's hearty "Achoo!" he took his right sleeve and wiped the snot from his nose all over his jacket. On the surface, you knew that this did not fall in line with the doctrine of perfection, and deep down, this was just about the only consolation you could have.

OVER THE YEARS, your mother has apologized to you, for this incident and others. She often says, "If I had only known how much that was going to hurt you, I never would have done it," or "I must have been out of my mind," or "Hey, early menopause, that one really did a number . . ." And these numerous times you have received her apologies, you always feel like they are heartfelt. Of course she would take that away if she could: she's your *mother*. And every time, you are left with frustration, because here your mother is, sincerely sorry, and still, somewhere inside, you are the devastated, inconsolable little girl, the one with a stiff upper lip and wide-open eyes, who wants nothing more than to cry out for her mother, but you can't, she can't, because this idea of the perfect mother, an infallible human being, someone who will never let you down and will fill you up with love—the one you think of in glowing predisappearance terms—she's not real. She's not even real.

You sigh, let your head drop to the side. There is a clearing in your mind, which you use to connect the standard psychoanalytic dots.

Oh, barf, you think.

You've told this same old story for so long, with so many therapists, on so many beige/leather/stuffed sofas. But this time, in this clearing, as your car inches toward the Midtown Tunnel and your entire being feels like it's being swallowed by this looming Manhattan skyline, this time those disparate dots—from a younger you to an older you—appear to be more connected, at least for the moment.

As you maneuver your car next to the toll collector's window, you look at the older woman in uniform, the winter winds breezing into her workspace.

"Gosh, I hope you get to go home soon," you say, as you lean out and hand her a five-dollar bill.

She looks at you and smiles, showing an expression more electric than her neon orange vest. As she leans out to hand you your change, she says, "I'm okay . . . but thank you, baby, thank you. God bless."

30

YOU TURN SIXTEEN: you can get your driver's license. You turn seventeen: you can walk up to the counter at a movie theater and confidently buy a ticket to an R-rated movie. You turn eighteen: you can get drafted by the United States military, legally buy cigarettes, and not worry about your older boyfriend committing statutory rape when the windows of his beat-up car start to fog on your Saturday night date. You turn twenty-one: you can finally throw out that ridiculous fake ID that that looks nothing like you when you want to go dancing at a club or buy a six-pack. You turn twenty-five: you can travel to faraway places and rent a car without additional fees because overnight your new age makes you less of a liability in the eyes of the powers that be. You turn twenty-eight, and what happens? All hell breaks loose, because this is the beginning of your Saturn return, baby.

Of course, you are not twenty-eight. You are thirty, and supposed to be acting like an adult. But when you scan back to everything that's happened to you since twenty-eight, when Saturn started heading toward its original placement in your birth chart, it seems like this was the point when you gave up on maturity entirely. In a flash, you thought: Proposal from boyfriend of five years. Reluctant, terrified acceptance. Sexy interlude with hot Czech boxer. Breaking up with your fiancé. Diving headfirst into a transatlantic relationship with someone who doesn't speak English, yet was remarkably adept at phone sex. Graduating from school with no plan for the future. Dwindling bank account. Ex-fiancé learns of your infidelity from his own mother as they are driving to a wedding. Resuming cigarette smoking after a seven-year break. Finding an agent. Sleeping with this agent and even making noises about the l-word, after a few short weeks. Relationship implodes, perhaps inevitably. Keep on the dating train. Meet a nice lawyer in Starbucks. Things with him evolve slowly, by design. All is well, until he disappears off the face of the earth, and your mind is taking careful stock of your road map, dwelling on each point with, "What if I had made a different choice here, at this very random intersection?"

Growing up. It's one of the oldest stories in the book.

But the truth is, you keep your downer thoughts to yourself, because the occasion is Paula's twenty-eighth birthday; the celebration has nothing to do with your own life's trajectory. You and she are at a tapas restaurant in Chelsea, sitting around a high table, snacking on oily Marcona almonds and catching up. Your visits with her have become less frequent, mostly because these days you find it excruciating to be with yourself in social situations.

Instead of sharing any of this, you say, "Girl, twenty-eight— well, I, for one, am glad you were born." No need to start talking uninformed astrology, for god's sakes.

Paula turns abruptly and says, "When he calls with a good excuse—and he will—don't take him back, okay?"

To an outsider, this statement might appear a complete non sequitur. But to you, her close friend, in addition to making perfect sense, these disjointed lines are what connect you. She says something seemingly random. You know exactly what she means. Hence, a bond.

"He's going to call you," Paula continues.

Your mouth is full of salty brandade, but you manage a "Yeah, right!" At this point, you expect nothing. Last week, you'd received a paltry text message from him that read, "Busy. Will reach out soon."

Paula pointed out that this text is the equivalent of an impersonal voice recording: "Please . . . continue . . . to . . . hold . . . Your . . . call . . . will . . . be . . . answered . . . in . . . the . . . order . . . it was . . . received."

"Whatever he says, just remember this feeling."

"Yeah . . . no . . . I mean . . ." you stammer, looking away. Your elbow is propped up on the table, and your palm is pressed into your face, your chin now grazing your collarbone. Quite frankly, you'd like to forget how you are feeling at the moment.

"Anyway, Paula, this is a celebration of *you*," you say, lifting your glass in an effort to change the subject. "May you have the happiest of years . . ."

AT HOME, YOU step into your apartment, now busy and bustling with your four new roommates—all of whom are nice, if transient. You wave hello to Yvonne, the twenty-one-year-old fashion student who likes to talk about the fact that all she ever does is sleep late with her boyfriend and go to late-night parties. Usually you are annoyed when she says things like this, because you work nonstop and this is the last thing you want to hear from the person who can't even seem to do her own dishes, despite all this alleged free time. But after a relaxing evening with Paula, none of the usual bitterness is even on your radar.

As you open the door to your bedroom, you are filled with okayness. There was life before William, and frankly, if you could just take a step back, you might see that life has, all in all, been pretty good.

Sitting on the corner of your bed, you open your laptop and check your email. There is only one message, from William. Your heart skips and your best instincts become louder: *Just remember, everything is fine, no matter what this message says.*

The subject line is "the bare facts," and this makes you very, very curious. You forget for a moment that you are so mad at him, because your chest is ringing.

Dear Suzanne,
For the last twelve days, I have been holed up in various hotels in Manhatten [sic], cocaine, $6K... I only saw the light of day when I ran out of money. The DA's sending me to rehab, but I'll call you when I get out. Lost my cell. Miss you,
William.

Your jaw hangs open. What? This . . . from the man you never saw have more than two drinks? How could this be?

You shut down your laptop immediately and lean back against the familiar pillows on your bed. You open your laptop again, sign in to your account again, just to double-check: *Did I read that correctly?*

Unfortunately, yes.

Your chest is tight, and you are scared, so scared that all you want to do is crawl under a rock. Prior to reading this, you hadn't even thought there was an "innocence" to which you could return. But now, imagining this man you care about stumbling through the city on a drug binge—for twelve days—you feel sick. This picture of William in some hotel room, doing God knows what, traveling God knows where, to step around junkies just so he can . . . Ugh. You're no stranger to substance abuse, but the two or three times you'd tried cocaine in your life, one night was just about all your nerves could handle. Twelve days? Twelve fucking days?

After thinking for another minute, you dial Dan. "You're never going to believe this, but, ah, I know why William hasn't called . . ."

"What?" Dan says when you read the email to him, word for word. "What?"

Yeah, it doesn't really compute for you, either. Not at all. You want to vomit every time you start to think of how he could have spent that much money in such a short time. Surely it wasn't only on coke.

Outside, the lights in your neighborhood are dim. Every other streetlight, it seems, is out. Not a good sign.

After a little while, Dan says, "Look, I know you might not be laughing about this right now, but someday you will."

"Really?"

This is not a rhetorical question. Because you don't want to laugh about this, not now, not ever. Fine, maybe at one point your strong suit was finding humor in even the most dire situations, but now this task seems impossible. Your humor, once

MUCH TO YOUR CHAGRIN

your lifeline, is dead in the water. Dead on arrival. Dead, dead, dead.

"Dan, he fucking spelled 'Manhattan' wrong. Who does that?"

"Aw, honey, you're going to be fine."

That's funny, you think, *because I can't imagine anything other than this block of ice in the middle of my chest.* You can't stop thinking of how awful it must have been for William. When you think of how awful you feel, though, you can't get past dwelling on "Manhatten."

Next, you call Henry, who is home working on a song.

He sounds very peaceful, and you hate to ruin his evening. But you are not through processing this new piece of information. When you tell Henry everything, he says, "What? Man, that is some crazy shit."

"I know."

"Six thousand dollars in twelve days on cocaine? That doesn't add up."

"Yeah." You are thinking this, too, but something about Henry's tone is extra concerned. "Wait, what do you mean by that?"

"Well, you know . . ." He doesn't want to say it.

"What?"

"I just mean, he must have been with prostitutes or something. You don't spend that much money on just coke in twelve days."

Gulp.

"Oh, God."

"Sorry. It's true, though."

"But Henry, that is not good."

"I know."

"No, I mean, for me. That is really not good."

"Why?"

"Well . . ." You really hate to admit this latest act of stupidity. Really. And especially to Henry, who is so protective. "The last time we were together we had unprotected sex."

"Oh, no," he groaned, making you feel a million times worse. "This is your health, your life. What were you thinking?"

"Guess I wasn't," you say, remembering that night, how in the moment when William pulled you closer to him, the thought that ran through your mind was, *What the hell?* And now that thought is here again, with an entirely different meaning. *What the hell?* You just have no idea about William and all the sorts of things he may or may not have been up to before his binge. You just don't fucking know.

"You can't take anything for granted," Henry says. "Don't you know that, dating in this city?"

You feel sick, knowing that it will be months before a doctor can give you a clean bill of health—or worse, news of some awful disease. Since you are a closeted hypochondriac, you skip right past all the self-flagellating and instead focus on your worst fear: you are going to *die.*

Just as you are in the middle of some stupid reverie about your funeral and what people might say ("She used to be a lot of fun, before . . ."), Henry interrupts, "Come over. I can rent a movie and we can just chill and eat popcorn."

This sounds so nice, and yeah, you really could use a hug, but you are too wound up to even put your clothes on and get on a subway to travel to Henry's apartment.

"Thanks, but . . . I don't think I can move."

You hang up the phone and try to sleep. But you can't. You wake up an hour after closing your eyes, with night sweats. Since when do you get night sweats? Since, well . . . you know . . . now. Now. Now. Now. You are standing on the edge, teetering back and forth, only you can never imagine falling, just the fear of it.

The next morning, you force yourself to take a yoga class, only the sight of your pale, gaunt face in the mirror for ninety minutes causes distress, not relaxation. Besides that, the carpet in the studio stinks. As the instructor speaks, your stomach remains tied in knots. You cannot stop thinking of William. You hope he's okay. No matter how many times you hear the teacher say, "Keep going! You are working to reach your infinite Self!" you're not feeling very . . . namaste. You'd rather lie down and close your eyes for a long, long while.

After class, you are in a checkout line at the grocery store. People are bustling all around you, doing Sunday shopping and getting ready for the week. Even though you only have a small pile of frozen fruit packages and green vegetables, you don't mind waiting behind a family with a huge cart overflowing with frozen dinners, cake mixes, and two-liter bottles of soda. You are thinking that you don't want to die, that you'd like a family to throw parties with someday, when the cashier asks, "Paper or plastic?"

"Paper or plastic?" you repeat, as if it's the gravest question you've ever been asked. Life or death, that seems like the real question. You can't handle this beautiful life and so what will it be? Life or fucking death?

As you burst out in tears, shaking your head, you reach for your wallet and try not to feel dumb for breaking down in public. The cashier looks at you with peering, concerned eyes and reaches her hand across the counter to still your shaking hands. "Is there anything I can do, honey?"

Although this makes you lose it completely, somewhere between your tears you look at her with red, bloodshot eyes; even though you manage to say, "No, uh-uh," that's not exactly the truth—because when she squeezes your hand, you feel the softness of her palm on your rough knuckles. Midday sunlight streams through the windows, causing you to squint. Your fingers folding around hers, you squeeze back.

31

LIGHT FILLS THE room. The hardwood floors gleam from a recent cleaning, finished with a lemon-scented oil conditioner. The books are stacked high in their place on the shelves, only now the doors are opened. The closet is thinner, having been depleted of old, worn-out clothing that you had thought you might wear again someday, even though the items were: silver lamé hot pants, a hand-knit sweater with an irreparable hole in the sleeve, a pair of threadbare, faded jeans that didn't fit anymore. A pile of opened bills sits on the top of your desk, paired with corresponding checks and envelopes, which now wait only for stamps. Music plays—airy and loud, filling the room. The melody is sometimes sad, sometimes lively, and always, always emotional. You need this, more than you know.

Outside, the sounds of uneven, shrieking laughter, running water, and the buzz of the dryer's finished cycle all meld together, holding up an expectation that life goes on: Whether or not you like it. Whether or not you're ready. Whether or not you are grateful.

* * *

YOU ARE SITTING on the floor, cross-legged on a white sheet, wearing your underwear inside out, and chanting next to a candle especially blessed by Lisa the Seventh Avenue Psychic for the very reasonable price of $150.

Iamstrong. Iamstrong. Iamstrong.

Desperate times call for desperate measures, and in your case, with your underwear inside out, this is especially true. In the weeks following William's email, you told the story to anyone and everyone you could. It's your way, storytelling. You hope that by recounting the details and making jokes about it when you can ("Oh, I can't meet up with you—that's the day my boyfriend's coming home from rehab . . ."), this will make everything somewhat okay. But in reality, nothing is okay here, and so you trotted your little chain-smoking self down to Lisa the Psychic, settled into her cramped red "office," which was separated from her living room by a flimsy cotton curtain (enabling you to hear the cartoons her kids were watching on TV), and Lisa, with her dewy dark skin and long jean skirt, told you things you already knew:

You're creative, but could be more creative.

You are good-hearted and give a lot to those around you. Not that you usually expect much in return, but lately you haven't been getting anything.

You're thinking a lot about doctors these days, but you can stop worrying because you are fine.

Sorry to say you haven't been lucky in love. You are lucky in a lot of areas, but love's not one of them.

The man from last year—the one everyone thought was so terrible for you—he wasn't as bad for you as everyone thought, but you still have to let him go.

*   *   *

BUT BETTER THAN Lisa's truisms, you think, as you inhale the thick scent of incense and garlic, is that Miss Lisa has handed you a prescription for your life, ready-made, with crystals, candles, incense—the accoutrements of this beleaguered path to wellness. She's provided you with a concrete (sort of) way to reassess what's actually going on in your life. So when Lisa tells you to sit on the floor with your underwear inside out, you listen—even though you feel completely ridiculous.

Somewhere, on the floor, probably at about the fiftieth "Iamstr—" you look out your bedroom window, to that owl, and actually think for a moment, "He's still there," before getting up and putting your robe on and sitting on your bed, the silk of your duvet cover grazing your thighs. You pick up your phone from the nightstand and sigh as you dial a familiar number.

"Dan," you say. "Can I admit something to you?"

"Sure. What's up?" His tone is curt. This is crunch time for his big studio presentation.

"This will only take a sec . . ."

Down to the type of candle you are burning, you describe the exact scene in your bedroom, just moments earlier.

"Yeah, so I'm supposed to sit here with my underwear inside out—oh, and it has to be white . . ."

"Hahahahahahahhahahahahahahahahahhhaaaaahhhhhaaah-hhhaahhhhhhhhhaaaaahhahahahahahahahahahahahahahaha-hahahahahahahahahahahahahahahahahahahahahahahahaha-hahaahahahahahahahahahahahahahahahahahahahahahaha-hahah!"

You can't help it; your ear glued to the phone, you start to choke out a laugh, too—not full-throttle and certainly not as gleefully as Dan, but you do laugh, and hear yourself thinking, *Good girl.*

A moment later you add, "Yeah, and the worst part is that she told me there's a black cloud over my aura that can be removed for the very small price of six hundred dollars."

"What?" Dan says, outraged. "That's shameless. She is obviously trying to take advantage of someone who's having a hard time. This isn't about an 'aura'—you know that, right?"

You don't actually know that. In this moment, you realize that, in your own head, Dan's words of wisdom have become substitutes for your own presence of thought. You mean, he's right—this isn't about a stupid black cloud over your aura. But when Lisa had mentioned this to you, your first response was not, *Bullshit!* It was, *Hmmm, so how can I get my hands on six hundred bucks?*

The truth is, ever since reading William's email, you'd likened yourself to being at a party—somewhat reluctantly, but then just as soon as you decided that dancing might be okay, someone pulled the needle off the record. Game over. Everyone's got to go home. But in your heart of hearts, it is this question of home that has perhaps sent you reeling on all these crazy, ridiculous romantic adventures. During a particularly numb moment following that email, you clicked onto one of those ads that pops up in your email account—this time the ad was for an ebook entitled *How to Get Your Ex Back* and so you started reading and the advice seemed pretty simple (focus on yourself first, start working out) but it wasn't until page twenty that you realized, rifling through your Rolodex of past relationships, *Wait a second . . . I don't actually* want *any of my exes back.*

Just yesterday, you opened your mailbox and spied a bright orange-yellow card amid the bills and odd swimming pool advertisements that came on a frequent basis to your Brooklyn address. On the yellow envelope, you saw William's name in the return address, from his rehab location in Pennsylvania. When you opened the card, you saw a bright sun on the front of it; inside, William had written:

> *Dear Sweets,*
> *Remember how I said I wanted to play more Ping-Pong? Well, it's great here—three tables, no waiting! . . . I'm sorry for not telling you what I was up against . . . I am truly sorry if you feel betrayed . . . Just dealing with the awful, painful circumstances here . . . I wish I could laugh a little more now . . . Gotta run as I have a Ping-Pong match with the house champ—a Korean doctor who spent all his $ on booze, whores and cars and is now being jailed by the IRS.*

Something about this touched you, profoundly (except, of course, the line about the whores, which made you gag and perform a hasty Sign of the Cross). You tried to let go of your questions, such as, *Why didn't he just tell me?* You don't yet know that when you see him for the first time after rehab, for lunch on Seventh Avenue at an outdoor café, he will tell you how grateful he is that you haven't lost your sense of humor. And you won't tell him that, for a time, of course you did, that you held your breath until that visit to the doctor, where he proclaimed you to be disease-free, and you, thinking of all your mental issues, thought, *Well, that's one way to look at it.* While some other woman might just chalk up this scenario to dating in New York and move on, the news had shaken you up, bad. Over omelets and salad, William will also tell you that when he wrote you the now-infamous email, he could even see the expression on your face as you'd presumably told friends that he'd been on a coke binge for almost two weeks. "I could see your face when I wrote it," he will say, chuckling. "I could hear you telling your friends as you said, 'Twelve days!' " This strikes you as oddly loving. Later, when you say goodbye to him, as soon as the door clicks shut, you will cry (because, yes, that's what you seem to be doing these days, making up for lost time, apparently). William has done for you what you haven't yet been able to do for yourself.

"DAN," YOU SAY, with a half smile, from the perch of your cozy bed. You are thinking of the time long ago that he bought black Dolce & Gabbana jeans with gold paint splattered all over the legs, and then tried to deny that he ever had a fashion crisis. "Dan, will you promise to laugh with me about this some other time? Like when I can actually see the humor of chanting in my undies?"

"Yeah, I don't think that's going to be a problem."

You giggle and wish him luck on his presentation before snapping your phone closed. Yeah, time to chuck that whole poor-me attitude—no more reliving the old, worn memories of Jack or blaming the state of your current life—yours, it's yours—on choices that your mother made.

Wah wah wah, you think, gingerly laughing at yourself for the first time in a long time.

Your mind skips rapidly by your recent past—the messy love life, the strained relationships, the dissatisfaction with your job, the extreme oblivion. All this time, you have been living in a diminished world, puffing up your chest and crying out, "No one's going to mess with me . . ." only it's absurd, really more of a joke than anything else, because no one's actually *trying* to mess with you. This little battle between you and the world, between your ego and what people think of you . . . it's all in your head, and when it crosses your mind that this is even more cause for shame, for shame . . . well, then it would appear that you haven't really been getting it at all, have you?

In the still of your room, you open your computer and take a look at the list of embarrassing stories that you have captured from other people. You measure this list against the embarrassing stories that you yourself have racked up in the course of putting this book together—although impressive, life imitating art wasn't your intention, at least not that you know of. Whatever was at work, you now realize that there was no way for you to ask other people to fess up without fully understanding yourself and what you find oh so truly mortifying. What is it that you have wanted to keep hidden from the world all this time? Well, that's suddenly a simple answer, Miss Know-It-All. After unwittingly dating a cocaine addict (and, um, actually, you found out later—much later—that the issue was most likely crack, not cocaine), there's something you need to know: it's okay to have been wrong—and even more okay to have been needy, very very needy. And of the utmost okayness to finally, actually, fully feel something, even if that feeling is shame.

For the last year, nearly every day, on your way to work, you have stepped over a bronzed Virginia Woolf quote embedded in the sidewalk on Forty-first Street: *If you do not tell the truth about yourself, you cannot tell it about other people.*

You will close up the *Oh, Shit!* shop, and in doing so, make room for something new, something unexpected, unscripted, and entirely organic. You will come to understand, eventually, that your greatest shame was not being able to connect with all the diversity within you—especially the parts that aren't so rosy—but then again, that's a silly thing to feel bad about.

You will stop asking other people about what embarrasses them, and perform an act entirely novel to you: you will mind your own business, and apply this aggressively to every aspect of your life.

In thinking back about what went wrong with certain relationships, you will not focus on how other people, like Annabelle or Jack, didn't live up to your ideas of who they should have been. Instead, you will finally acknowledge your own regret—and it is profound—for not being honest with the people about whom you cared most. You are so sorry.

When friends call upset, you will not imagine what it is like to be in their shoes, because you are not. Instead you will focus on listening. When a coworker starts to complain about her day, you will say only, "Sounds rough"—and stop there. When your friend calls with relationship drama, you will not offer her any advice about what might work the best for her. Because, if you have learned anything, it is that we ourselves always know. This whole time, you have known that you were trying to avoid writing your own script. You have known somewhere deep down that you were playing by everyone else's rules—not because you are lazy, but because you have been, quite simply, afraid to tell the truth about you.

* * *

WITH YOUR NEW MYOB mantra in hand, you will sit patiently, try and do all the right things—eat well, start exercising, quit smoking—until the picture of who you are comes into sharper focus. You will become sure, even as a wide-open horizon looms before you. But before long, it won't be looming, it will be inviting. And you, my friend, you will be there, ready, opening yourself to what's right in front of your eyes—what's been there this whole time. The spindly branches on a tree, reaching skyward after a long winter. Your favorite cat in the whole wide world, Gidget, as she stretches out on the floor, dives for a long string of red yarn, and throws herself against the French door upon which her feather-toy hangs. The sugary sweet scent of red velvet cake coming from the bakery at the end of your block. Stepping out of the subway, looking upward, to see brownstones and trees and small children tagging along with their parents. And, as everything glimmers, you will be there, confident, willing, ready to begin.

"EVERYTHING"

Everything—

a bumptious, stuck-up word.

It should be written in quotes.

It pretends to miss nothing,

to gather, hold, contain, and have.

While all the while it's just

a shred of a gale.

—WISŁAWA SZYMBORSKA

AFTERWORD

BUT WAIT, DEAR reader. There is one more embarrassing story left to tell. Approximately seven months after I'd decided to stop collecting embarrassing stories, I emailed Phillip and asked if he wanted to have coffee.

Sure, was his reply, and every time he sounds even remotely pleased to hear from me, it gives me pause. *Did he just forget everything?*

So we met up for a coffee and pastry at the gourmet café at the base of my office building. When I told Phillip that I worked in the Chanin Building, a well-preserved structure from the Art Deco era with ornate details on both the inside and outside of the building, his response was, "The Chanin Building! I hope you sing every day on your way in to work."

When the time came for coffee, here I was, descending in the familiar elevator, saying a not-so-silent prayer that I would be free from clumsy maneuvers and other accidents. *This will be fine. This will be fine,* I told myself, until I almost believed it, too.

When Phillip, who had been waiting at a table, stood and smiled, I paused, looking over both of my shoulders. Surely he wasn't smiling at *me.*

After a quick greeting, I ordered a tea and sat with him, picking at a glossy fruit tart and chatting, mostly about writing. I had seen Phillip twice since the omelet burning. Once, just after William went to rehab, I saw Phillip for a short coffee and told him of my woes. Then I saw him read at a festival in Brooklyn and said a quick hello.

After a little while, Phillip took a sip of his coffee and said carefully, "And what of your love life?"

My love life. Months ago, when I had first mentioned William's surprise drug addiction, Phillip told me, with a mischievous smile, that I was "just like" Candide, moving from one adventure to the next. He then asked me why I thought I always went for inappropriate men. I rolled my eyes and laughed. "Well, if I knew that . . ." I could have given him a million party lines. *Oh, I just wasn't ready for anything and so I attracted this. Oh, I am still working on those old abandonment issues, so it's more comfortable to be with someone who's not reliable. Oh, I'm still working out my tangled knots with Ted. Oh, I'm a distant Aquarian, who has petrified herself with the very* (shudder!) *thought of commitment.* Oh, and how could I forget this one: *I am paralyzed on this tightrope between loneliness and an all-smothering togetherness.*

Three months after William returned from rehab, I started dating him again—moving slowly at first, and last. We didn't work out as a couple, because ultimately I knew that it wasn't entirely his drug problem that stopped us from moving forward from our reliable, cherished Saturday night dates to a more intimate, I-had-a-terrible-day-at-work-and-you-are-the-only-one-I-want-to-see kind of relationship. It was me. When

I told him this, he said, "Oh, great, and I bet you want to be friends, too?" Which, incidentally, I did.

When Phillip noticed my eyes moving back in time, he added, "How is he doing, the one who—"

"Went to rehab?" I interrupted. "He's great. But we just broke up. I—"

"What?" Phillip's jaw dropped. I could see him thinking, rather loudly, *How could she have gone back to him?* I had wondered myself, many times. But William was lovely, always lovely, and we were easy companions, at least through a summer filled with beach days and lobster rolls, evening walks around the park, picnics on the lawn. It was all very . . . nice.

Phillip was now looking at me with much concern. After a moment, he said, "May I offer you some advice, from your 'Uncle' Phillip?"

"Uh, sure."

"Someone once told me . . ." he began. Now, I've heard him say this a few times. I am not sure if someone ever actually said such things to him, or if he's just trying to make strong words more palatable for my ears. For an acquaintance, he's good.

"When I was dating inappropriate women, someone said, 'Phillip, you're so smart in certain areas of your life. Take some of that intelligence and apply it to your love life.' And this is exactly what I would say to you."

I sat there in real-time, suddenly looking around the café, interested in all these folks taking midafternoon coffee breaks and paying one dollar per mini chocolate éclair. I felt my breath draw in and then release. I put one hand on my stomach and listened as it floated in and out, in and out. Phillip gave me a stern look. After scanning the café once more, I turned back to let myself look at him, let him look at me, and I did not crack one single joke. There was no punch line ready for arrival. No nervous laughter. No charming smiles or clever deflections.

Whatever it was that he saw—emotions, irrational thinking, self-involvement, bad choices, neediness, longing, imperfection—whatever it was, it was okay, absolutely okay. And just a fraction of the whole.

I felt my spine and its nervous tap, tap against the chair. I did not look away or flinch or even contemplate changing the subject, all of which would have been fine, of course. But after a spate of very loud adventures, I was ready for a little peace.

Months after Phillip's advice, I was approaching the Verrazano Bridge in a pristine rental car, rifling through my feelings about the night before, when I had seen Jack for the first time since we broke up. We had bumped into each other on the subway and he later suggested via text that we "catch up," like old friends might. Only, we aren't old friends, or even friends at all. But for reasons not entirely known to me, I am one of those people who has a hard time resisting an opportunity to "make nice."

Many of my other relationships from this particular time had already normalized. For example, I often bumped into Marco. He worked in the neighborhood where I practiced yoga. Every time I saw him, the mood was happy, void of expectation and awkwardness. We always kissed, but never on the lips. Every few months, Dudley and I had brief phone conversations. Ever the trainer, he often asked, "You eatin' enough? You stayin' out of trouble, girl?" (And yes, I knew enough not to call him back until I could answer honestly in the affirmative, on both counts.) Still practicing law, William had since left New York; we still emailed and talked on occasion. Once he'd written, "Sometimes, I think we could have made it." I'd written back, "But don't you remember how you wanted someone more nurturing? I am so not a cookie-baker." (Even though, actually, I am.) But all that was beside the point. There was just no way. By the time we broke up, I'd already started moving in another direction.

Over the course of the last year, I'd quit smoking, slowly tapered off my antidepressants, began working out again, quit therapy, and eventually made the decision to stop drinking, too. Ever so slowly, color began to seep back into all the corners that had so abruptly turned black and white. And then on Easter Sunday, just when I was beginning to think about forgiveness, Jack had appeared on the subway platform.

Approaching the Verrazano, I found myself drifting back to the night before, when Jack had come to meet me in Brooklyn. We'd spent a few hours talking about his career, my writing, our families, everything except our prior relationship. Neither of us said, "I'm sorry." (Wasn't that obvious?) By not rehashing what was already long dead, we seemed to be affirming that even though our breakup was a little rough, hey, life goes on.

As I rolled down the car window, I couldn't help but think how much of Jack I had missed during our brief time together. Sometime just before that first kiss, I had begun substituting Jack-the-real-person with some one-dimensional knockoff, whose only relevant quality fast became whether or not he was going to shower me with indiscriminate praise. Cool spring air filled the car, and I remembered a time, not too long ago, when I would have argued against the very concept of regret. *Who has time for regret?* I might have said. But now I was beginning to understand differently.

Looking ahead, I realized that the right lane of the bridge was closed. A line of orange cones signaled the closure, guiding my car toward the center lane. Half paying attention, I noticed the blue-sky day, one of those perfect, perfect blue-sky days. I felt a lump in my chest, a lodged feeling of . . . something.

Long ago, I had cried plenty about the joy that Jack and I had lost; I didn't think that seeing him inspired this sadness, at least not in a predictable sort of way. What I felt on the bridge was markedly different, less specific to one relationship between two people.

No cars were letting me in. I sat there, hunched over the wheel, frustrated that I couldn't move. Tears started to well, filling up my eyes to the brim. Instead of demanding a detailed justification for every single emotion I had, I just cried—what the hell, right? And then the word "mourning" came to mind. I was in mourning—mostly of the time that humans, in general, waste. In my rental, on this long bridge, situated between two massive towers, I felt very small.

When I looked up, in my blurry vision, I saw a hearse. A hearse on a bridge. (You can't write this stuff.) The cars that wouldn't let me in were part of a funeral procession. A funeral, on this loveliest of days. Every car filled with a distraught person, the traffic slowed. One of the drivers finally motioned me in, and before I could say, "Bizarre!" I was part of the procession, too—crying right alongside everyone else, suspended on the Verrazano, somewhere between Brooklyn and Staten Island, somewhere in this long, imaginary corridor between the delicate processes of looking back and leaping forward, between what I think and who I am, that extended realm where dreams are not only possible, but sometimes involuntary.

Although I should have been concentrating on the road ahead, I couldn't help but look at the view—the Upper and Lower Bays, the Statue of Liberty, the constant Manhattan skyline, ships crossing underneath, piers dotting the coastline, more blue sky than I'd seen in a while.

Words from Cicero came to mind: "Not to know what has happened before one was born is to always be a child." *This sadness and mourning, they do not belong to me,* I thought, letting the sun stream through the windows, even as I cried. *Not at all.*

Soon enough, I pulled up to the toll collector at the end of the bridge and held out a crisp ten-dollar bill. I saw, in his eyes, everything I had just released back into the world. Had he asked me what the matter was, I couldn't have said a word.

RECENTLY, I DODGED through the crowded streets of SoHo, making my way back to the subway after a yoga class. But first I had to eat. Armed with a container of to-go sushi, I stopped on the tourist-filled corner of Prince and Broadway, hoping to find somewhere to sit while I ate. Sometimes, after yoga, I eat on the subway, which is kind of disgusting, given the stale air and God knows what else that's hanging out in those stuffy cars. But this night was temperate and clear and I didn't have anywhere to rush off to, so I crossed Broadway and settled on the makeshift bench created by Prada's large window. Feet planted firmly on the sidewalk, I watched with interest as people stopped to check out the fashion display. An older white-haired woman paused in front of the window with her younger lover, looking over my head to say, "I like the gradation of that patent leather heel, but I would never wear that, see."

Shifting back and forth, I saw a young man sitting to my right. He was wearing a blue polo shirt and tapping his fingers on his jeans-clad legs. I pulled out the package of sushi from my bag, lifting the lid and placing it next to the container of food on my lap. Despite being spill-prone, I always put the ginger, wasabi, and soy sauce in the empty lid, mix it up, and then dip with the cheap chopsticks.

The young man was looking at my ritual, and so I said, "Beautiful night, huh?"

He nodded. "Yes, it is. Good dinner?"

He spoke with a Spanish accent. Turns out he was visiting from Madrid. I was there once. I told him about how I walked into what I thought was the Prado with great fanfare—taking pictures, loudly gushing, "Beautiful entryway!"—only to discover it wasn't the Prado. It was a bank. A very nice bank, but a bank nonetheless.

He asked me what I do in the city.

"Uh, I am a writer," I said, wiping soy sauce from the corner of my lips.

"What do you write?"

"Uh, I just wrote a book." I got up to reluctantly place my sushi trash into one of those big, overflowing piles of trash. Once I was sure that it was not going to topple to the ground, I turned around to take my place at the window next to my new young friend.

"Well?" he looked at me impatiently. "What's the book about?"

I paused for a minute. *Aren't I done talking about embarrassment?* My gaze moved beyond my new friend, toward downtown, where I could see the sky becoming a hazier pink.

"Peanut butter bonbon?" I asked, pulling out the box of specialty chocolates I had planned on sharing with friends. Somehow, this just seemed like a sweet moment for chocolate. Besides, he was a guest in our city. I had to offer this man *something.*

"Yes, thank you," he said, pulling a perfect brown square, topped with just a dash of sea salt, out of the lavender box. I took one, too, and bit into half, wishing that I were either alone or in the company of a very good friend so that I could say, "Mmmmmmmmm!" really loud. Apparently, when Ted and I were dating, I made that sound a lot in his presence. On more than one occasion, Ted said, "Is the bagel really that good? It's the same exact one you have every day." Oh, but it was! It really was.

I told my new friend about *Oh, Shit!* and about how in collecting other people's embarrassing stories, I had unconsciously started to accumulate my own, on more levels than I could even count.

"Life got a little, uh, out of hand."

"I don't like New York," the young Spaniard said, wrinkling his nose. "People are in such a rush. I cannot believe that people actually stopped to talk to you. On the street?"

"Yeah. It was kind of cool."

"How is that even possible? Nobody even bothers to look where they're going, they're too busy working."

I conceded, "Yep. The pace is quick here."

After a minute, I added, "But you'd be surprised. People talk."

"Wait," he asked, reaching for another chocolate, "so your life got crazy because you were asking about the embarrassing stories?"

"Mmm . . . crazy? Yeah, I guess you could say that."

This guy wasn't wrong in suggesting it was crazy, but I was now thinking of that precious year in different, more reverential terms.

Although I had trailed off in thought, my young friend looked excited, more eager than before: "Well, I have this idea."

He was motioning with his hands, focusing more closely on me now.

"Because you were asking people to tell you about their most embarrassing stories, then it seems like there is an easy answer," he said.

"Yeah?" I asked, looking at him with zero expectation that this could be the answer. Hadn't I done this a million times over?

Turning more intently toward me, my new friend began to gesture with his left hand, lifting it toward the sky, like his words were an offering to the gods. Or me.

"You need to ask people about their happy stories. Simple."

BLESSINGS

THOUGH MUCH OF this book portrays a period of isolation, the reality is that I have always been blessed with vast amounts of love and patience from friends and family. Even if I wasn't seeing that love during this particular period, I know it was there. Therefore, it gives me great pleasure to acknowledge the deep gratitude I have for all of my friends, past and present, for your support, companionship, and joie de vivre (which I am so for, by the way).

I would also like to gratefully acknowledge the following people, who made specific contributions to the creation of this book:

Kenya Lynn Murray, for laughing me through many a dark moment and citing the Rules of Karaoke and Life, when appropriate.

Karen Walsh Rullman, who is both family and dear friend, for bringing to this project your characteristic warmth and genius narrative powers.

Phoebe Damrosch and Sarah Norris, as writers, your thoughtful insights at many a critical juncture—including after you read this manuscript in its most raw form—are greatly appreciated.

As friends, you helped me make lemons out of lemonade, far too many times to count. Thank you.

Real-life Jack, upon whom Book-Jack is loosely based, for telling me all I needed was the right arc. I trust that you know how grateful I am for the brief period of time our lives intersected.

Sarah Szurpicki and Julie Asher, for reading early drafts and offering some much-needed reassurance about my decision to share this story. Your encouragement means more than you know. And an extra dose of gratitude to the fabulous Julie, for insisting that I talk about "the book" the one night I really didn't want to.

Cameron Atwood, for reminding me that it's "better to ask for forgiveness than permission."

Seth West, for your steadfast love of life, the absurd, the absurdly beautiful, and me.

Ted Riederer, for believing in me and then pointing me square in the direction of New York.

Hillary Enselberg, for being on the case and in the process, spending hours on the phone living up to your nickname.

Melissa Fallon Miller, for being unfailingly supportive through all the Three Seasons. I couldn't have asked for a more ideal witness to my original embarrassing moment.

Raquel Quinones, for pointing out that I was attracting embarrassing situations and for suggesting *Oh, Shit!* in the first place.

Emily Williams, for reading early chapter outlines and being a true friend.

Maya Whiteley and Jason Tobin, for providing much needed refuge—both during and after this year—in the form of good company, good food, and understanding.

Stefan Block and Diana Spechler, for being the best first-book friends a girl could ask for.

JoAnna Nocera Chatfield, for always encouraging me and supporting me in my writing efforts. For this and so much more, thank you.

Dalton Conley, for your careful consideration of the subject matter, including helping me to brainstorm on the more theoretical aspects of this topic.

Phillip Lopate, who never batted an eye in the face of breakage, spillage, and declination. Thank you for your utter kindness.

Christina Case and Robyn Delman, practitioners of (positive) voodoo magic, for your pivotal support. It worked!

Angela Balcita, my dear and honest reader, for your generosity and your fabulous sense of humor.

Hilary Robertson, for good cheer and expert guidance, especially with regard to the cover.

Jose Ayala, for being so very supportive.

Stephen Dolben, for your loyalty and unbelievable generosity of spirit.

Jessica Mazo, for reading the very first pages! And being such a great listener.

Brian Farnham, for gleaning the essence of the book from an hour of my rambling and then going out of your way to introduce me to Laura.

Sabine Hrechdakian, for giving me solid advice every time I found myself in a certain type of professional jam. I must owe you a thousand dinners by now.

The faculty and administration at Sarah Lawrence College, for instilling in me a keen sense of space and possibility, as well as the love of revision. Special thanks to Vijay Seshadri, for your one-of-a-kind pep talks; Alice Truax, for caring so deeply and giving so much, including the suggestion that I write this story from a distance; and Fred Strype, because you rock.

My AHA family, for providing plenty of maternal support during the writing of this book. Special thanks to Joy Chaillou.

Sherene Schostak, for cowriting *Surviving Saturn's Return*, and for your estimable way of being both loving and fierce.

Bethany Birkett, fellow Cancerian, for teaching me to draw from the highest sources, always.

My beloved yoga family, especially Raffael Pacitti and Paola Arinci, for cracking the daily whip, with love.

The writers at Serendipity, for going on countless journeys with me.

Annie Belfoure and Erin Edwards, sirens of the Foxy Den, for your fine company, ridiculous patience (because I practically burned a hole in that green couch), and, of course, your love. I'm humbled by the good fortune of having you in my life. Thank you, thank you, thank you.

Dearest T, for keeping my real secrets.

Jeanne and Brian Smith, for opening your home and hearts.

Mary Ann Guillette, my dear, for doing your darndest to find me stories and giving me thorough, expert design guidance. And for your heart always being in the right place.

David Guillette, for your supportive, psychically timed phone calls and for making me laugh in that way only you can.

Annie Guillette, whose generous ear both comforts and inspires me. You are beautiful, inside and out. And I am lucky.

Dan, for practically everything, especially the oft-cited "We'll be laughing about this someday soon." When I try to think of an adequate way to acknowledge the depths of your contributions, I'm stuck. So I'll just go with what you suggested: "Without you, Dan, this book wouldn't have been remotely possible or half as funny." Nothing could be truer.

Martha and Ray Guillette, my exceedingly patient parents, for so much love and encouragement, for your fabulous senses of humor, and for giving me many precious freedoms—none of which I take for granted. (And let's not forget the material!) Mom, thank you for teaching me the fine art of talking to strangers. I learned from the best.

The entire Atria team, including Judith Curr, Kim Curtin, Felice Javit, Jeanne Lee, and Isolde Sauer, with special thanks to Emily Bestler, Sarah Branham, and Laura Stern, for making this process truly wonderful. Sarah, I am beyond appreciative (but not surprised) that our book found its way to your desk. For your dead-on intuition, your thoughtful and thorough edits, and your lovely, lovely way—not to mention all the hard work—I am so grateful.

Laura Dail and everyone at the Laura Dail Literary Agency, including Tamar Rydzinski and Madeleine Desmond, for taking such good, loving care of this project. Laura, I'm in awe of your instincts, your editorial talents, and your just-right blend of warmth and professionalism. Thank you, thank you, thank you.

I would also like to acknowledge all the elements that made for a thoroughly enjoyable (and occasionally even ecstatic) revising process: handmade chocolates from Kee's, especially the black-and-white sesame seed dark chocolate truffles; croissants from Marquet; L'Artisan Parfumeur's Timbuktu and Passage d'Enfer; Zodiac Dance; and the music of the following artists, which provided me with good company during what might have otherwise felt like long hours in front of the computer: Beethoven, LCD Soundsystem, Lucero, Mary J. Blige, Faith Evans, Death Cab for Cutie, Citizen Cope, Sam Cooke, Crowded House, Regina Spektor, Radiohead, Amadou and Mariam, Mahler, Minnie Driver, Sia, ELO, the Swell Season, and The The. And let's not forget the beloved Gidget, who reigned queenlike over the entire writing process.

Finally, I would like to thank each and every person who assisted so valiantly in the collection of embarrassing stories—you are friends and strangers alike. I accosted you on street corners, in elevators (ahem, Ken G.), at parties, and often via email. I will always be grateful to every single person who considered my request, for you were open to my unarticulated longing. Thanks for indulging me and, of course, for making life so fun.